A true story of horror

The Irish Republican Army,  ests,
became involved in murdero
Troubles in Northern Irelanc
rebellion.

A watching world was sickened as acts of depravity played out on their television screens. The conflict soon spilled into England and support for the Republicans spread around the world to countries where the Irish had emigrated or been despatched as convicts.

The IRA became infected by criminality with money was raised by robbery and extortion. Bombing and shooting innocents in England, and torturing and killing defectors in its own ranks became the norm. Britain sent soldiers to Northern Ireland to stop the excesses by both sides that had killed and injured many thousands. That much is history...

In 1970, Britain's MI6 thrust into the bloody fray a young former commando, the ideologue Maurice Tansey, born in Britain to Irish Catholic supporters of the Cause. This is the true story of his life-threatening years as Britain's first and only spy in the Provisional IRA.

To maintain his cover, he admits he participated in bombings, and murder in association with well-known IRA heavies...

More killings in Northern Ireland in 2010 prompted Maurice Tansey to risk the telling of his incredible life story to author, historian and former national newspaper editor Michael Tatlow — feeling strongly that the public should no longer be denied his secrets.

MIKE TATLOW

Difficult circumstances in the wake of his father's death caused Michael Tatlow to leave school aged fifteen in his native Tasmania, Australia. He earned a living trapping rabbits, snaring kangaroos, and fishing for shark in the Southern Ocean. He was also the state's surf swimming champion. In rough seas at different beaches, alone Michael saved four people from drowning.

At eighteen he became an Australian newspaper reporter, then a journalist correspondent in Britain, the United States, Canada, Vietnam and much of Europe. A year as a feature writer for Sydney's *Sunday Telegraph* followed. As a young man, he broke his spine resulting in a year in hospital, during which time Michael twice received the last rites. Fully recovered, he became the *Sunday Telegraph*'s News Editor and Acting Editor, then the Chief of Staff and Pictorial Editor of the city's *Daily Telegraph*.

Returning to Tasmania in the 1970s, Michael became head of Australian Broadcasting Corporation Television News and, rated as an historian, began writing books. He is the author of the non-fiction books *Bloodhouse* (with criminal Darcy Dugan), *A Walk in Old Sydney, A Tour of Old Tasmania, A Walk in Old Launceston, A Walk in Old Hobart* and recently the fiction crime thriller, *Pike's Pyramid.*

He lives in Hobart, Tasmania, and has a son and daughter, and six grandchildren.

MAURICE JAMES TANSEY

Big and likeable Maurice Tansey was born in his family's home in post-war Birmingham, England, on Valentine's Day, February 14, 1947. His strictly Catholic working-class parents imposed miserable conditions on Maurice and sister Maureen, four years his elder, and brother Kieran, four years younger than him.

Maurice was educated at a local Catholic convent and was a Mass altar boy for some time, until a priest caught the youngster sampling the altar wine.

Although indoctrinated to be *a good Irishman*, he developed loyalties to the British Crown. Maurice, aged nineteen, rebelliously ran away from home and joined the British Army. He was an heroic paratrooper for three years in many places, including Denmark, Malaysia and Hong Kong.

His long-time anguish at the killings in the *Troubles* in Northern Ireland was sharpened when he was stationed in Belfast for three months. Back in England in August 1970, a Secret Service officer and Army intelligence officers assigned Maurice to be their first spy in the IRA in Belfast. His diabolical years there are recounted in *Days of Fear.*

His cover was blown late in 1974. Both IRA and Loyalist assassins hunted for him and his wife and two young boys. They fled to the relative safety of Australia, but even there he received telephone and mailed death threats from Irishmen.

Since, Maurice has remarried. He acknowledges publication could endanger him and his family but strongly believes that his story must be told.

Paratrooper Maurice Tansey in 1970.
Behind his left shoulder is the notorious Divis Flats building, where he later attended IRA planning meetings.

Published by
CUSTOM BOOK PUBLICATIONS
FIRST EDITION

Author's Note

Maurice Tansey dug deeply into his remarkable memory – recalling times he had blotted from his mind for years – to re-live many of the events.

His decision to let the public know about his dark secrets from Northern Ireland and elsewhere was sparked largely by recent British judicial hearings' failure to expose the truth about events such as the lead-up to Bloody Sunday and the mass killings on Bloody Monday.

He has revealed his story to me at considerable risk to himself and his family. This gallant and momentous decision was in the face of threats to kill him made by vengeful extremists of the Irish Republican Army and the Ulster Defence Association, in both of which he became a troubled leader. For these and legal reasons, some names have been obviously disguised. Dialogue cannot record precisely the wording of conversations, but truly reflects the essence of what was said.

Maurice, with his official army record of service, has sworn a statutory declaration as to the truth of this book.. For many years, dire memories of Northern Ireland have stained his mind, tormented his nights. After trying in vain to bury those horrid memories, recent events prompted him to relate to me with absolute frankness, and along with his good records, the story of his dramatic life. I hope this book is his panacea, and my gratitude goes to him.

My thanks for their help go to Maurie's supportive wife Joan and their daughter Roisin; and to Jay Pring, Bruce Terrens and Marie Di Benedetto. Literary agent Keelane Lake was a diligent enhancer of this book. I am grateful to Custom Books for their excellent preparation of this book. A valued reference, confirming Maurie's extraordinary memory for names, dates and places, was Tim Pat Coogan's authoritative book *The Troubles*, published by Random House.   M.T.

DAYS

of

FEAR

The true story of the life of Maurice Tansey as a spy –
as told to author & historian
Michael Tatlow

For all the innocents...

Introduction

The conflicts of Ireland that set the scene confronting a young paratrooper-turned-spy.

The people of Ireland have occupied their green and fertile isle since at least 8,000 BC. The romantic, tribal, music-loving and spiritual race replaced their indigenous Celtic religion in favour of Christianity when it was introduced by St Patrick about 600 AD.

A century of invasions by the Vikings began two hundred years later, leading eventually to the invaders' harmonious assimilation, with no rancour about religion.

More than eight hundred years of English occupation of Gaelic Ireland began with the unprovoked arrival in 1169 of a mercenary army under *Strongbow* – Richard de Clare, the second Earl of Pembroke. In more than one-hundred and fifty years of military campaigns, nearly half of the population of Ireland was slain. The English Crown asserted control of the island in 1534.

Outraged that Catholic Ireland generally rejected the new Church of England that had accommodated another marriage by King Henry VIII, an army led by Oliver Cromwell – the Puritan – marauded the land for four more years from 1649.

Religious differences became the new division as thousands of English and Scottish Protestants settled there, driving the Irish from their farms. Protestant supremacy in Ireland was confirmed when Dutch and Danish mercenaries with English and Scottish soldiers led by William of Orange won the gory Battle of the Boyne in 1690.

The eighty-five percent Catholic majority suffered severe economic and political hardship when, late in the 1600s, they were banned from the Irish parliament. Anglo soldiers and settlers, and more specifically the Protestant Church of Ireland, took charge despite assistance for Ireland from Roman Catholic Spain and France. For more than a hundred years it became illegal to practice Catholicism.

Irish Catholics doggedly resisted the rule of the United Kingdom of Great Britain and Ireland, established in 1801. They were still banned from sitting in the parliament and their language discouraged, until the Catholic Emancipation of 1829. A key tenet of the new rule, however, was that more Catholic farmers were banished from their land in favour of Protestants. British-ruled Ireland around Dublin became known as the Pale.

Thousands of Irish were despatched as convicts for generally-trifling crimes to America, never to return home. After losing the American War of Independence, the British claimed Australia as the new land of internment for the wretched men, women and children jammed into the Crown's prisons. Fear and the violence forced more thousands of free Irish to flee to America, Canada, Australia and elsewhere.

The Potato Famine of 1845-52 was a grim reaper, causing awful change to the Irish demographic. A third of the population was largely dependent on potatoes for food when rampant blight ruined their crops. More than a million died from starvation and disease. Another million of the desperate emigrated to all parts of the world in one of the greatest diaspora in history.

Throughout the famine, thousands of shiploads of meat and vegetables from English-owned farms went across the Irish Sea to the British. Many Britons regarded the Irish as inferior, stupid and a vulgar lot, despite their plethora of fine scholars, authors and composers, and performers of their distinctive music.

Generations of bitter conflict followed.

Irish Republicanism gained momentum with the 1905 formation of the political party Sinn Fein – Gaelic for 'we ourselves'. The Easter Rising of 1916 saw the birth of the Irish Republican Army. It fought three years later in the two-year Irish War of Independence. Seething emotions in the once-romantic land of the Irish Gaels –Protestant neighbour versus Catholic neighbour – fired the Irish Civil War a year later.

The thousands killed included Irish Republican Army leader Michael Collins, founder of the Irish National Army. The Irish Free State Republicans won, but sectarian bigotry between Catholic Nationalists and Protestant Unionists continued to fester.

In 1922 most of Ireland – twenty six counties – seceded from the United Kingdom to become the independent Irish Free State, now the Irish Republic, centred on Dublin. Six north-eastern counties remained under British rule, becoming Northern Ireland, with Belfast as its main city.

Republicans, led by the IRA, wanted the six counties back. Dominant Protestants in Northern Ireland resisted with equal violence.

These rival paramilitaries brought on the Troubles, which simmered throughout World War II and into the 1950s, exploding into outright armed rebellion in 1969. A watching world was sickened as acts of depravity – bombs targeting innocent civilians – played out on their television screens.

The conflict spilled into England, with support for the Republicans spreading across Europe, to the United States, Canada, Australia and many other countries to which Irish had emigrated or been despatched as convicts.

The IRA became infected by criminality; raising money through robberies and extortion, bombing and shooting innocents in England, and torturing and killing suspected defectors in its own ranks. Britain sent soldiers to Northern Ireland to try to stop the excesses by both sides that in recent years had killed thousands and injured many more.

In 1970 Britain thrust into the bloody fray a young former commando, the ideologue Maurice Tansey, born in Britain to Irish Catholic supporters of the Cause. Maurice's amazing, life-threatening years as Britain's first and sole spy – and an IRA leader – in the Provisional IRA personified Ireland's horrors. The turmoil of conflict between his loyalty to the land of his birth and his affection for his Irish Catholic ancestry savaged his sanity.

Relative peace has prevailed since the signing of the political Irish Agreement on Good Friday, 1998.

But hated persists and pockets of violence still flare.

1. Oh, to be a spy...

March 1970

A car-bomb exploded fifty metres in front as British paratrooper Maurice James Tansey drove his commander along the busy Falls Road in Belfast. The canvas roof of the Land Rover was dangerously down.

The blast added to the death toll from a bombing nearby a few hours earlier. Body parts were scattered about.

Rifle-bearing Maurice had just turned twenty-three. Under his Red Devil beret, he leaped from the vehicle into the mayhem and cursed. The bombers, it seemed, had cleared out. the soldier picked up a child's bloodied shoe figuring it must have belonged to a toddler. He shook it. Onto the footpath fell a bare, bloody and pink foot wit five tiny toes.

Sickened, shaking with rage at whoever exploded these bombs in Northern Ireland's *Troubles*, Maurice walked among dead, wounded and shrieking victims shrouded in the pall of smoke. He could not find a possible owner of the foot.

Holding the bloodied foot by its tiny toes, the grief-stricken private ran to a medic helping a wounded woman into an ambulance.

'This was in a kid's shoe,' he said. 'Have you got a patient it might belong to?'

'Don't think so, soldier. Can't wait. I've gotta go.'

Maurice was irritated by the medic's lack of concern. 'Well, take it to the hospital. If a little boy or girl is there, a lower leg blown off, it could be sewn back on.'

'Oh, okay then.' The medic casually placed the pink bleeder on the floor of the ambulance and slammed the door shut. Maurice searched again among the corpses and the wounded, fearing the rest of the child had been shattered and the shoe was blasted away.

He returned to the Land Rover, his boss in the back seat saying nothing about the awful find. 'This crazy war, it breeds callousness, even in non-fighters,' Maurice muttered to himself as he started the motor.

The young man from Birmingham was relieved that the bombers in this Catholic enclave would not be, as usual, his fellow Catholics. They would be Loyalists. And why, his mind persisted, why doesn't the army ever know in advance of these brutal bombings so we can prevent them? Surely Britain has spies planted in both the IRA and the Loyalists.

They must be pretty useless spies, he decided.

If Tansey was an undercover spook, he was sure he could do more than he was now as a soldier to save the lives of innocents, get more IRA and Loyalist terrorists bundled into jail.

Spying was what the Special Air Service, his country's elite band of soldiers, had trained him for lately. Thanks to his pro-IRA Irish parents, he had the right background. The SAS liked his skills, his enthusiasm but Maurice had the feeling that the espionage mission he hankered for had been cancelled. Day and night, he wondered why.

Driving away from bombed Falls Road, unrepaired ruins of buildings reminded Tansey that during World War II virtually-defenceless Belfast had copped more German bombs than even Coventry, near his family home in old Sparkhill, Birmingham.

He recalled reading about two-hundred Luftwaffe bombers blitzing the city, killing nearly a thousand people and leaving a hundred thousand homeless. Outside London, it was the war's most destructive night of bombing in Britain.

The Germans did not, of course, bomb the neutral Irish Republic, which nonetheless had many men and women in Britain's armed services during the war.

Knowing of big, blue-eyed Tansey's special training with the SAS, the private's combat skills, Major Jones, his company's commander in Belfast, had assigned Tansey to be his driver-cum-bodyguard. But the driver felt that the Land Rover's canvas soft-top, nice for a sunny Sunday drive in a peaceful country, was a risky choice in the Troubles. Major Jones was a prime target for IRA, even Loyalist, assassination by bullets or bombs. Tansey had a good rapport with his boss, but kept his reservations about the soft-top to himself.

The private's notion to get out of the army sharpened when he was directed again to drive to the home of Protestant Jones' lover, in a largely Catholic-controlled ghetto in East Belfast. Tansey had been surprised to learn she was a Catholic.

In uniform, his red beret prominent, Major Jones went inside the girl's home. Maurice parked the vehicle around a corner a block away, as directed. He was the sole paratrooper who knew about the commander's sexy affair.

Nowhere around this place was an army vehicle with a uniformed soldier at the wheel safe from the attention of a sniper. Tansey tensely watched rooftops and windows for suspicious movement in the quiet street. He was a tempting target – a bull's eye. A few men walking by in the fading light slowed and looked at him keenly without speaking. Some hastened their pace as they moved on. *Hurrying to tip off a gunman?*

After waiting an hour and fifty-five minutes, images of a little boy or girl who had lost a foot preoccupied Tansey as he returned smiling Major Jones to their barracks at the former Albert Street textile mill, behind the notorious Divis Street block of flats. It was a short distance from both the bombed Falls Road and the Shankill Road, lately the scene of more riots and killings.

Maurice knew today's Falls Road bombers would be off drinking somewhere, bragging about their outrage. He hungered to get his hands on the demons.

As soon as he was inside the barracks, he telephoned the hospital where, he hoped, that poor child's foot had been re-attached. After the call was diverted to three different departments, a doctor came on the line.

'Late this afternoon, Doctor Jensen,' said Tansey, 'an ambulance delivered to the hospital a tiny foot, blown off a really-little child by a bomb in the Falls Road. Were you able to find who the foot belongs to?'

Jensen paused. 'Sorry, soldier, but we didn't get a foot like that. It must still be in the ambulance. In any case, I don't know who it would belong to… and we're busy here. Gotta go.'

'Can you check where the foot is? Have a look in the ambulance?'

'I don't have the time for that. And I don't know which ambulance.' The doctor paused. 'Hold on for a moment.'

Maurice heard paper crinkling.

Dr. Jensen said, 'I've had a look at the casualty list. A girl, aged about two, was brought in this afternoon. And, yes, her injuries included a lost lower leg. Soldier, I'm afraid that soon after the girl was admitted unconscious, she died.'

Maurice went to bed. He was too upset, too angry at the escaped bombers, to see his girlfriend as planned.

After another day's patrolling and chauffeuring, Maurice had a colleague cover for him so, in violation of a curfew, he was able to scale two high fences in the dark, scamper over a roof, and get out of the barracks. He went through and under fences of barbed wire, then dropped down a four-metre wall into a dead-end side street. He crossed bombed Falls Road, then pro-Protestant Shankill Road, in order to get to Crumlin Road.

He clambering over burnt-out vehicles and barricades and sneaked into Cliftonpark Avenue. His girlfriend Carol Brown rented the downstairs flat there in a two-storey house. She was a Presbyterian and a divorcee, with a son, Allen, aged four. The young soldier was in love with the gorgeous blue-eyed blonde, the same age as himself. Carol and Allen, Maurice hoped, would one day be his ready-made family.

She was a friend of Toni, the bride of Maurice's closest mate, fellow para Bob Rossan. Carol had met then flirted with holidaying best man Maurice at the wedding reception in Belfast early in 1969. Affection had blossomed into love in a few days.

He left Carol before daylight to get back to the barracks, where his dog tags remained. He carried nothing to connect him with the military.

As usual, he was stopped, searched and questioned by Protestant and Catholic vigilantes at different check points. He could not tell either side that he was an off-duty paratrooper. He presented as a labourer, a Catholic to the Catholics, a Presbyterian to the Protestants. A Loyalist aimed a pistol at him but a smiling Tansey got through. His spy-type training and passable brogue of the North were his best assets in those confrontations.

When not driving his boss, he was engaged in riot control, manning crucial flash points and guarding busy public centres, sometimes with the Protestant-dominated Royal Ulster Constabulary. Regular assignments were to run VCPs – vehicle control points – and search vehicles for bombs and militants on the lists of the wanted. At night he helped secure critical facilities including power stations, fuel depots, rural reservoirs and pump houses.

One evening he joined some colleagues for off-duty drinks in civilian clothes at Mooneys, a busy hotel in Belfast's Arthur Square, around a corner from Donegal Square.

His good friend Michael Doherty was returning to their table with a tray of drinks when he bumped into another table. Drinks spilled on a man sitting there, who swore, picked up a broken glass and hurled it at Michael.

It struck him on the neck. Maurice rushed to the scene, pushed the big offender to the floor and took off his own shirt. He wrapped it around the wound, which spouted blood. A jugular artery had been severed, he feared. He carried Michael to the back seat of a car that was parked outside.

He yelled at the man behind the steering wheel. 'He's badly injured! We're soldiers. Please, get us to hospital… bloody quickly.'

He pressed the shirt against his friend's neck as the car sped to the hospital. Blood, however, kept spilling during the five-minute rush. As para Michael was placed on a trolley, a doctor checked his pulse.

'Your friend is dead,' Maurice was told, implacably. He raged with anger at the killer, who he wanted to deal with personally.

Michael's shocked and grieving mother rang Maurice. She thanked him for trying to save her boy's life. She wanted to see Maurice when he was back in England. The killer, meantime, was charged with manslaughter.

Not able to get leave to attend the funeral in Hampshire, Tansey was again annoyed that the army made no provision for anyone's religious faith. before being recruited, he had not missed a Sunday Mass since he was aged three. Since, Maurice had not stepped inside a church for years. His sense of religion had waned. He kept his Catholicism a secret from his fellow paras. Otherwise, he knew, he would be taunted and have to fight the offenders. He did not dare wear the holy medallion his mother had uncharacteristically given him when he quietly left home to join the army. The medal, blessed by a Pope, was hidden in his locker.

One openly-Catholic youngster in his regiment had been so harassed by ridiculers of his church, who reckoned priests had buggered him, that the private tried to hang himself in a shower recess. Maurice had bashed the recruit's three main harassers into submission.

His only religious strife so far had been when a priest caught him, aged ten, taking a sinful sip of sacred altar wine in his church's sacristy. Maurice was sacked as an altar boy.

He was concerned about abounding allegations that Catholic priests and monks carried out brutal and sexual acts on boys and girls in their care in Ireland and England. He was to soon witness and learn of even more outrageous conduct by clerics in the province.

Most Catholics in Northern Ireland welcomed the British Army, seen as their protectors from the more numerous and stronger Protestant factions. Catholics regularly opened their homes to Maurice and his cohorts, plying them with cups of tea, sandwiches and cakes, and he loved their Irish stews.

After three months in Belfast, his deployment there ended. He was returned to their barracks at Aldershot in Hampshire late in June 1970. He walked through the barracks gates, pleased that he had not shot anyone dead in Belfast.

He wondered if another letter about him was on the way to his battalion commander from the Department of Defence.

2. You'll be our top spy...

August – September 1969

Ten months previously, Maurice had been in the army two years when he was summoned to face the commander at Aldershot's Browning Barracks. He had saluted and stood anxiously at attention. Usually a mere private entered this hallowed room only if he faced disciplinary punishment.

Sitting behind his desk, the colonel had held up a sheet of paper. He said portentously, 'This is from an intelligence chief in the Defence Department in London'.

Maurice had thought MI5 or MI6.

'This man at the top thinks highly of you, young man. I agree with him. You've applied yourself outstandingly as a soldier. You're intelligent, skilled, versatile, and as tough as old boots.'

The colonel had guffawed. 'No. Sorry. You're as tough as nails... and as sharp.' He directed the private to be seated. He put down the letter, which Tansey was clearly not allowed to read.

'You have impressed the officers you have served under,' he was told. 'You must officially leave the army... quite soon.'

Maurice's puzzlement evaporated when told that, in the meantime, he would receive special training and a briefing. He faced an important and secret assignment.

'No doubt you've a fair idea of what the assignment is,' the commander had said, smiling. 'Private, you'll be our top spy.'

The colonel had walked around the desk and shaken the awed young man's hand. 'I wish you well and good luck. As well as your skills, it's luck that will keep you alive soon.'

Standing in the parade ground half an hour later, Tansey had been excited. Surely he was to be a spy in Northern Ireland. For months he had desperately wanted to cut the toll of deaths of innocents there. He wanted to infiltrate, hopefully wreck them from within their murderous outfits on both sides of the Troubles. He had felt that he was a good enough combatant and deceiver to go undercover despite his God-fearing childhood being largely free of training in the sin of lying.

A few days later, wounded soldiers returning from Belfast had told Maurice about a bloody re-ignition of the Troubles. The new Provisional IRA had become a major force to tackle. It had split maliciously from the old IRA, which for years had been mainly a punching bag. The Provisionals were fighting back effectively at gangs of anti-Catholic Unionists and the Royal Ulster Constabulary. Bombing and shooting outrages had become near-daily events.

A week after his session with the commander, Maurice was transferred from the Parachute Regiment to the 23 Special Air Service's Territorial Regiment and sent to the Stirling Lines, the main SAS base, at Hereford. It was named, he learned, after Captain David Stirling, who secretly began the elite service of elite soldiers in North Africa during World War II.

3 Is your dad in the IRA?

From October 1969

A day after arriving at Hereford, Maurice was ushered to the sanctum of the officers' mess located in Nissan hut. Seated at a table with cups of tea, a plate of cake, glasses of beer and wine, were a uniformed major in his forties, a captain of about the same age and two younger lieutenants.

They had ominously and abruptly asked him all sorts of questions about his family. Daring to ignore a question, he asked the ruddy-faced major, 'Sir, what's this all about? Is my family in strife?'

Did they suspect, he wondered fearfully, that his father and Uncle Matthew, who commuted between their home in Birmingham and the Irish Republic, were in the IRA?

The major smiled thinly, glancing at his sombre colleagues. 'No, there's no strife, Private. Not yet, anyway. It's to do with a special, top secret and important assignment that certain parties in London consider you're worthy of. They feel you have the skills and credentials required for a dangerous, and a pioneering role in our worst hot spot.

'You are not to tell anyone about this, Private.'

The hot spot was Northern Ireland, Maurice felt sure.

'You are an outstanding young soldier. Your efforts at home, and in Denmark, Malaysia, Singapore, Hong Kong were splendid.

'But first, Private, we need to test you… What side gets your strongest loyalty or support? The Crown of England, to which you have sworn allegiance… or, considering your Irish Catholic family, do you support the Republican rebels of Northern Ireland?'

Tansey managed to look affronted.

'Sir, my mother and father migrated from the Irish Republic to Birmingham and married there. They contributed to the war against Germany. Mum drove trucks and Dad supplied building materials, repaired bombed premises.

'Dad's still a building contractor. He keeps in touch with our folk back in County Galway and Roscommon. As a kid, I went there with him on holidays lots of times. There's some anti-British feeling around there, sure. But all the Tanseys in Britain are loyal to the Crown, gentlemen. I hold firm to my oath of allegiance.'

He had cultivated a fond regard for his Irish Republican father, despite the old man's drunken thrashings of little Maurice, sister Maureen, young brother Kieran and their Mum. If those interrogators had got to the truth, they would have chucked father Nicholas in the slammer, and probably also good old Uncle Matt.

He was careful not to show his disgust at the conduct of some of his Red Devil colleagues; the rapists, the thieves, the brawling boozers… and at the stupid directives from some of the officers.

Tansey, the muscled hulk, then his regiment's champion of unarmed and armed combat, had been relieved to see glimmers of satisfaction around this table of his seniors. But the two lieutenants had looked aggressive.

All these officers would be from SAS Military Intelligence, he had figured. Smart bastards whom he had best not cross.

Maurice had volunteered that he knew Belfast quite well from holidaying there a few times with his army mate Private Bob Rossan, a Protestant whose family lived there.

'I'm horrified at all the years of bloodshed from the Troubles,' he had continued. 'I'd like to help put an end that. To deal with those mad bombers. The killers of innocents here in England, too.'

He had kept to himself what he then felt was a bias – his critical views about cruel excesses of Northern Ireland's Loyalists, the Protestant militia, and the Orange Order. They wanted the land Britain had invaded to remain under British control. The British Army, he felt, was the Loyalists' key ally.

Maurice was not told the names of any of the interrogators. The major had concluded the session by saying, 'We'll have you back in here in a few days, Private, after we've thought about it. Meantime, Resident Staff Sergeant Geordie Tasker will begin your course of special training for what London is contemplating.'

Tasker had been waiting for him at the door. The rugged-looking sergeant, aged about thirty-five, gripped the private's hand. 'So you survived the grilling in there?' he asked with a grin.

'Sure, Sergeant. It was okay, but I don't really know what it's about yet. I've gotta be back in there about the end of the week.'

'Okay. They tell me, Maurice, that something bloody big's in store for you. From now, you're excused from normal training exercises, from arctic and desert warfare, from scuba diving, from more parachuting and all that stuff you don't need training for, anyway. And I hear you're pretty good at my speciality. That's the martial arts, mate.

'It's my job to run you through a damned intensive program of training for that special assignment. It's going to be for a few months, I reckon. For a start, let's go for a walk to the pub and we'll have a beer or three. Not at the sergeants' mess, where they'd wonder what I was doing in there with a private. At the pub, it'll be just us.'

At the quiet bar, Tasker told Maurice his instruction would include skills at deception and how to make and explode basic little bombs, like the IRA used. He would be shown photos of suspected IRA terrorists and needed to memorise their names, districts and pubs in Northern Ireland where rebels hung out. Maps and photos of the province, especially Belfast, would have to be mastered, along with the brogue of the place.

Tansey by then was sure he would be planted in Belfast. *Terrific!*

'I don't need the map reading,' he told Sergeant Tasker, who put down his glass of Guinness. 'And I can talk like a native of Belfast. I've been there a lot on holidays, and tripped around the province – up to Londonderry, for instance – down south of the border to Manorhamilton, and all around the republic.'

'You still have to do it,' Tasker informed him. 'Them's the rules.'

In those days, pubs closed for a short period in the afternoon. The pace of drinking hastened as closing time approached. The grog taking a hold, Geordie taunted his trainee with increasing vigour about anything he could think of. Maurice could see that his Staff was girding for a fight… a test. Geordie had obviously felt he was better at martial arts. His trainee felt differently.

'That's enough crap,' Tansey had said. 'Okay, if a fight's what you want, you're on. We'll go outside.'

The Staff surprised him with a smile. 'No, there's no need, Big One Five. That's what they call you in the paras, isn't it? 'Cause you weigh fifteen stone?'

Tansey had smiled into his drink. 'Yeah, I was the biggest in the gang. When I had to lug heavy gear up steep hills during the Hong Kong posting, training with Gurkhas, I was called the Platoon Horse.'

'Sorry, mate. I had to find out if you've got the fuckin' guts to fight me. One more pint before we go.'

Maurice's dictum since his first, his successful and last fight at school with a bully, an older kid, was – never take a backward step. In combat, he never took that backward step – except from his father when he was a boy. The rule had earned him the respect in the army that he needed.

After three long days' training, he had been summoned back to the officers' mess. The seated four still did not reveal their names. He figured that his new posting must be an undercover job, one in which, if his cover was blown or the enemy captured him, he could not reveal their names under torture?

Maurice had decided to be reasonably frank with them this time. The dialogue went like this:

Q. 'Were you ever aware, through your family, of planned violent activities by the IRA?'

A. 'Sort of. Uncle Matt lived at our home in Birmingham for a few years when I was a kid. He's back in the Irish Republic somewhere now. He and Dad used to have meetings with IRA men, in pubs and private homes, when we were in Galway. Meetings I was usually excluded from.' He named a few locations and men he remembered, his memory seemingly impressing them.

Q. 'Were you aware of any shipment or method of smuggling arms or explosives into Ireland?'

A. 'No, apart from the locals sometimes mentioning cargoes of some sort arriving or due to arrive by ship. When or where, I never knew.'

Maurice tried to wipe from his memory his father's and uncle's regular despatching to the IRA of gelignite from their construction sites in Birmingham. Telling the officers about that would surely have landed Dad and Matt in jail. As a kid in a pub in a village in Galway, six-year-old Maurice had been intrigued when a drinker thanked his father Nick for 'that box of jelly'. That it going to Ireland explained why, he felt, jelly was seldom served at home. Weeks later, back home, Maurice had found out what an explosive that jelly really was. About then he had also realised, remembering how all those men deferred to his uncle, that Matt was the leader of the Galway gang of militant Republicans.

Q. 'Do you know that your Uncle Matthew Tansey is highly regarded in the IRA? That he is a major supplier of money for them? Where does your uncle get the money?'

A. 'I assumed Uncle Matt was important at the meetings I was excluded from. I was sent out of pubs to my dad's car or to the donkey cart. Uncle Matt threw a few functions, as I recall, and got cheques now and then… from our relatives in America, I think. There are quite a few Tanseys in the States, mostly my father's brothers and sisters, and their folk.'

He did not reveal that his American relatives often held fund-raising events and raffles in their Irish communities to benefit the IRA. Nor that his dad's oldest brother was a fire brigade chief in Chicago. Sister Geraldine, who was wealthy, lived in Miami. The youngest sibling, Kitty, lived in Boston. To the boy, America had been the magical source of all things good – peace, pretty girls, flash cars, cowboys and lots and lots of money. Talking to his friends, Uncle Matt often thanked Uncle Sam. Young Maurie had assumed that Uncle Sam was a Tansey, and a millionaire.

Q. 'Where does Matthew Tansey live now?'

A. 'I don't know exactly. Probably County Galway. I haven't seen him for about three years, not since I joined the army.'

He was not going to give them the address of bachelor Matt's favourite boarding house. Compared with aggressive Mum and Dad, his uncle had been such a soothing influence when he lived in Birmingham and such fun in Galway. The thought of further betraying dear Uncle Matt had been repugnant.

Q. 'Did your father approve of Matthew's IRA work?'

Maurice remembered chuckling at the inquisitors.

A. 'Dad was raised in the Republic, surrounded by people who hated the British. I suppose a bit of that rubbed off, but…'

Q. 'Is your dad in the IRA?'

A. 'No, I don't think he's a member. He talks a lot about the Troubles, but I think he's keener on Irish football.'

Q. 'Were you ever aware of IRA activity by residents of England?'

A. 'I think there were a few Republican nutters at Dad's regular drinking hole, the Mermaid Hotel. Our Sparkhill, you know, is the Irish part of Birmingham. Dad took me to the pub sometimes. But, again, I was excluded from talk about the Troubles.'

What he had felt was the key part of that second session came after a meaningful glance at the major from the captain, who asked, 'Are you aware of your father's friendship with Mr. Roy Hattersley, MP?'

Tansey had smiled. 'I certainly am.'

Q. 'How? Have you met Mr. Hattersley? Did you hear him in any IRA talk?'

A. 'Roy Hattersley and Dad were real mates, and probably still are. I met him at the Mermaid before he was elected to the Commons, when I was aged about thirteen. Talked a bit with him several times after that. I reckon he and Dad, usually with Uncle Matt, still got together every week or so after I joined the army. With Dad's mates, they drank at the Mermaid and other places. And, sure, IRA talk was common.'

Q. 'Do you think Mr. Hattersley had any connection with the IRA?'

Maurice had laughed. The major frowned at the questioning captain.

A. 'He's the Deputy Minister for Defence, of course. I'm sure there was no IRA connection. As a politician, he sort of went along with the tone of the conversations about the wicked Loyalists. Siding with the Loyalists in the Mermaid would have brought on a brawl.'

The captain had lurched forward in his chair. '*Wicked* Loyalists?'

Tansey found another grin. 'Ah, no Captain! That's far from *my* view. It's what my uncle reckoned. I've already told you I strongly, damned strongly, support our army's role in Northern Ireland.'

Maurice had been uneasy about how his questioner knew of his father's and Uncle Matt's mateship with friendly Mr. Hattersley. He had wondered if these officers really thought the Deputy Defence Minister – who had sent soldiers to Belfast – might be a member of the IRA. Had Military Intelligence tuned into them at the Mermaid? The young soldier had sensed that he would have more dealings with Roy Hattersley.

The major finally had told Tansey he had been successfully assessed. 'With a bit more training you'll be ready, Private. Being a Catholic and your family's IRA connections are assets.'

'Ready, ah, assets for *what*, sir?'

The man at the head of the table had glanced about at his colleagues and smiled enigmatically. 'A special assignment overseas. All in good time, Private.'

Two weeks later, a saddened, astonished and puzzled Private Tansey had been despatched to Belfast with other Red Berets in the 2nd Battalion of the British Army's Parachute Regiment. Crossing the channel, he had felt sure he would never go back to the Troubles as a spy.

4. Is it on again?

July 1970

Red Devils returning to the Aldershot barracks from the Troubles some six weeks after Maurice's three months of soldiering in Northern Ireland – told him the general mood of grateful hospitality he had experienced there from Catholics, never Protestants, had changed lamentably. They now saw British soldiers as the enemy. It was because the army had protected from Republican objectors, the Orange Lodge members on their yearly Orange Day parade in July through Catholic districts, which celebrated the English Protestant victory over Irish Catholics at the Battle of the Boyne. The scene of the vicious conflict by the River Boyne was in the republic, near Drogheda.

Maurice was amazed at the provocative celebrations of a battle that had taken place nearly three hundred years ago, in 1690.

He had seen on television, along with people around the world, hundreds of marchers flaunting themselves with bands and orange bunting. Thousands more watched from footpaths, buildings and their homes. Several riots broke out.

During a solitary evening stroll in the countryside near Aldershot, Maurice considered complaining to his good, and old friend Roy Hattersley, the MP for Birmingham Sparkbrook in the House of Commons for the past four years. When Maurice's dad had taken the boy to local pubs, kindly Mr.. Hattersley had fussed over him.

Early in 1969, Hattersley, as Acting Defence Minister in Prime Minister Harold Wilson's Labour Government, sent scores of troops into Northern Ireland. His plan to get in touch with the MP stalled when Maurice recalled him heatedly sharing his father Nicholas' and other drinkers' sympathy for the North's brutalised Catholics. 'The militant

Loyalists are bloody murdering bullies, religious nuts,' he remembered the politician saying.

Did Roy Hattersley know his Defence Department had considered making Maurice Tansey a spy in the North? If Hattersley knew, he would have told Nicholas; already outraged about his son being in the British Army. If he had any notion of Maurice becoming a spy, his dad would have told the IRA.

Maurice anxiously wondered, *Did that happen? Is that why the undercover job's been cancelled?*

Peeling buckets of potatoes at the barracks, the bored and disappointed young man considered a means of getting out of this force. A week after Belfast, Michael Doherty's mother came to the barracks, as promised. She thanked him for trying to save Michael's life after the smashed glass struck her son's neck. She gave Maurice the Bible on which Michael had sworn his allegiance when joining the army. To the inactive Catholic, it was a generous gesture.

The next day, his commanding major at Aldershot summoned the private to his office. Until the major smiled at him, Maurice wondered what he had done wrong. A few long and wispy hairs hung from each of the officers' ruddy cheeks. Facial hair, other than neat moustaches, was taboo in the army. Floppy moustaches and beards were encouraged in only the Air Force and Navy. Maurice wanted to walk around the desk and pull out the major's strands, the cause of regular sniggering by the troops.

The commander praised Tansey's skills from his specialist training now months ago and his record in Belfast.

'You've been chosen for a very special and undercover assignment,' he announced. *Strewth*, Maurice thought, *what the hell's going on? This is an echo of the past. Now after I've paraded all around Belfast in uniform!*

'It's because of your skills,' the officer continued. 'Also your Catholic upbringing in Birmingham, where you mixed mainly with the pro-Irish Catholics. You will be told more about the assignment later. For now, you're to resume that special-skills training.'

Maurice felt stunned as he left the room. *Hell, will it be in Belfast?* Under his red beret, he had met hundreds of Catholics and Protestants there. The good news, if the job was to be in Belfast, was that lovely Carol and cute little Allen would be waiting there for him.

SAS soldiers now called the flared conflict in the province 'the new Troubles'. He wondered if last month's problems had prompted the renewal of the plan to get him cloak and daggering there. He hoped Roy Hattersley did not know about this.

He resumed training with Staff Sergeant Geordie Tasker at the 23 SAS Shirley Barracks, on the outskirts of Birmingham. He spent a few boisterous days and nights being harangued by two aggressive sergeants at IR – Interrogation Resistance.

Strapped to a chair under an intense spotlight – guns and bayonets wielded around him – he enjoyed denying that he was a British soldier. 'I'd never be a part of that rabble of goons,' he told them, smirking.

Maurice refined his considerable skills and knowledge of guns and rifles used by the IRA. He could face situations, he was told, where he would use such weapons in attack or self-defence against Republicans or Loyalists militia or both.

At the firing range, he often thought of his father's shooting lessons in the cellar at home after the death of the owl Dad had planted down there to kill the rats and mice. Because of his father's fury at Maurice joining the British Army, he had not been to his old home in Sparkhill for more than a year.

His new skills in making bombs, he was told, should make him valued by the enemy. He became competent in handling Semtex. He already knew the highly-explosive substance could be moulded into shapes to suit almost any purpose, like planting under vehicles or bridges. The SAS trainer, Tasker told him that most of the IRA's bombs were made in back rooms and sheds in the Catholic ghettoes in Belfast such as the Falls Road.

His fitness training included carrying a heavy pack on a dash up a steep mountain in Brecon, Wales, and beating to the peak his embarrassed mountaineering instructor.

A week after the climb, he was summoned to the main dining room in the officers' mess at Aldershot. Clearly in charge of a bunch of seated officers in uniform was a distinguished-looking gentleman aged about fifty, in a grey suit and a tie of blue silk.

The man looked like a spymaster. Tansey surged with hope. *Is this it? Is that the top spook who wrote the Defence Department letter about me?*

'

5. We have a deal, son.

August 1970

'At ease, Private,' said a colonel. 'Take a seat.' He gestured to a chair facing them across from the long table.

The civilian had short, greying hair with bright blue, alert eyes. His suit looked like Saville Row. Maurice felt immediately that this gentleman was of the sort depicted as the assigner of James Bond 007. The deference the others showed towards the civilian indicated to the young Tansey that the man had considerable influence and power. He sat in the centre between the colonel, a major and two lieutenants,. Tansey did not know any of them. He decided, they would be part of the SAS secret intelligence and counter-insurgency team, known irreverently among the soldiers as The Kremlin.

Maurice knew the civilian had to be from the almighty National Security Service, the domestic counter-espionage organisation MI5, or the Secret Intelligence Service, MI6, the more aggressive military section that had agents planted around the world.

The more Maurice thought about it, he decided it was MI6. Perhaps this smiling and learned-looking man was its director. MI6, Maurice learned, was a corporation of spies. MI5 was the catcher of spies.

No others were in the big room. The officers silently looked at the civilian, who we will call Bernard.

Smiling, he said, 'Maurice, you have been selected to be Britain's first undercover agent to be planted in the IRA in Northern Island... Our *only* one.'

Maurice was elated as he faced the man. But that could not be true, could it? Surely British spies, moles, snoops or spooks had been over there for ages. 'Good. But *really*, sir?'

'Indeed, Maurice.' Bernard had a plummy, West London accent. Most of the officers nodded. 'Military Intelligence and Special Branch officers are over there, but not inside the IRA.'

The men across the table again had not been introduced to him. If he took on this job, if his cover was ever blown, if he was tortured and questioned... Of course, the British would want to be able to deny at any time that he was their spy. He would not be provided with any documentation. He would be alone... but he wanted to help save innocents across the Irish Sea.

'You are more likely to get to the heart of those swine than any other we have assessed,' Bernard continued. 'I have seen your record of achievement in the army, reports of the extra training and questioning you received months ago. They are impressive.'

Bernard looked left and right at the others at the table. 'You are an outstanding combat soldier, outstanding in armed and martial arts. And,' he beamed, 'you are intelligent.'

The snob Bernard obviously thought intelligence was rare in the paras, Maurice noted.

'You uncle and father's involvement in the IRA, and your local knowledge should stand you in good stead there. Notwithstanding those family connections, we know your loyalty to the British Crown is absolute.'

Well, nearly absolute, Maurice thought. He would never be a traitor to the army. He had long wished, however, that it was more objective about the stricken North. Not so brutally pro-Protestant as so historically it was. After all, the objective was for the invaded North to remain part of Britain. Therefore, Republicans were the enemy.

The colonel took over. 'Your immediate departure from the army, Private, an early discharge by purchase, at your own request, and on payment can be arranged,' he declared.

Maurice's heart sank. The cost would be £330, he knew. Heaps more than he had.

They saw his disappointment. 'Don't you worry about the payment, soldier,' the colonel grinned. 'Instead of the customary procedure, the army can pay the money back to itself. No financial burden would go to you.'

They waited again for Bernard, who sipped at a glass with a slice of lime floating in what Maurice assumed was gin. The Londoner studied the young soldier closely.

'So, Maurice,' he said auspiciously, 'the assignment would be for three years or thereabouts.' Maurice gave a slight nod. 'Do you agree to undertake it?'

'Yes, sir,' he said firmly. He skipped thinking about implications for himself. A mere private would instantly say yes to any request from this hierarchy. 'It would be an honour, sir. I hate all that senseless killing of innocent people over there and want to help minimise it, bring militant killers to justice.'

All across the table smiled, nodded at one another. They would be thinking only of the IRA, Maurice felt. Not Loyalists.

Bernard said, 'Thank you. That's a fine motive. I am confident you will be of truly significant service to Great Britain.' He leaned across the table and shook Maurice's hand. 'We have a deal, son.'

He consulted a notebook. 'We are aware that you have a girlfriend in Belfast. Carol Brown. I understand she is a Protestant but not really opposed to the Republican cause.'

Maurice was surprised that they knew about her.

'It's up to you and her, of course,' Bernard smiled, 'but we recommend that you marry Carol. Then you would not need to provide false details by applying for a permit to acquire employment at a place we have in mind for you. If, as a recent immigrant, you applied a work permit you would have to name your last employer. Married to a local, you would more easily pass as a local yourself. Your local accent is quite good, I understand.'

Maurice nodded, looking again at the officers chewing biscuits from several plates in front of them.

Bernard drank from his glass and said, 'Soon after settling in Belfast, ideally married to Carol, you should seek employment at the Michelin Tyre Factory. Your work as an auto mechanic before you joined your father's construction firm should qualify you well.'

Bernard looked pleased with himself. 'Several workers at Michelin make up a major cell of the Provisional IRA, and we have the means to grease the wheels…'

Some of the officers grinned at the pun. 'Grease the wheels, so your employment there would be fairly certain.

'Being a Roman Catholic is essential in the IRA. After a while, let it drop to the right people that your Uncle Matthew is in the IRA. That your father is a strong supporter. That members of your family raise funds for the IRA in the United States.

Bernard looked questioningly at the impressed Maurice but he kept a blank expression on his face. *Does MI6 also know Dad sends them gelignite?*

The Londoner continued, 'Maurice, never ever reveal to anyone over there that you're ex-army. That's important. Tell them you have firearms skills, and especially that you know about explosives from when you worked at your father's demolition sites.

'Your family connections and skills should impress the leaders of the cell. Make them keen for you to join the IRA. The Provisionals, that is. But they cannot be made aware of it.

'So,' said the smooth tongue, 'do you agree to undertake all that? A wedding and the Michelin job?'

'I do, sir. I want to.' Regardless, he ached to marry Carol. 'But, sir, a lot of people in Belfast, militants and paratroopers included, know I'm a soldier. Couldn't I just tell the IRA that I've left the army, or deserted, or been discharged dishonourably for some foul up? For being pro-IRA, even?'

Bernard glanced with raised eyebrows at the colonel, who pursed his lips and slightly shook his head. 'That would not be credible,' the civilian said solemnly. 'Too dangerous. They hate British soldiers. It's where a spy could come from. Simply keep away from your acquaintances there, including soldiers, who'll know you were a para.'

Including Carol? incredulous Maurice asked himself. He felt that his life was being placed in more peril.

The major told Bernard, 'Nearly all of Private Tansey's company are back here now.' Bernard appeared not to be interested in that.

Maurice said, 'Okay, I'll keep my time in the army a secret.'

He felt again that he, a mere private, aged twenty-three, could not dispute the word of these heavies. He well knew that more than fifty of his paratrooper friends were still in Belfast and Londonderry, regularly confronting IRA militants and their associates. His being able to save innocent lives over there was worth the risk.

For his own survival, he decided right then, he would trot out a line of having left the army in disgust if ever challenged about it by those he was spying on.

The session in the officers' mess then became an instructional briefing of sorts.

Bernard told Tansey that he was to relay directly to London any information, the names of prominent members of the Michelin cell and others if and when he became an IRA trusty. To tell London where weapons and explosives were kept. He was importantly required to report likely targets for the army and dates of upcoming IRA attacks. Also, he was to pass on similar information he happened upon about what militant Loyalists were doing.

London, Bernard said, wanted to know the times and places of arrivals of ships carrying weapons and explosives to carry out atrocities. Where bombs were made.

'Report anything you feel the Secret Service should be made aware of,' Bernard added.

Aha, Maurice noted to himself, *that's MI6, all right.*

He was told that his information to London would be relayed promptly to the army in Belfast for precautionary or retaliatory action.

With the others clearly in support, the spymaster said that to be a credible Provisional, Maurice would inevitably take part in atrocities, including bombings, individual and multiple murders, perhaps torture.

'There's no alternative,' he said adamantly. 'In your case, Maurice, they would be the actions of a soldier at war. Not crimes. Do you understand and accept that?'

Maurice was concerned but not surprised. 'I don't relish the thought, sir. Killing innocents is repugnant to me.' He saw a few of the officers exchange looks of dissatisfaction. *Bloody thug-masters*, he thought to himself.

'Yes, sir, I understand and agree,' Maurice concluded. 'I'll try to minimise it, but if the necessity comes along, I'll have to be part of the bloodshed.' He looked around the group again. 'But what if I'm caught committing a major crime with the Provisionals or whoever and get charged by, say, the Royal Ulster Constabulary or even the British Army?'

'If that happens, Maurice, we'll find a way out of it for you,' Bernard promised. 'We can stop you being charged in the first place. I *guarantee* that. Like a soldier at war, you will never be convicted of a crime committed as part of your spy work.

'We do not need or want you to report to us about criminal activity you face getting involved in. Nor of past law breaking, unless you can give us the names of guilty associates. We want to know mainly about imminent violence, the what, where, when and who, in time for us to prevent it and have the offenders and their leaders arrested.'

So, the young soldier pondered, *I'm licensed to kill, like J. Bond. Time might tell.*

He was told that he could tell the Provisionals at Michelin and elsewhere at first that he was not likely to remain in Belfast for more than a year or so. If newly married, say that he intended taking his wife and her son to live in Birmingham. It probably would not happen, but it was not the sort of thing an aspiring spy would say. That would make him a more credible volunteer.

'In fact, returning home later could put you in touch with IRA activists in England,' Bernard said.

Like Dad! Maurice had a sudden feeling that he would be an experimental pawn in a world of horrors, putting his life on the line more than in the army. A sucker who was expendable, whose real role could be denied.

No one here had mentioned what salary, or expenses reimbursements, he would get. Had they forgotten about that? He did not think he should ask. If he did, they might see him as just a money grabber. Saving lives in Northern Ireland was more important than making money. He would manage somehow, and surely the Secret Service would somehow get pay packets to him over there. There would also be income from working at the Michelin works.

Bernard instructed him to mail his information by express post to Private Bag 9, Victoria Street Post Office, 110 Victoria Street, London SW1. No alternative was offered in Northern Ireland.

'We will act rapidly and comprehensively on your information,' Bernard asserted. 'But not always. Our prompt action on everything you learn would indicate you were spying on them.'

Maurice looked at stern faces across the table. 'No phone number in London, sir? For emergencies?'

'That would be too risky. The enemy has means of accessing telephone traffic.' If the rebels ever rumbled him, and he was fleeing to save his life, Bernard added, he could go to a safe house at 178 Kings

Road, West London. No safe house was offered in Northern Ireland. He kept to himself the fact that he had one – the home of Carol's mother.

Maurice withdrew a pen from a pocket to note the Kings Road address and the post office bag number.

'No, no writing, thank you,' Bernard directed. 'Commit the details to your memory, which we know is exceptional.'

'Who's to be my contact, I think *control* is the word, in Belfast, sir?'

'It's safer for you not to have any direct liaison there,' the civilian said curtly.

Maurice was surprised. 'Not one of the Special Branch or Military Intelligence people over there that you told me about?'

'No,' Bernard told him with a frown. 'The role of those officers is not much of a secret. They are followed sometimes.'

'Do I get a dead drop, a secret place where I can drop messages?' the private pressed uneasily. 'A phone number to call from a public box only in emergencies?' This was bloody important stuff. Surely for them, absolutely for himself.

Bernard smiled again. 'So, you know a bit about the spy trade, Maurice. But I must say no again to a Belfast dead-drop or a phone number. Your security is paramount.'

Bernard pressed back on his chair and looked, eyebrows raised, at the officers. 'I think we're finished here. You can go now, Maurice. You'll soon be in Belfast. Congratulations and thank you, young man.'

They engagingly drank to him. A few shook his hand as Maurice left the mess.

As he left the building in the dark, his mind brimmed with questions about the future, with information that he was prohibited from recording on paper. *Is that all the briefing I'm getting for working in that place of horrors?* Did they know Tansey was not leaving the army entirely? He would automatically be in the Army Reserve, but unpaid, for nine more years. He decided to keep that to himself for now. *So much for my security.*

Just before four in the afternoon, three days later, he was summoned to the adjutant's office. 'All is in place for you to leave us,' he was informed. 'You're now *Mister* Tansey, not Private.'

Maurice had checked the duration of his active service. This was the end of it after three years and twenty four days. He signed off on his Regular Army Certificate of Service and surrendered his dog tags.

At five minutes past four in the afternoon of Tuesday, 4 August 1970, he went to the barracks' accommodation block and grabbed the bag he had packed.

He had an army travel warrant to Belfast. Using that would be a bit risky, he figured, if the IRA ever checked on his means of transport to the province. *Oh well, it saves some money.*

He hurried to Aldershot's railway station. From there, he phoned Carol. He told her he was finally fed up with the army and had resigned. He wanted to be with her. Could he go there? Right now?

She sounded enthralled. 'I'll be waiting with open arms,' she said. 'Stay with me. Forever, darling.'

On the way to Liverpool's ferry terminal, questions about Roy Hattersley, MP. still played on Maurice's mind. The genial man was no longer the Deputy Defence Minister. Not since the Labour Party lost the election to Edward Heath's Conservatives two months ago. Had that change, he wondered, suddenly brought on the spying job?

An schoolmate of Maurice's had lately told him he had twice seen Hattersley and Nicholas Tansey together at a pub. Why would Hattersley, even now an Opposition heavyweight, and a boozy builder in Birmingham, meet so regularly?

Would Nicholas not be furious when Acting Defence Minister Hattersley signed the Army Board Order last year, sending troops into Northern Ireland? Perhaps the Minister had restricted the number being sent.

Perhaps his father had influenced the involvement of – Hattersley – while the Birmingham MP was still a Minister – in the recent disbanding of Northern Ireland's pro-Loyalist police force. Those hated B-Specials had harassed and slain Republicans for fifty years. In one of his last acts in Government, Hattersley had agreed to the formation of the Ulster Defence Regiment in an attempt to create a non-sectarian replacement for them.

Labour's rising star Hattersley had been re-elected in Birmingham, with an increased majority, on June 18.

The demise of the B Specials, Maurice believed, followed their brutal ambushing of hundreds of Republican university students on a peaceful People's Democracy hike from Belfast up north to Derry, in January 1969. The Bs belted the students with clubs, iron bars and bicycle chains.

That night, B Specials in Derry's Bogside, celebrating the plight of the students, had rioted drunkenly. They smashed up pubs, houses and people. Maurice had been amused to read of a concerned resident who dialled nine-nine-nine to complain. He suddenly realised he was calling the police to complain about the police, and hung up.

Last October, Loyalist rioters in Shankill Road, where Maurice had holidayed so often, had killed a policeman.

He smiled to himself now with the view that Hattersley had not known, hence his dad did not know, that Maurice would soon try to be a spy in the IRA. If his dad had known, he would have phoned his son to abuse him before reporting it to the IRA.

Still, there was still the likelihood of meeting up with IRA men who recognised him as a soldier, of confronting a former colleague in the paras in the street, a pub, anywhere when he was with IRA men.

As the ferry left the wharf, he thought of disguising himself with plastic surgery. But ingrained and reckless optimism, fomented by the army, prevailed. He could not afford such surgery, anyway.

If a militant found out Tansey was a spy, it would quickly be a matter of Tansey's life or the militant's.

When he took a seat in the ferry dining room for dinner, there at the same table sat his immediate past company major, the one who had alerted him to the coming meeting with Bernard and the officers. He still had those wisps of hair on his cheeks.

He said he was going to Belfast to attend the trial for manslaughter of the man who had slashed the throat of para Michael Doherty in a hotel in Belfast's Arthur Square.

Maurice told the major, 'I was there. Mike was a close mate. He died on my lap in a car racing to the hospital.'

He was surprised he had not been summonsed to testify at the trial. But it was probably just as well. Perhaps MI6 or whatever had prevented it. Publicity from ex-soldier Tansey's evidence would ruin his chance of becoming a spy.

In bed that night, it occurred to Maurice that perhaps MI6 had despatched him to the core of the Troubles as a Red Devil last April to test his loyalty to the Crown.

6. Brawlers, drunks and cobras

August 1970

Privates Tansey and Geordie Smith had been their company's toughest two men when their battalion was training for jungle warfare at the town of Kota Tinggi in Johor, Malaysia. The soldiers of the Queen were often an unruly rabble.

Weeks were spent on arduous tasks in Malaysia's wet and infested jungles, without washing, shaving or changing clothes. They had to survive on basic ration packs… and drinking contaminated water.

Soldiers were regularly ill. It was part of the training, they were told. Maurice, however, coped pretty well. He for once had thanked his tough upbringing. One evening after a jungle exercise, a mighty fire was lit in a clearing. Untold gallons of beer were drunk, bringing on wild brawls, some of them between mates. Red Devils staggered all about the place.

Well into the night, Maurice had imbibed enough. He sauntered off to the privacy of his bivvy, his makeshift tent.

He was asleep when Sergeant Peacock pulled back the flap and yelled, 'Out you get, Private. It's time for you and Geordie Smith to square up. We're gonna find out who's the best.'

This meant a bare-knuckle fight. It was the army's way of grading the toughest in the company; at the same time providing entertainment for the drunks.

'I've got no beef with Geordie,' a yawning Tansey said from his pillow. 'He's a fair enough bloke. We get on pretty well.'

Peacock was swaying from the affects of grog. 'If you don't fight Private Smith, you're weak. You'll be a wimp to the ranks. Get to clean out the shit holes.'

Tansey left the tent in his jungle green shirt and pants and went out to the still-huge fire. Geordie had joined the paras a year before him. The fellow heavyweight stood there, waiting. At six-feet-six, he was taller and a bigger than Maurice, and he did not look as drunk. About seventy braying soldiers surrounded Smith.

He strode up to Maurie, without speaking, and threw a punch. Maurie countered it, but had decided not to employ his karate skills. It was a blow-for-blow affair for about fifteen minutes, men cheering and booing the pugilists. Some were laying bets on who would win.

Tansey paused when he had his opponent by the throat, sprawled backwards over a log. He knew it would be called weak if he let go of the struggling, defeated Geordie, with whom Maurice had no quarrel. He and Geordie were supposed to fight until one of them was knocked out. Maybe, he felt, Geordie was now a hospital case. *The company major or some other cheerers or booers here should be pulling me off him.*

Geordie Smith was barely breathing. Maurice's clawed hands were strangling the blubbering guy to death. To this day, Maurice believes he would have then been a killer had he not let his victim go.

That, he felt sure, was the end of it. He turned away from Geordie to face the mob, still roaring for blood. Behind him, Geordie had the strength to get up and king-hit him on the back of the head. Tansey was on the ground when Smith approached, about to kick. Tansey leapt to his feet. The fight was on again.

They eventually knocked one another senseless, unable to do any more than sit on the ground, dazed and staring at one another through eyes that were bloody slits, throwing round-arm punches that barely made contact. It was a stalemate. Most of the mob booed the fact that there was no winner.

But Tansey and Smith were joint company champs. An okay result, Tansey had felt.

The next morning the fighters were summoned before the company commander. He ordered them to shake hands and make up, which they had already done privately. The commander was annoyed, as if the fight was something they themselves had started. They were told to report to the medical officer, who was suffering from a hangover.

Tansey had severely-swollen punching hands. The two went to Singapore for x-rays. Maurice had two broken bones. Geordie, also with fractures, spent a few days in hospital.

At the outset of their R & R soon after, Maurie was with a group of paras in civilian clothes who strolled along the streets until they were opposite Singapore's Britannica Club, for military personnel. They joined a few American sailors who were watching two Indian men charming their snakes with flutes.

An American said, 'You must be goddam British paratroops. We've been warned by our ship's captain to stay clear of you Red Devils. If not, there's a good chance of a fight, and you lot sure as hell can run faster than us.'

Most of the paras laughed with pleasure. It was a compliment.

One hypnotized cobra was performing, but one of Maurice's group, Driscoll, began kicking a charmer's basket to force a reappearance of the other snake, which had retreated. An agitated charmer, waving his flute, pleaded with Driscoll to stop. The soldier kicked the basket all the more.

The cobra suddenly, angrily, reared from the basket. Its wide and flat head waved menacingly as it hissed.

In a flash, Driscoll grabbed the cobra and bit its head clean off. He spat the head to the ground. It was a mere extra step for Driscoll, Maurice felt, from the regular pastime of roaming around in the jungle in Malaysia, grabbing cockroaches, spiders and ginks and eating them. Driscoll and others were showing how tough they were.

'We ain't payin' you nothin',' Driscoll yelled at the mortified Indian, who had lost his means of livelihood. 'Your bloody snake was too slow and too lazy. Get another one.'

The Americans were agog. So were Private Tansey and a few of his fellow soldiers. Other paras thought it was a neat prank.

The Americans remained there, compensating the distraught Indian with money, while the British soldiers crossed the street and entered the club. More of their regiment's personnel were drinking there. Maurice's group of about twenty pulled a few tables together for a day of boozing.

Driscoll stood and declared, 'This is where the boys are separated from the real men'.

Each handed Driscoll a wad of money. The self-appointed treasurer detailed the rules of this engagement. Until they all left the club, no-one could leave the table. Additional drinks would be ordered when a few glasses were empty. So they had to down their beer at the rate of the fastest few drinkers. No one could have more than one glass on front of him.

'When you want a piss,' ringmaster Driscoll continued, 'do it in your glass. That glass a piss has to be drunk. Spilling beer or pissing on the floor gets you a belting when we go.'

Maurice wanted to leave. He realised, though, that with both his hands bandaged over the broken bones, he would be an easy mark for the rest of them.

As the afternoon proceeded, those with small bladders were the first to urinate under the table into their glasses. Many paras demanded more beer. But all glasses first had to be empty. No beer was left. So, in a clockwise direction, glasses of urine were handed around the table. Every man had to drink from them.

They downed mixes of beer and urine for more than an hour until one of them announced that he was feeling crook. He urgently had to vomit.

'So, weak bastard, spew your guts in a pint glass,' the ringmaster directed. Soon after, the only glasses not empty contained urine or stinking vomit. A waitress who came to the table gagged and hurried away. It looked like she, too, was about to be ill. As Maurice now recalls, he must have been depravedly drunk to join the others in swilling those disgusting cocktails. Finally, most of them needed to have a crap or vomit, or both. Except for those who were unconscious. Maurice had a horrid vision of a glass of dung.

'The ceremony's over,' Driscoll slurred.

After a rush to the lavatory, the clowns staggered from the club as the club staff and other military personnel drinking there watched in sickened awe. Maurice's next memory is of waking on the grass with others from the fest in a large traffic roundabout during Singapore's early-morning rush hour.

He was ashamed at being so weak and easily goaded. It would not happen again. Officers from their company had been at the club but no disciplinary action was taken.

During another R & R break in Singapore, Geordie arrived at their billet and handed Big One Five Maurice and another friend two cut-throat razors. 'Put them in your pockets,' he said. 'We're going into town to fix up a bunch a fuckin' Chinese merchant seamen. Last night one of them called me an English shit. The others laughed. We're gonna give em a lesson.'

Maurice was alarmed, reckoning to himself that Smith had earned the insult. But there was no way he could back out of this without a brawl. Maybe, by being there, he could prevent major casualties. Surely the razors were for show.

Geordie led them to a seedy bar in open-market Boogie Street. It was a haunt of shady characters, including transvestites – local male dregs dressed as gorgeous whores, carrying knives, set on robbing their customers. A sergeant had warned the paras about those catamites. Never, they were told, never go with one with an Adam's apple.

The three, in civilian clothes, bought beers and sat where they had a view of the entire public premises. Four Asian seamen arrived and sat a short distance away.

Geordie said, 'There they are. I'm gunna fix up that bastard.'

He opened his razor. The handle was in the palm of his right hand. The blade glinted between the first and second fingers. The seamen sat and gaped as the big soldier ran straight at their table.

'Take this, you fuckin' cunt!' With one massive swipe, Smith completely opened up a sailor's face from his forehead, through the left eye, across his nose, cheek and neck.

'Christ!' cried disgusted Maurice. He ran to his colleague who stood glaring at his victim. 'His eye's hanging out. No more of that!' The victim's mates sat stilled; shocked, fearing a similar slashing.

'Let's go before the cops come,' said Smith. The three soldiers bolted to the exit as women screamed. They ran in different directions.

Tansey dashed along a series of alleys. He finally burst into a brothel. The madam insisted that he hand over some money for the services of a pro. This was no problem to him. A back room of a knock shop was probably a good hiding place.

He explained to the young Chinese girl, as best he could, that all he wanted was to spend a little time with her. No sex, thank you. It would have been impossible in his state of mind. He sat on the bed.

The razor fell out of his pocket to the floor. As he picked it up, the girl's smiling curiosity about this client's non-interest in copulation turned to trembling, open-eyed fear.

She sat, barely daring to move, for nearly an hour until Maurice sheepishly left and found a taxi. He had the driver stop on a causeway. He went to the edge, as if urinating, dropped the razor to the water and continued to the barracks.

Geordie and their companion at the razor slashing were there, quietly drinking and smoking as if nothing had happened. The next day, news of the outrage spread through the camp like a gale. The Asian seaman was in hospital, one eye lost, his face distorted for life. Everybody knew a British soldier had done it.

The army hierarchy immediately covered for Geordie, telling inquiring police it could not have been him. Private Smith was on guard duty that evening, they claimed. It was something the officers did a lot, to protect the 'good name' of the force.

It was as though the brass were quietly pleased, Maurice felt, that their men were the toughest thugs around. And the local police did not want to annoy the British Army by pressing to prosecute one its soldiers.

There were similar outrages by Maurice's colleagues in Hong Kong and Denmark.

7. Into the bloody fray… '

From August 1970

As the ferry passed the Isle of Man, a few hours from Belfast, Maurice acknowledged that he had experienced much less thuggery among paras in Northern Ireland than on other postings.

Low pay forced a lot of Red Devils to pawn watches, gold bracelets, pornography, anything of value – sometimes stolen, but often bought duty-free while on foreign assignments. The receivers were mostly publicans, who traded the items for drinks and food around Aldershot and nearby Guildford. Sometimes the traders were prostitutes.

Maurice had narrowly avoided death outside the Military Licensed Club when a large jukebox smashed to the ground beside him. It had been hurled through an upstairs window during a brawl.

Soon after the ferry from Liverpool berthed early at Belfast, Maurice left a taxi in nearby Cliftonpark Avenue. He walked into the arms of waiting Carol and picked up and hugged an excited little Allen.

'Of course, my love,' said Carol. 'I told you that on the phone.'

He kissed her again. 'Later on I'm going to try to get a job at the Michelin tyre-making factory. But to do that, I'll need to be married to a certain beautiful girl who's a local.'

'So,' she said, 'let's do it!'

That night he impressed on her the importance of none of their friends knowing he had been in the army. Both Catholics and Protestants would detest him for that. Carol promised to keep it a secret. Also secret would be the fact that he was a Catholic. Mixed marriages were virtually banned in the province. They generated hatred from both sides. Carol agreed to tell anyone who asked that he was, like her, a Presbyterian.

If word of that got to the Provos, he could tell them that Catholic Maurice had lied to Carol so she would marry him. Cripes, he mused to himself, what a devious, dodgy business he was getting into.

He soon confirmed that he had been lobbed into the nub of a community of terror and mayhem. Worse, it was, than when he was there as a Red Beret only two months ago. The expanding Provisional IRA, fighting back at marauding mobs of Orangemen hell-bent on ravaging the Catholic population, had re-ignited the Troubles to unprecedented levels.

Falls Road, where he found that child's half foot, had copped more attacks, with deaths and countless injuries. The attacks were reprisals for a fiery assault by the Provisionals on a rally against 'Popists', sponsored by the anti-Catholic bigot, the Reverend Ian Paisley.

Maurice knew Paisley had been jailed recently for organising an illegal and menacing demonstration. He had been released during an amnesty for predominantly-Protestant prisoners guilty of political offences.

In the past seven months, the new Loyalist Ulster Volunteer Force and Unionists of the reborn Orange Order had exploded bombs and shot Catholic families throughout the North. Maurice understood that all Northern Ireland Members of the House of Commons were Loyalists, as were all of the Government MPs of Northern Island. It was the result largely of gerrymandering of electorates to deny power to Catholics, many of whom were unemployed, still denied public housing and proper schooling.

Paisley was the most forceful influence against a constitutional solution. The 44-year-old Baptist had recently co-founded and now led the Free Presbyterian Church of Ulster, the radical Democratic Unionist Party and the Ulster Protestant Volunteers, who ran vigilante patrols. The UPV set up street barricades against Catholics and made lists of IRA suspects, many of whom were later slain.

Maurice Tansey expected that he would be on that death list. He knew Paisley had celebrated the death in June 1963 of the universally-popular campaigner for Christian unity, Pope John XXIII. The night after the death, a big audience in Belfast's Ulster Hall cheered as Paisley told them that the flames of hell were licking around the dead Pope.

Three years later, Paisley co-founded *The Protestant Telegraph* newspaper.

Also that year, after their bombing and murders around the province, the Ulster Protestant Volunteers had openly declared war on the IRA, saying 'all known IRA men will be executed mercilessly and without hesitation'. That, Maurice felt, had prompted the formation of the Provisionals.

Not long before he returned to Belfast, four thousand Catholic protest marchers were batoned and kicked to the ground by Paisley's Unionists and the Royal Ulster Constabulary.

Catholic Cardinal Conway had received about £24,000 from a Northern Government fund to alleviate community distress, administered by the Red Cross. Word in the army was that a goodly slice of the money purchased weapons and explosives for the new Provisionals.

The Catholic Bogside district in Londonderry City, a little over an hour's drive north-west from Belfast, had had a spate of nasty riots. Police cars were stoned, shops and pubs blown up. Counter-attacks from the RUC followed. Some 15,000 orderly Republican marchers confronted police in Derry, getting through the barricades after half an hour of bristling exchanges of abuse.

Those events and the re-arming of the Provisionals set the climate that maybe-soon spy Maurice Tansey, aged 23, had landed in.

No Catholic of the North could go to bed at night feeling really safe. Nearly every night, Maurice and Carol heard bombs exploding. For the first time, he was glad she was a Protty and thus not a prime target.

With no army severance pay and no money arriving from the Secret Service, he needed an income until, he hoped, he got that job in the New Year at the Michelin factory. He did not want to depend on Carol's salary as a secretary in the Ear, Nose and Throat unit at Belfast's Royal Victoria Hospital.

He decided to become a professional window cleaner. The thought had entered his mind during an army exercise in Wales. On a cold night under a sickle moon, he had stood in rain in a trench more than knee-deep in icy water. He looked down at a distant town of Merthyr Tydfil, with lights shining brightly. Hey, he had thought, all those windows had to be cleaned now and then. Becoming a window cleaner would be cheap and easy. Better than soldiering.

He borrowed an old car from a friend of his para mate Bob Rossan, placed a few classified advertisements in a newspaper, and became a self-employed window cleaner. His extension ladder went on the roof rack.

He worked only in Catholic areas. It was easy and reasonably enjoyable, and gave him a feasible reason to be seen about regularly, mixing with Catholics, not attracting suspicion. His income, in cash, was adequate. He was pleased to read in a newspaper that the killer of his mate Mike Doherty with a glass in the pub had been found guilty of manslaughter and sentenced to several years in jail.

Maurice's SAS training had included learning the history of the Irish Republican Army. It had been the name of several armed groups in Ireland from the 1800s. It was used by Fenians who launched raids in Canada in the 1860s.

The IRA had long been rife with internal disruptions, resulting in splits. One followed the signing of the Anglo-Irish treaty in 1921. Supporters of the treaty formed the core of the Irish National Army. Detractors still called themselves the IRA.

When the Republic of twenty six counties was established in 1922 in the wake of the Irish Civil War – six counties making up British-controlled Northern Ireland – the IRA, wanting the whole island for the Irish, fought its cause in relatively insipid ways. Early in 1969, the IRA still largely observed a ceasefire it had begun in 1962.

Accusing their more-pacific colleagues of failing to protect Catholics in the North, of timidly accepting the division of the Emerald Isle, frustrated militants spawned the aggressive Provisional IRA, flaring the Troubles.

If militants recognised window cleaner Tansey as a British soldier, he feared, they would strike without even asking him about it.

If he told his future Provo contacts about his IRA family, as Bernard had advised, surely the Provos could check with his father or Uncle Matt. Proud about him becoming a Provo, they would say they were pleased Maurice was no longer a paratrooper. Exposed, he'd be, as a liar.

High-level militant Republicans had demonstrated time and again their effective means of knowing what was going on in Britain. This applied especially to the British Army. Its ranks included boozy loose tongues in pubs, the occasional betrayer, even moles for the Republicans, who were notoriously ruthless with *their* suspected traitors.

And it was on the official record that M. J. Tansey was still in the Army Reserve. *Dammit, experimental pawn or not*, he declared as he wiped bird shit from a window, *I'm going to succeed.*

Feeling that he was now a true civilian, he enquired about getting the Michelin job in October 1970, two months after moving in with Carol. Personnel officers interviewed him and gave him aptitude tests. He had the feeling that they had expected him to apply for a job in this city of rife unemployment.

MI6 must have greased the wheel, applied pressure of some sort on the echelon of Michelin management. Maurice told the personnel people that, despite being a new arrival in the province, he would not be needing a work permit. He would soon marry a local girl.

He and Carol left the flat and rented a house, a more comfortable place, with a garden in front and back, in Thirlmere Gardens, by Antrim Road, which ran off Cavehill Road, North Belfast. It was nearer to the Michelin factory.

They married at a small ceremony in a registry office on 21 December 1970. As was his custom, Maurice left the marital bed at 6.30am the next morning to jog for an hour to the top of Cavehill. However, he sprained an ankle when he had covered about a kilometre. He limped home.

To find Carol fornicating in bed with Maurice's friend, their best man, who had overnighted in the house. He will be called here Phil Evers.

The limper was aghast. But their best man did not cop all the blame. His randy bride had drunk a lot of grog at the local pub lately and maybe cavorted there with men. Maurice assumed she had thrown herself at the bastard Scot, who had travelled from England for the wedding in response to Maurice's invitation. Evers was a para, recently promoted to corporal. He had not met Carol until the day before the wedding.

Fuming Maurice threw Evers out of the house. The adulterer's case of clothes was dumped on top of him as he lay groaning on the path. Luckily for him, Maurice felt, Evers had only a blackening eye.

The new husband's love for Carol was shattered. She tearfully claimed she couldn't help herself; pleaded for his forgiveness. They decided not to have a honeymoon.

His anger settled. He decided to still give the marriage an honest try. She was his means of getting a work permit, acceptance into this ragged community. Carol at least was a superb cook. He enjoyed eating her roll-mops of marinated herring. And he loved young Allen.

Maurice formally applied in mid January 1971 for the job at the Michelin works at Mallusk, on the northern fringe of Belfast. The personnel officer importantly asked him to name his religion.

'I'm a proud Catholic,' Maurice declared. The officer ticked a box on a paper in front of him.

He was deemed ready for a coveted six-week course to become a skilled tyre maker. Few trainees made it through the first week. It required accuracy, speed and stamina. Those completing the course gained permanent spots upstairs on the main production line.

Maurice joined the elites there, doing piecework with automatic tyre-making machines. After the first hour at it, his speed improving, he knew he would earn big money by Irish standards. Considerably more than the army had paid him, even allowing for its free accommodation. He no longer needed to be a window cleaner.

Michelin's huge work floor had dozens of tyre-making and finishing machines. Each was operated by one man. The loud and piercing noise, heat and the stench of hot rubber, made it difficult to communicate with his fellow workers. Only the very fit or crazy would last at this for long, Maurice was sure.

The company allowed three twenty-minute breaks during each eight-hour shift. On his first break he went to the staff canteen. Here, he knew, chatting with colleagues a few times a day, he ought to get a sniff of that cell of Provos.

As he stood with a plate of sandwiches, he introduced himself to a wizened man behind the counter. Food server O'Grady said, 'Being new here, you cannot just go and sit wherever you like. Our staff are a bit clubby.'

O'Grady looked around. About 100 men, a few women, were seated at tables for four. One long table had about twenty diners. The server pointed to the far end of the big room. 'Go to that vacant table over there, mate.'

It was not until Maurice's second week at Michelin that O'Grady smiled and directed him to a table for four that had an empty chair. 'But first, ask if it's all right to join them.'

He took his plate of food to the table and stood, looking at three men he had met on the top floor. 'Take a seat, fellah,' he was told. 'Join us.' The canteen's seating system, he guessed, was copied from prisons. He could be questioned for weeks, his personality assessed, before promotion to a status in which he could sit wherever he liked; get a chance of a Provisional revealing himself.

Meantime, he tried to accept Carol's infidelity. Maurice's concern had risen since that awful morning after the wedding. She was playing the field, particularly when he was on night shifts. Tolerance of his bride's conduct turned to bitter disregard after she twice staggered home drunk, her clothes in disarray, bra in hand.

Maurice became more attached to little Allen. To the boy, the big man from England was his much-needed dad. The two regularly kicked a soccer ball around the back yard. When Maurice was home on an evening, he put Allen to bed and read him tales from books.

Divorce was not an option. It was, in any case, alien to Catholics. The real reason he was in Belfast, and married, was to get into the Provos. He appreciated getting a candled chocolate cake but did no more than smirk at her sexy overtures on his Valentine's Day birthday on February 14.

News reports of atrocities in the province – one and more nearly every day – sharpened his hunger to reduce the Troubles.

Some sort of clearance seemed to be granted in the Michelin canteen. 'You go sit wherever you like, young Maurie,' server O'Grady told him. 'To any table for four. You might be able to join a special group one day.'

Maurice's curiosity intensified about that long table of men, who often seemed to talk conspiratorially. That twenty had the run of the room. On Wednesday, 24 February 1971, O'Grady smilingly informed Tansey that he was invited to join them.

About half of them whom he did not know introduced themselves. The banter was cheery, covering football, the bitter weather of winter, a bit about politics. Some mild criticism of Britain, with which he quietly concurred.

A solidly-built man, reddish hair, blue eyes and a square face, a few years younger than Maurice, came to his side as they were leaving the table. 'Remember my name?' the redhead asked, smiling.

'Ah, Martin?'

'It is. Martin McGuinness. I'm the union rep here. Welcome to Michelin, Maurice. You come from a good Irish family. Look, I know you've got to get back to your machine, but we ought to have a few drinks together.'

This man had checked him out. But how much? 'A good idea, Martin. Tonight?'

'Good. How about after work at six at the local pub on the Ballyclare Road?' His accent was from the north of the North. Around

Derry, Maurice felt. That pub, he remembered, was nearby, in a busy shopping strip.

'I'll be there. But how do you know about my family?'

McGuinness grinned. 'I'll tell you at the pub, eh?'

Was this it? As he thought about it in the din back upstairs, the name sounded familiar. But Martin McGuinness was not listed in the IRA rogues' gallery he had examined at the SAS barracks. Heck, Martin didn't seem to be much more than a smart-arse kid.

McGuinness was seated, drinking Guinness with another man, when Maurice arrived at the pub on time. There were about thirty customers. McGuinness' companion was writing in a notebook while McGuinness talked. The other man closed the book when they saw Maurice coming.

8. You'd be a fine, Provo.'

March 1971

The new tyre maker got himself a pint glass of the black stuff and spent ten minutes chatting in the pub with the two men about work. Yeah, he told them, he was happy at Michelin.

McGuinness now was an engaging sort of fellow, self-opinionated, with flashes of probing intensity, Maurice felt.

'So, what made you come to live in all this uproar, this rioting and killing, in Belfast?' McGuinness asked.

'It's the home of Carol, who I wanted to be with. We married a couple of months ago, four months after I got off the ferry from Liverpool.'

'I come from Derry,' said McGuiness. 'A stone's throw from Celtic Park, where brother Tom and I play Gaelic footy. Tom's brilliant. He'll play for Ireland one day.'

'You're pretty good at hurling,' observed his companion, who had been introduced as Paddy, who also had the brogue of Derry.

McGuinness said, 'Well, I'm a keen player, anyway. I go fishing when I can and I'm a fan of the Derry City Football Club. And you, Maurice?'

He told them he was born and grew up in Irish Sparkhill in Birmingham, where father Nicholas had his own building construction business. His mother and father met there during the war, after having to leave stricken County Galway to find work.

On getting out of his Catholic school at fifteen, he completed an apprenticeship in motor mechanics, then worked for his dad. In the cellar under the house, his dad had taught him the skills of handling handguns and rifles; at building sites, how to use explosives.

Maurice summarised his career playing soccer, rugby and badminton, mountain climbing, hunting, amateur heavyweight boxing. He did not mention martial arts. For a while, he added, he had been an altar boy. Until he was caught swigging altar wine.

The two men laughed. *In nomine Patris*,' McGuinness recited. Maurice instantly recognised it. In the name of the Father, the words spoken for the sign of the cross. *Et Filii et Spiritus Sancti*,' he responded. A test. Martin's smile indicated that Maurice had romped home.

As a kid he had gone many times to the Republic, he said, mostly to Galway, with his father and Uncle Matthew Tansey, to stay with relatives. Since arriving in Belfast, he had run his own little business, cleaning windows. Nods from the two men indicated that they knew that.

'We're about the same age, I think, Martin,' he added. 'I turned twenty four ten days ago.'

'Happy birthday to yooo,' they chorused, raising their glasses.

'You've got a few years on me, Maurice,' said the redhead. 'I turn twenty one in a few months, May twenty third. It's the anniversary of the day Hitler said he'd invade Poland.'

'Bad anniversary, Martin, but it's a big date for *you*! I'd like to be at the party.'

'That'll be celebrated with the folk in Derry. But there'll be an event in Belfast soon after. I'll let you know where and when, my friend. You can join us for a celebration before then, in a few weeks, for Saint Pat's Day, March 17.'

McGuinness paused, took a sip of Guinness. 'I don't drink a lot. Seeing all the damage booze does to the Irish, I'm likely to join the Abstinence Association not long after my twenty first.'

'Good luck with it, pal,' said Tansey, grinning. 'You'll see that I'm not a heavy drinker, either. Usually, anyway. My father was a hopeless, a vicious alcoholic. And I don't like the way grog addles the head.'

He had decided never to get drunk in Belfast. If he got into the IRA especially, he had to keep alert. He could hold his drinks well but, boozy, there was always the risk of blurting out something that could cost him his life. Strangely, MI6 Bernard had not warned him about that.

Both men nodded approval. Non-abstaining Paddy looked at his empty pint glass. 'Three more?' he asked.

'I'll stay with this one for a while,' said McGuinness.

'I'll have another, thanks,' said Tansey.

While Paddy was at the bar, McGuinness lowered his voice and said, 'I know about your Uncle Matthew and Nicholas, your father. Surely you know of their involvement with the IRA?'

Maurice thought about it for a moment. This was a recruiting session. Jackpot! 'No offence, Martin,' he said firmly, 'but I don't want to talk about that. It's private family business.'

The young union rep from Derry looked down at his half-full glass, smiling approvingly.

'Anyway,' Maurice proceeded, 'how do you know about Dad and Uncle Matt?'

As Paddy returned with two drinks, McGuinness gave his fellow Derryite a confiding nod. 'Maurice, I hope you don't mind that we've done some checking. Irish Catholic Republicanism is in your genes. You're one of *us*.'

He looked about the bar, ensuring no one was listening or watching them. 'I can tell you now that we're Provos.'

Tansey looked startled. 'Provos? The Provisional IRA?'

'Indeed we are,' said Paddy, brown-haired, looking about thirty.

'That's easy to say. Look, I'm not accusing you two of lying, but how the hell do I know that's true?'

'We don't have ID cards!' McGuinness smirked disarmingly. 'Nobody lightly claims to be IRA when he's not.' The two recruiters exchanged more smirks.

'Like Marty, I was in the Official IRA,' said Paddy. 'He joined as a nineteen-year-old and didn't know for a while much about the Provos forming and splitting away from the softies until after the IRA convention in December '69. The Officials are a bloody weak-kneed lot. Just about complicit, some of them are, with Brits and damned Orangemen; and with fucken Paisleyites.'

'Yes, the Officials are the Irish Ran Aways,' McGuinness jested. 'And yes, it's the Provos who brought on the real Troubles in '69, last year and now. We've taken the fight right to the Loyalist swine, Paisley's nutters and their mates in the RUC. There's still a lot to do.'

'Okay, I agree with that,' said Maurice, putting a hand on McGuinness' shoulder. 'It's my dearest wish that the whole of this bloody beautiful Emerald Isle is returned to the Irish. The treatment of Catholics, of generations of us in the Republic and the North, was and is disgusting. Jeez, some of the tales I've been told...

'Yep, Uncle Matt and my father are in the IRA, all right. The Official one, I fear, now I think about it. But their hearts would be with the Provos. They're sure not chickens.'

McGuinness said, 'Matthew Tansey is a big raiser of funds for the Cause. Both in Ireland and when he lived with your family in Birmingham. I look forward to meeting him one day. He's still in Galway, I suppose, where he gets considerable funds from the United States. I'd like that money to go to the Provos now.'

Tansey smiled, implying enthusiasm for that. But he could not undertake to find Uncle Matt and ask him to do that. Matt, of course, knew about his Red Devil days.

'Most of the American money comes from my folk over there,' he said. 'Do you know the source of gelignite from England?'

'Your Uncle Matt gets the credit for that,' said Paddy. 'But I have a notion it comes from your builder father.'

'It does. Or *did* for a long time.' The undercover novice paused, feeling the chance to find out something. 'Dad's great mates with our Birmingham Member of Parliament, Roy Hattersley. You'd know he was Deputy Defence Minister until the last election. I met Roy many times when I was a youngster.'

McGuinness held up his glass and clinked it against the newcomer's. 'Roy Hattersley's a fine bloke, a supporter, but I shouldn't talk much about him. We applauded, though, when he put those Loyalist thugs, the B Specials, out of business before Labour was defeated.

'They were latter-day Black and Tans. But it's turned out to be a useless gesture. Thousands of thugs from the Bs joined the replacement mob, the RUC Reserve. Then after it became operational, appropriately on April Fool's Day last year, the Loyalist thugs joined the Ulster Defence Regiment. The regiment, with government backing, is as rotten now as the B Specials were.

'Maurice, mate, you should be one of us. You look pretty tough. Any brawls, I'm on your side. With your skills with guns and explosives, you'd be a fine Provo.'

'Well,' the young man from Birmingham said, his glass touching their two, 'my family would sure be proud of it if I was able to step in. But now that I've married Carol – .' He stopped himself from blurting about her unfaithfulness.

'Our plan is to go back to England in two or three years, away from the confounded Troubles, with her young son Allen, a terrific kid. Perhaps also a baby by then. But that, the baby or clearing out, mightn't happen.

'Regardless, I'd like to lend a hand at, say, smuggling gear for you across the border, and from landing places on the coast. My bushcraft is okay. And I think I could stitch up anyone who tried to stop me, with my fists or a weapon. I've done a bit of karate.'

Maurie was pleased to see more nods of approval. 'Oh, Dad would be chuffed, but I wouldn't want him or Uncle Matt to know about me helping the Provos. Full of grog, they'd brag about it to their Irish mates in half the pubs in Birmingham.'

McGuinness said, 'Okay, and thank you. I'm sure you're a man of action. There'll be jobs soon. Meanwhile, have you got a handle on what's going on?'

'I think so, but I don't get the paper every day. News about the Troubles is terrible stuff.'

'It is,' said McGuinness. 'And we're evening things up. Eventually, we'll force the Protty bastards, depleted no end, into an enduring peace treaty. Next big step, a united Ireland run by the true Irish… Home rule.'

He told Maurice the Provos now had more than 300 active fighters and a thousand auxiliaries. Some of the auxiliaries were women, supportive doctors, and many priests. There were scores of safe houses throughout the North. 'And recruits galore! But you, Mr. Tansey,' he added, 'you have rare qualities that we want. Do you know how to make bombs?'

'My father's an explosives pro who always wanted me to be a true Irishman, supporting the Cause. Like handling guns, he showed me how to make bombs, all right. I made different sorts as a hobby for a while.'

He was ready to elaborate. *Hell*, he thought, *do they know about my time in the army?* If they ever did, he had that ready response. He had left it in disgust. Had been ashamed to talk about being a British soldier. If need be, he could trot out a litany of specific reasons for despising the army. Only a few would be invented.

McGuinness confidently told him that guns and explosives were coming in steadily from the U.S. and Europe, and especially from Libya's Colonel Gaddafi. One vital lot of weapons had even got past Customs at Dublin Airport a year ago. 'But the Unionists, the damned Loyalists, that is, have more than a hundred thousand weapons, licensed by the Government because the thugs are in phony rifle clubs. Catholics can't get gun licences. What a sick joke!'

The brawling between the Provisionals and the Officials had flared nastily a year ago, McGuinness said, when the Provos took on with nail bombs and guns a Royal Scots riot squad as it terrorised people, violated young Catholic girls, by the Falls Road and all around Ballymurphy.

The mention of the Falls Road lurched a sad vision into Maurice's mind again of a little foot, dripping blood.

McGuinness said, 'Nearly forty enemy soldiers were injured big time over a few days. Couple of Scots were killed. Provo casualties were less.'

'The Scots rats,' the redhead said. 'They used CS gas. A canister of it was fired into the home of Dominic Adams, who still has an awful voice impediment from it.

'Dominic's the young brother of my friend and inspiration, Gerry Adams,' he added. 'After that outrage, the British army boss here, the Director of Security Operations, General Sir Ian Freeland, announced that anyone they found using a petrol bomb, for God's sake, would be, and I'll use the idiot's words, he said they'd be "shot dead in the streets".'

He took a swig from his glass. 'That inflamed matters, probably making Freeland sorry he made the threat. The British army in the North is a hopeless mess.'

At his own request, a stressed Freeland had stepped down from the post and left Ireland. His replacement was Lieutenant General Vernon Erskine-Crum.

'That change was only three weeks ago,' Maurice observed. He was bursting now to tell them some of his own experiences of the army's clumsiness and thuggery.

'You know how the stress of the Troubles has got to Crum?' McGuinness asked.

Maurice nodded. 'He's in hospital from a heart attack he had about a week ago. After less than two weeks at the job.'

'What a shame!' McGuinness happily sipped again at his Guinness. 'Not that I expect relations with the Brits to get much better with that snooty snob Freeland gone, and now probably his replacement going, too. Glad you keep an eye on things, Maurice.'

Tansey silently recalled that – with the Provos striking – the Troubles had ignited a month after Freeland took over in the North, at the time of the Orange Day parade in July '69. When Red Devil Tansey served there, the Brits had 6000 soldiers in the province.

'So Gerry Adams is a friend of yours?' he asked as casually as he could. Adams had been high on the list of IRA suspects at the SAS. 'He's a Provo, too?'

'We're not really close, but I'm sure we will be,' said McGuinness. 'Gerry's in Sinn Fein. He's a future leader of the province, methinks. He was a barman for a while after leaving grammar school. He's likely to marry a great girl called Collette very soon, if he hasn't already. He sided with the Provos when we split from the Officials, I'm glad to say.'

Maurice saw McGuinness' wink at Paddy. 'As for Gerry's actual membership of the Provos, my friend, it's a touchy subject, given his political ambitions. Let's just say that Gerry's a fine man, and a valued part of the brotherhood. He's about eight months older than me.'

So, Adams was really a Provo, Maurice felt. Not, it seemed, a declared one.

He was told the two men's version of a plethora of ugly events lately, regular gelignite explosions in Belfast on Friday nights, the Rape of the Lower Falls; the vicious and bloody riots in the Clonard area, in the city's west. The Troubles had come to a shocking pitch in the north of the city on February 3, a month ago.

Paddy said, 'Provos and other Republican rioters fired steel darts, lobbed petrol bombs and grenades on soldiers hiding behind shields. The soldiers hailed rubber bullets, also *real* bloody bullets, on civilians. A firearms novice in the Official IRA named Billy Reid got hold of an automatic rifle. Then the bugger emptied its magazine at random. He killed a young ensign, Bob Curtis, of the Royal Artillery.'

'Yes, I know,' Maurice said softly. 'Carol and I live just a bit west of there, off Antrim Road. I heard explosions that night.'

'Heck. I think Curtis was the first English soldier shot dead in Ireland in ages,' McGuinness said earnestly. 'It was a mad act. Regretful. It's brought on more army violence and also rioting in all six counties of the province. Two more civilian deaths followed that. It's when Chichester-Clark made the public claim that Northern Ireland is at war with the Provos.

'Bloody nonsense. We're at war, right enough. But against less than a quarter of the population. That's the activist Protties, including the stupid Orangemen who swagger through Catholic streets in their July parades.'

Maurice told them he knew of Major James Chichester-Clark, a firebrand politician, the leader of the Ulster Unionists. On that sobering note, the three decided to go home. They had been in the pub for two hours. Two pints of Guinness to McGuinness, four to Maurice, six to Paddy.

'So glad to have you on board, Maurie,' said Martin as the three shook hands outside the front door. 'I'll be seeing you again soon. At work, and then on the real business.'

On the way home, walking in chilly moonlight, Maurice reflected that McGuinness saw himself as a Provo commander, at least at Michelin. Did the young man really have the authority to make him a Provo? He dared not contemplate about what his first assignment – the 'real business' – – might be.

He was relieved to find Carol at home with Allen. She was roasting a chicken. 'Been to a pub' was the explanation she readily accepted for his lateness.

Maurice got on well with the regulars at the long table at Michelin's canteen. Their trade union rep McGuinness was seldom there. About two weeks after the recruiting session, Martin McGuinness sidled up to busy Maurice at his noisy tyre machine.

'Can you meet me and some others at the same pub tonight?' Martin yelled in his ear. 'At seven?' Maurice nodded, and smiled.

'Good. There's a matter we need to act on.'

'I'll be there,' said Maurice as a new tyre left the machine. He was now a gun operator, making more than two hundred tyres a shift. In excess of any of the other workers there.

With Carol employed full-time at the hospital and Allen attending the Mossgrove kindergarten, which was a short walk from home in Newtownabbey, near Glengormley, across a field and over the main Antrim Road. Maurice could do as he pleased on his work-free week days.

When he walked into the bar, two men he did not know were with McGuinness. Martin introduced them as Michael and John. After one quick drink, Martin seemed anxious about something.

'We have a mission,' he said. He led them out of the pub to his white or cream Ford Cortina sedan, parked nearby in the street. 'A killer has to be dealt with.'

9. IRA Tansey: murderer or soldier?

March 1971

A Provo leader who Maurice knew – we will call during that night Mervin – sat at the steering wheel. Maurice sat beside him. Michael and John sat in the back.

'There's a man we're pretty sure assassinated one of our volunteers just lately,' said Mervin. 'He's likely to be drinking at his favourite hotel. First we find him.'

Maurice wondered to himself what was in store. Mervin reached under the seat, produced three Taurus revolvers and handed one to each of them. He did not have one for himself, from what Maurice could see. Mervin looked at the new recruit. 'I hope you know how to use these.'

Maurice's smile said he did. 'Are we on a *killing*?'

Mervin nodded. He drove to a two-storey hotel at Corr's Corner, near Newtownabbey. Michael said he knew their target by sight. He and Maurice went inside, guns in pockets, to see if he was there.

Michael looked around the bar. 'No,' he said, 'we'll look in the lounge upstairs.

'Bingo!' he confided quietly as they walked into the big room. 'There he is.' He pointed towards a tough-looking man of about thirty sitting alone at a table. 'Go and tell (alias) Merv he's here, on his own.'

Is this for real? As he hurried to the Cortina, Maurice felt that this might be just a test of his mettle. The initiation. Not a killing, surely. This young Merv seemed to be a self-appointed boss.

'Good result,' said Mervin. 'Have a drink or two with Mike and wait for the bugger to leave. Follow him out. I'll park near the front door. Get him into the car, quietly as you can.'

He and Michael were on their second drink when the man they were watching checked his watch for the umpteenth time and walked out of the lounge. It seemed he had been waiting for someone who did not turn up. Maybe, Maurice guessed, a mate of Merv's had made a phony arrangement to meet there.

The two were close behind him in the dark when their prey strode to the footpath. Michael dug a revolver into the man's ribs. Maurice gripped the man's arm from the other side.

'Into the car, bastard,' Michael instructed bluntly. John, standing outside the car, opened the back door.

'What the fuck?' their victim exclaimed.

'Get in the car,' Michael repeated.

He was pushed onto the back seat. Michael followed him in, while Maurice went around the car and sat at the other side of the prisoner, who cried objections as Michael frisked him.

'No weapon,' gunman Michael reported to Merv, who sat silently at the wheel, looking ahead, as John sat beside him.

The car sped along Ballyclare Road and made a sharp turn left and north from the city along the B90 Manse Road, which went from Newtownabbey to Carrickfergus. They usually called it Mountain Road. Mervin remained silent during the fifteen-minute drive as the man in the middle yelled at them, his fear mounting. 'What the fuck do you buggers want? What's this about, damn you? What do you think I've done? Tell me, and I'll have an answer. Please, bloody *please* let me go! I'll never talk about this.'

Maurice could see that the alleged killer knew that at least a beating loomed. After going about three kilometres along the road, Merv turned into a gravel track. The car went slowly down a steep incline and halted in the dark at the base of a disused quarry. No one else was there. Merv murmured something to John. The two left the front seat. Michael backed out, pointing his gun at their victim's head. 'Out you get.'

Wishing he knew the name of the prisoner in a blue jumper, Maurice followed him onto the dark and stony ground.

The prisoner stood and faced Mervin as John, from behind, fired a shot into his spine. He lurched forward and reeled to the ground, screaming in the moonlight. From two metres away, Michael fired a bullet into the victim's neck. He slumped face down in the dirt. Blood poured from his back and neck.

'Right, Maurice,' said Mervin. 'Finish him off.'

The big man from Birmingham was appalled. This was out and out murder. 'What? No questioning about the assassination?'

'We know the shit did it,' said their leader, glaring at the quivering form on the ground.

Maurice wanted to know who their victim had allegedly killed. Was this wretch on the ground an Orangeman? A real killer? With two pistols smoking near him, the new recruit did not ask. It was his Provo test time. 'He's probably dead already.'

'Make sure of it,' Mervin instructed. 'In the heart or head.'

Maurice bent over the now-inert body. 'John, help me turn him over, face up. I don't like shooting from behind,' he said to the man who had just done that.' He shot the man in the chest.

'Well done, boys,' their instructor smiled. 'Let's get well away.'

They simply left the body there, not even bothering to wipe footmarks in a patch of mud. Maurice was the only one to wipe his fingerprints from the revolver before Mervin put the three of them back under the seat.

Maurice knew too well that such killings were commonplace in the North. Not wanting to get involved in investigations, people mostly walked past a body or bleeding victim. RUC officers were too scared to enter 'no-go areas' in Derry and Belfast to look for crooks.

'Well, what was our man in the quarry?' Maurice asked in the Cortina on the way back.

'He was a murdering bloody Loyalist,' Mervin said candidly, not taking his eyes from the road. 'He tried to penetrate us.'

In bed that night as Carol slept beside him, Maurice was beset by guilt. He had shot a man whose name and background he did not know. Why the blazes wasn't their victim told what he was accused of?

The sole positive thought Maurice could muster was that he had passed his initiation. What the hell, he wondered, would he have to do for the Provos to maintain his credibility over the next few years? He had expected to be involved in smuggling, riots, shooting at armed foes of the Provos. Not a cold-blooded slaying like that.

He remembered vividly the words of MI6's Bernard. He was a soldier at war, on an assigned job. Not a criminal. To establish and maintain credibility with the Provos, he had no choice but to be a bloody slaughterer. He was a combat soldier, not a murderer.

He hoped their victim was in fact a killer. That he was already dead when that bullet splattered his heart. Maurice knew he was quick enough with a gun to take the alternative – shoot instead his three partners in the crime.

To this day, Maurice wonders what, if anything, the police did to find the man's killers, given the forensic evidence – bullets, their casings that Michael and John had tossed from their revolvers, tyre marks, foot marks – left at the quarry.

If Martin McGuinness' car was ever impounded, the guns in it could be matched to the bullets. Surely at least the RUC Special Branch would soon know, or already knew, Martin was a Provo. But, in the centre of nearly-daily violence, the finding of a shot-dead body usually attracted only cursory attention from the police.

In the Michelin canteen and at hotel bars and a restaurant over the next week, Tansey gained a closer friendship with engaging Marty McGuinness

Two weeks after the quarry murder, Maurice express-mailed his first letter to London. It announced that he was now a Provo. It related details he had been told about most of the Provisionals' weaponry coming from Libya, including two delivery points and the date of an expected shipment.

Feeling guilty for dobbing in his new friend, Maurice also reported that the leader of the Provos' Michelin cell, also a Provo heavy in Derry, was trade union rep Martin McGuinness. If their victim in the quarry was really a murderer, the new spy reflected, the killing was reasonably justified. Vigilante justice. He did not tell London about that.

He waited in vain to hear news of action, even condemnation by British politicians of Libya and its dictator Colonel Muammar Gaddafi, who had violently gained power in a coup late in '69. He was glad to find out, though, that the navy had intercepted the cargo of armaments from Libya to which he had alerted MI6. Those on board were arrested.

In a pub a few weeks after the letter was mailed, Martin introduced Maurice to another Provo. He assigned them to 'deal with a mob of rioters'. McGuinness was not with them when a third Provo slowly drove the two past a group of Loyalists – mostly men, a few women – standing on the footpath. They were yelling obscenities about the IRA in front of a Republican pub in the Crumlin Road.

The other Provo's rifle fired about ten bullets at the scattering rioters. Maurice lifted his aim, so his lead went above their heads.

The car sped away, dropping off Maurice at a bus stop, from where he went home to Thirlmere Gardens. The radio the next day reported that drive-by shooters had killed three men and injured many by the Crumlin Road.

He did not report his involvement to London. It was not in his brief. He had been told to report forthcoming violence that the army could prevent or minimise, and who would participate. Both those horrid jobs had been on no notice. If only he had a phone number for London…

He and Carol seldom went out together at night, although she was still a regular drinker in assorted pubs when he was at work at night. She was a cheap drunk. Such a ready lay, he sadly acknowledged.

Maurice was surprised over the following days that, in the wake of his passing their tests so far, he had not sworn an oath of allegiance to the Provos at some sort of initiation ritual.

Perhaps they had forgotten. Perhaps it was because he and Martin had clicked so spontaneously and that his family's IRA work was known to many Provos. And he had implied at the recruiting session with Martin and Paddy that he didn't plan to stay in the province for long. They might have thought of him at first as only a temporary volunteer.

He later attended a few formal swearings-in of volunteers at an old gymnasium in West Belfast. They were private affairs, with only about five PIRA men present, and lasting a few minutes.

The master of the ceremony told each recruit that he had passed their tests of security and loyalty to the Cause. That Martin McGuinness, sometimes another leader, had found him to be a good recruit. That he must behave responsibly and always obey the Provisionals' orders and regulations. That volunteers who engaged in loose talk faced at least dismissal. Disloyalty or traitorism could result in execution.

The recruits simply had to agree to the requirements; acknowledge with a 'yes' the fate of failure. No document was signed. Men always held up the flag of Ireland between the recruit and the man in charge, below their eye lines.

Maurice had learned lately that Irish nationalists introduced the tricolour when they were fighting for their freedom from England in 1848. Although widely flown, it was not officially recognised until their Easter Uprising of 1919, early in the War of Independence. The flag was written into the Republic's constitution in 1937. Its bright green rectangle was for the native people, the traditions, of the Emerald Isle. White in the middle optimistically represented the hoped reunification of the isle, enduring peace between the sundered population of Irish and pro-British settlers and soldiers and their descendants.

Maurice had read that the last rectangle was orange, probably in generous recognition of old Ireland's oppressors and Loyalist hero William of Orange, whose troops won the Battle of the Boyne.

As a youngster, however, Maurice had never known that last colour as anything but gold. His father had kept a flag folded on his desk at home, waved it about on St Pat's Day and when friends were there to see All Ireland hurling and football matches on television.

The last rectangle of the Tansey flag, like those displayed now by the IRA, was more the colour of gold than the official flag's orange that Maurice had seen illustrated in a magazine and flying above some buildings. His folk in the Republic when he holidayed there as a kid always called the flag the green, white and gold.

'It's gold,' a Provo told him in a pub when Maurice mentioned the colours of Ireland's flag. 'We'd never fly the fucken colour of those screwball Orangemen invaders.'

Maurice guessed to himself that the Loyalists flew the traditional version, orange. But he had never seen even that on a Loyalist or Northern Government building. Their flag was the Union Jack.

He said, with a grin, 'It's a wonder the damned Orangemen don't drop the green bit from our flag, or put it last and change it to dirty dark and yellowy green, like baby's poo.' His companion was not amused.

As he and some Provos from Michelin were about to leave for an initiation a few days later, Maurice said it was time he, too, was formally sworn in as a Provo.

'Jeez, you're getting high in the ranks,' said the man who would run the event. 'And you haven't been sworn in yet? Well, we'll do you today.'

About a minute later, they were summoned to get to the scene of a bombing by Loyalists that had killed a woman and injured six civilians. The Provos' hunting failed to find the bombers. Maurice did not remind his colleagues again of his non-initiation.

He joined twenty two other Michelin Provos to celebrate St. Patrick's Day on the evening of 17 March 1971 at McGurk's Bar on North Queen Street. They called it the Tranmore Bar. Maurice, in a green jacket, had walked by celebraters on the way to the pub but it was less of an event in Belfast, he saw, than in Birmingham's Irish Sparkhill. Less than in New York City and Sydney, hosts to yearly televised St. Pat's Day parades.

There was no parading of Catholics that he knew of in the North. Targets, they would be, for Paisleyite Orangemen and their assorted confederates, who sometimes killed Catholic protesters at Orange Day parades.

Two big bouncers, whom he now knew, frisked at the front door men and women they did not recognise, regardless of their greenery. Maurice was pleased to see the security. Catholic pubs were prime targets. McGurks would be an obvious one tonight.

He enthusiastically joined in the merriment but drank sparingly. Three of the celebraters were men he had seen kill people recently. *Oops, four of them*, he corrected, *counting M. Tansey.*

There was general anger at the Orange Lodge parade two days ago in Catholic suburbs, again protected by British soldiers. The big talking point was that the British Army's GOC in the province, Lieutenant General Erskine-Crum, died that day in hospital. It was a month since his heart attack, less than two weeks into the job. The Provos and others drank to the Republicans' success in stressing the general to death.

A man at the bar, Harold, said the word in the army was that the interim GOC and Director of Ops, war hero Lieutenant General Harry Tuzo, would remain at the job.

Martin McGuinness, who had arrived soon after Maurice, agreed. The Provos had good information about the army, Maurice realised. They drank to the prospect of Tuzo being the next to stress out.

Maurice was privately annoyed by the talk of violence. But he enjoyed the session, especially the music from a fiddler, guitarist, pianist, drummer and a woman singer. They performed traditional ballads of Ireland and a few modern airs. He joined with gusto in singing his old favourites, *Tim Finnegan's Wake* and *The Mountains of Mourne*. When pouring out *Galway Bay*, they used the original lyric, 'Yet the *English* (not the strangers) came and tried to teach us their ways…'

McGuinness sidled up to him. 'You're doing well, Maurice. Now you're a real Provo, a damned good one. I want you to join in our planning sessions. Okay?'

'I'd like that, Marty.'

'Good. You'll be hearing of a meeting to attend very soon.'

Their leader from Derry raised his glass, clinked it against his new mate's, finished the drink and went home. London would be rapt about this elevation, Maurie mused.

In the morning three days later, he found a quiet spot at home and penned a one-page note to the London bag number. Again feeling awkward about not having a name to write at the top of it, he settled for Sir/Madam.

It informed Bernard or whomever that Tansey the spy had become a planner of Provo activities. The note gave the names of five more Provos he had mixed with.

They included the two with whom he had shot the terrified man in the quarry off Mountain Road but Maurice still refrained from recording the murder. Nor did he mention four shootings he had participated in with other men. He reminded himself again that those events were specifically not in his brief and he had learned of them only hours beforehand.

He walked from Thirlmere Gardens to the central city post office in Royal Avenue to express-mail it. But, being a Saturday, the place was closed. The letter box there was no good. He had to pay in the office for the express delivery. Walking home, he reflected that his messages to London would go quicker by carrier pigeon.

He mailed the note on the Monday morning, anticipating that the five names would be added to London's list of militants. There might be some arrests.

To perform well for his anonymous bosses, get information about planned atrocities and their objectives in plenty of time for the army to prevent at least some of the horrors, Maurice was keen to get involved in those Provo planning sessions; their day-to-day preparations.

In a back room at a pub, he learned that a Provo bomb-making garage was in a back street off the Falls Road, behind Saint Dominic Grammar School, close to Cavendish Street. Also, after being asked at work by Marty to be there, he joined six Provos in a private room in a pub. They planned a car bombing in a busy Belfast street where and when Loyalists would gather for a party.

His news to London resulted in several troops raiding the garage where the bomb was waiting in a hitherto no-go area for soldiers and the RUC. Soldiers also were there waiting when Provos drove up with a yet-to-be-fused bomb in a van outside the house where the Loyalist party had begun. Four Provos he had named were jailed.

Maurice hoped the Provos did not link him to the arrests, as the bombing was decided on at the first planning session he attended.

Over the following few weeks, he passed on to London specific details---the where, when and who – of six planned car-bombings in public places in Belfast and Derry. He was frustrated by the blasts often being planned only a day or so in advance.

Despite his hurrying to the nearest post offices, expecting his expressed letters to be in London the next day, the Secret Service or whatever would be finding out about them only a day, sometimes only a few hours, before the bombs exploded. Sometimes afterwards.

He hoped they checked their mail box every morning and afternoon. Why the hell did he not have a dead-drop in Belfast for alerting a local control, who need not know his identity?

He also gave London the names of two more bomb makers, who soon after were arrested. The bombs which he saw were highly-lethal, made from fertiliser soaked in diesel oil. They were usually made only a day of two before they were ignited. The detonators and timing devices were inserted minutes before the stolen vehicles housing the bombs were in place for their deadly demise.

Maurice participated in two bombings that killed three people. No army patrol was at either event, to his guilt-ridden relief. He had told London sufficiently in advance but did not anticipate to them that he was likely to take part in the atrocities.

He understood that, for his own safety, MI6 did not want to react to all of his information. Two more planned bombings he had alerted London to were averted by obviously-informed army patrols swooping on bomb-loaded vehicles.

But, oddly to him, the troopers arrived after the drivers and fuse-setters of one bomb had left. Perhaps London had been late letting them know. He was sure that at least the British Army would respond quickly to any tip of a planned outrage.

10. The extortionists, dismemberers

May 1971

Soon after eleven one night, when Maurice's car was being serviced at a garage, three Provo mates from Michelin said they would give him a lift home to Thirlmere Gardens. It was near the home of their driver, Jimmy McCabe, who was not related to Maurice's sulphuric father's mate, Irish patriot Eddie McCabe.

Jimmy said he would take a different route from normal by going left off the Antrim Road into North Circular Road. He wanted to minimise the possibility of confronting an RUC or army road block. A stash of weapons was in the boot.

They had been stopped a few times at such blocks on the usual route Jimmy and other Michelin men took to go to and from their homes in the city's predominantly-Catholic western suburbs.

Near New Lodge, a few blocks from Maurice's drop-off point, they were stopped by a road block staffed by armed British soldiers. He cursed anxiously in the rear passenger seat, fearing the troopers would recognise him.

'What the fuck do we do?' Jimmy asked urgently. 'They'll find the gear in the boot and we'll go to jail.'

'Go off left there,' said Tom, beside him. 'Into New Lodge Road.'

'Nah,' Maurice replied. 'The army will be up there, too. Or these ones will radio ahead.'Jimmy, however, sped the car to the left. They flashed past a couple of soldiers but, after a kilometre, more soldiers were ready in front of them. They went into a narrow street that turned out to be a dead-ender.

'At least we're in Catholic territory, with time to arm ourselves before they get here,' said Jimmy as he left the car. 'Let's get the guns.'

Each of the four grabbed a weapon and abandoned the car. Maurice chose a Beretta 9 mm semi-automatic pistol with a full magazine of bullets. His life was in peril, but he was not going to aim his shots at soldiers if they arrived. They ran in the dark to near the end of the quiet alley. A lane up there looked a good place to hide in.

But before they reached the lane, a Land Rover full of soldiers arrived and began firing at them. The four returned fire while still running. They stopped, stunned, as they came under fire from ahead. 'Has the army surrounded us?' cried Tom.

'No,' Maurice called as he fired again, above the soldiers' heads. 'The new shooters must be Catholics! They think we're Loyalists.'

They crouched behind a car in the alley, being shot at from guns in front of and behind them. Tom, crouched next to Maurice, was shot in the back from what they hoped was a Catholic barricade.

Jimmy screamed at the shooters behind them. 'We're Catholic IRA. Provos! Trying to get away from the bloody British Army!'

A man's voice boomed as the fusillade from there stopped. 'Okay. Come on up to us. We'll cover you as you go.'

The soldiers stayed behind their Land Rover, firing a few shots in reply to firing now directed at them from the barricade as the escapees, Maurice carrying unconscious Thomas, scurried to six men with rifles behind a low wall of bricks. One applied first aid to Tom's back before he declared that the man was dead.

'I'm Jacko,' the evident leader told them. 'We live near here and heard the commotion. Thought you were damned Paisleyites. Glad we could help. With your mate dead, stay with us for a while, in case the army gets up behind us. But it's not likely. They'll cop resistance if they do. You're in a tough area, a no-goer for Loyalists.'

The three survivors did not tell their saviours that it was they who had killed Tom. Gunfire was exchanged sporadically until the first glimmer of dawn and the soldiers drove their vehicle away. The street was quiet.

The locals showed the way to drive Jimmy's bullet-riddled car along a network of narrow lanes to safety. Tom's body was in the boot with the rest of the guns. The car, high on the army's and RUC's wanted list, was used in a street bombing ahead of a boozy and musical wake for dead Tom. Using Gaelic, Maurice figured, the locals called the wake a faire.

Hundreds marched behind the coffin to Milltown Cemetery for Tom's funeral.

Maurice was pleased that his letters to London had prevented the slaying and injuring of a lot of people, mostly non-combatants. That was the pro side. It was the con side that kept him awake at night.

By late in May 1971, he had counted nine dead, two of them children, who would have been saved if the Secret Service or the army had acted on all his alerts. Surely, he felt, Belfast's army top-brass now knew there was a snoop in the Provos.

Usually at strategy meetings in back rooms of pubs, Maurice learned in advance of the exploding of small parcel bombs left in Protestant-patronised cafes, restaurants and pubs. Parcel jobs had been more-commonly used in the years before car bombing. Careful not to be too inquisitive, Maurice never found out at that time where and by whom those sinister little killers were made. His alerts to London, however, resulted in the arrests of a few bomb planters.

The abuse hurled at the meetings about the Reverend Paisley often made him wonder why the cleric was not targetted. But such an assassination would inflame the Troubles to new heights, causing the determined targetting of IRA leaders.

He and McGuinness, who missed some Belfast meetings when he was in Derry, drank less than the others at the planning sessions. A few Provos there said they would love to get an opportunity to slay 48-years-old British Army General Sir Anthony Farrar-Hockley.

The general had just been on television naming Provo and Official IRA leaders, including militants Maurice had named to London. The general blamed the leaders for an outbreak of bombing and shooting in Belfast's Clonard district. He had threatened forceful retaliation.

Maurice had had direct contact with the gracious general when Farrar-Hockley was a brigadier in the young spy's paratrooper days. Farrar-Hockley had escaped many times from prisoner-of-war camps in North Korea, where he had been brutally tortured.

Most soldiers and the public knew him as Farrar the para. To the Provos, he was Sir Horror Fuckley.

'We ought to track the bastard's movements and stick it to him,' said a young man named Billy. 'The Clonard flare-up was the doings of the Loyalists. We only retaliated.'

They agreed to organise an assassination of the general. Soon. The Officials would be after him also, they were sure.

'Billy's just reminded me of something,' said Martin McGuinness. 'You remember me telling you, Maurice, how the Official IRA's Billy Reid got hold of a machine gun and recklessly killed a Brit soldier in the Ardoyne? Ensign Robert Curtis, it was. The first Brit soldier killed in the North in fifty years?'

'Sure do,' said Tansey.

'Well, Reid has just been killed. By the army, I think, who were stalking the silly twit.'

Maurice next morning mailed to London an urgent warning to be relayed to the general. Farrar-Hockley quietly left Ireland a week later. As a result of his letter, Maurice assumed. He had probably saved another life.

That alone, he later figured, should justify his being a spy. General Farrar-Hockley was destined to be NATO's Commander in Chief, Allied Forces, in Northern Europe.

IRA ire at the army, its frustration perhaps at Farrar-Hockley leaving before the assassins could get to him, was reflected many months later when a bomb was planted at Maurice's former HQ at the Parachute Regiment barracks at Aldershot.

But the bomb setters wrongly placed it near a kitchen. It killed a Catholic chaplain, a gardener and five civilian women. Maurice had not known in advance about it, the work of the Official IRA. He hoped London did not blame him for them not being warned.

He sometimes visited, with Carol and Allen, the home of Carol's mother in Hillview Drive, off Ballyclare Road, near Glengormley. It was a comfortable residence, where he was made welcome. It was his safe-house in waiting.

More and more violence was planned in lowered tones at their big table in the canteen at the Michelin factory during the twenty-minute breaks from work. He now felt he was a real spy. And a sleazy pedlar of hate and violence, and a killer, in the interests of Britain. Still, he had anticipated this. He drew satisfaction, however, from calculating that his alerts to London had prevented close to a hundred innocent civilians from being killed. They were about 50/50 Republicans and Loyalists.

He now felt sure that Bernard and the officers who put him into this had not lied. He must be Britain's first and only undercover agent planted among the North's Republican militants. A deniable and expendable one.

A gullible pawn? Perhaps the Brits had not found anyone else qualified and crazy enough to take this on, he guessed. Although he had given London his home address and phone number, they had not contacted him. Nor had he received any payment.

A quick way of getting involved with more Provos, Maurice decided, was by selling his car. Not having one. For now, anyway. With no public transport on that route, he told the men at the canteen table, it was a hassle to have to walk to and from Mallusk's Michelin.

Regular transport to and from work was arranged immediately. Fellow Provo employees worked out a roster to pick him up and drop him near home at the intersection of Old Cavehill Road and North Circular Road. It hastened him becoming one of the boys, hearing more about planned violence.

In return for these rides, he bought his drivers and their companions a few drinks after day shifts. His largesse was appreciated. He became a regular at Provo-patronised bars and clubs like McGurk's, the Glen, and the Crown in Victoria Street.

As requested, he planted several small incendiary devices in department stores. He did it as late as possible on Saturday afternoons, soon before the stores closed. This reduced the chances of the bombs being found. More importantly to him, they were set to ignite hours after the stores were emptied of customers and, he hoped, staff.

The devices ranged from the size of cigarette packets to cigar boxes. He generally tried on garments then returned them to the racks with the devices in pockets. Sometimes he hid primed explosives in ladies' clothes sections after lifting garments from racks. When staff asked if he needed assistance, he said he was okay; just looking for a gift for his wife. A couple of times he sneaked a bomb under cushions on sofas in furniture departments.

He seldom had time to warn London, but was enormously thankful that the destruction he caused in the stores did not kill anyone. The practice, aimed at causing havoc, continued for only a couple of months until shop security was upgraded.

Maurice was glad he had not been questioned by officialdom. If the army had grabbed him, at least a few paras would recognise their Big One Five.

He often heard Provos mention money they collected from shopkeepers, restaurateurs and even banks to buy weaponry. It would be protection money, extortion, so the money takers did not bomb the premises.

Maurice suspected that much of the money was pocketed by the collectors, as were some of the proceeds from the Provos' robbing of banks and post offices. He was particularly disgusted with this common-criminal aspect of the IRA.

Before they were married, he had driven Carol and Allen across the province's south-west border to stay for a Saturday night in the marvellous old town of Manorhamilton, North Leitrim. He had enjoyed visits there when a para, on holiday with colleague Bob Rossan. The family posed as Catholic tourists from England. Tourism was important to the Republic's economy but, Maurice knew, in the North tourism was nearly nil.

They stayed in a comfortable hotel built of local stone. After Carol and Allen went to bed following a splendid dinner and good craic, Maurice had some drinks with the engaging publican, who had lent him a fishing rod to catch a salmon in a nearby stream. The publican confided that he was a long-time Republican whose support for the Cause had waned lately. Since he was forced to part with £50 a week to IRA men from the North.

The man said his hotel might be bombed out of business if he did not pay, or if he reported them to the Garda, the Irish Republic's national police service.

A couple of local men joined the two of them at the bar. In reply to his question, they told Maurice the town was named after a rotten bloody tyrant, an Englishman named Sir Frederick Hamilton.

In the 1620s, the English had seized the town and surrounding countryside from the old and popular clan of rulers, the O'Rourkes. The whole lot, every little farm nearby, was given to Hamilton by the English rulers as a reward for his contribution in England's recent European wars. Hamilton had used local slave labour to build nearby Manorhamilton Castle, the ruins of which Maurice could (and did) explore.

Under Hamilton's rule, the town became a community of desperate peasants. Most of the meat and vegetables they produced was shipped to England, making the local dictator wealthy.

Hamilton regularly sent sword-slashing horsemen, former English soldiers, to the town to kidnap any pretty girl they saw in the street or at the town market. Not one of the girls was seen again. Hamilton locked them in his dungeon, and raped them whenever he liked, Maurice was told.

When he tired of a girl, she was given as a plaything for his personal guards. Then she was murdered – burnt to cinders or buried in the grounds of the castle. Over nearly twenty years, the fuming locals said, a hundred girls fed Hamilton's lust.

Rebellions by groups of locals were brutally repelled, until one lot sneaked into the besieged castle in 1642. But Hamilton escaped with a bag of money through a secret tunnel and went to Scotland.

The place was now being restored as a tourist magnet, with a display that would tell the awful tale of tyranny that followed England's plundering, at least in part because the Irish would not join the new church of the Protestants.

Maurice now knew that the Republic from Manorhamilton to the Atlantic coast, including Sligo, was a favourite holiday retreat and hiding place for IRA activists based in the province. The district was nearly free of Loyalist terrorists.

One spot on the coast, Bundoran, in County Donegal, was a special reserve for Provos in hiding. It was also a regular destination for shipments of ammunition, guns and explosives. The area was destined to loom as the scene of a horror that shocked the world.

When Maurice returned to Manorhamilton with his family a few months later, two Provos he knew were at the bar, ending a terse conversation with the publican.

The militants looked surprised to see their big colleague. They promptly left, enabling Maurice to make out he did not know them. They were staying at Bundoran, he assumed, and were collecting extortion money.

Back in Belfast, Maurice felt that the risk of him being killed had mounted but, since he first jumped from an aircraft with the paras, he was prepared for an early death. That time, he had only half-expected the 'chute to open.

Sure, he would fight all the way if his life was imperilled but he still did not expect to live beyond about the age of 35. He had at least ten more years to go. His fearlessness in those days, he much later reflected, was dumb. The result, it was, of the way the army trained its men.

June 1971

By now Maurice had found out how brutal PIRA punishment could be. Even for what he deemed minor misdemeanours.

About midday one Wednesday, after he had completed a night shift, he was in a pub with a few Provos, chatting about recent activities.

Michael, of quarry murder infamy, asked four of them to go with him to the Cracked Cup Club, in the Lower Falls.

The men, including Maurice, strolled up to Joe Donnelley, a small, young Provo who was drinking there. Donnelley was genially asked to accompany them outside. The man followed them to the street without any fuss.

He was pushed into the back seat of their car and taken to a residence by the Stratford Gardens in the Ardoyne, West Belfast. The five of them went to the kitchen. Donnelley was told that he was an 'earwig'. Maurice was not told, nor did he ask, what Donnelley had done wrong. Clearly, he had revealed a Provo secret to the wrong person. Maybe he had bragged in a pub about a job he had been on.

'You're a rotten gobshite, Donnelley,' said Michael. 'You've got a big mouth.'

Two men, nearly as big as Maurice, bent their victim head-first over a sink. 'Mickey's gonna make sure ya never hear too much again,' he was told. Michael produced a hacksaw. He sawed off Donnelley's left ear while he screamed in pain. The severed ear was thrown out the back door, where two dogs fought over it.

Stricken Joe was given a towel to press against his ear hole to minimise the spilling of blood on the carpet on the way out of the premises.

'You're fooken lucky you didn't get a bullet, or lose the other ear, too,' said his main tormenter.

Late in June, Maurice happened to stroll into the same property in the Ardoyne, which he suspected was a scene of bomb making. He was after firm evidence he could relate to London. Two men there said his timing was a handy fluke. They were about to punish a boy aged 17 for sexually molesting a fourteen year-old girl on her way home from school. She had told her parents about it. They informed the Provos.

The two took Maurice to a garden shed, where a scared-looking lad was tied to a chair. Maurice looked on, trying to conceal his alarm, as the teenager, crying his apologies, was freed from the chair.

His right hand was held on a metal workbench and covered with a wooden cheese board. The lad screamed as the board was bashed nine or ten times with a lump hammer, a heavy metal job that surveyors used to drive pegs into the ground. The hand was a smashed, bleeding mess. Maurice was sure every bone was shattered.

'That's just a damned warning not to rape a girl again,' the boy was told as he stood, trembling and horrified.

'I didn't rape her!' he cried, not daring to look at his hand. 'I just felt her up.'

'You piss orf,' the hammerer told him.

It was a torture that bystander Tansey could not have participated in, regardless of the circumstances. That sort of lusting on behalf of complainers, he reflected, had been the foundation of the Italian Mafia.

The PIRA commander in his part of town had lately instructed members of his unit to remove the fingers of a man, in his mid 30s, for having 'sticky fingers'.

He had allegedly stolen money from the till in a pub that was popular with the Provos and where he had been a barman for many years. The whole thing, Maurice was told, was over in a flash. The barman's right hand was held down on a chopping block while a meat cleaver did the bloody damage.

The man was left with half of one thumb. No fingers. The injury made him unfit ever to work in a pub again, or any place where money was handled. The spy from Birmingham felt it was contradictory for the outfit seething with thieves to do that.

Later, Maurice was one of four ordered to attack a military foot- or vehicle-patrol by RUC or British soldiers in the Lower Falls. It was suggested that they select their victims, drive ahead of them and wait in ambush.

Before that could be done, they were to travel south from the Ardoyne to Andersontown to get ammunition, which was in short supply. They entered a smart-looking house, compared with the others in the neighbourhood. The ammunition was hidden in a hole in the kitchen wall behind a cabinet.

With it, the four proceeded on their daytime assignment. It was completed without any of them being injured. Maurice again fired above their prey but the ambush crippled, maybe killed, two RUC men.

Martin McGuinness had recently given his buddy Tansey a .22 Taurus revolver, possibly the one with which he had shot the man in the quarry. In case of a raid at home, and to keep Carol ignorant of it, he hid the gun in a roof space under an insulation batt.

It took him only seconds to get hold of it, reaching above a railing that ran along the top of the staircase. The gun's presence, sometimes on jobs for the Provos, gave him a small amount of security. It might be his lifesaver.

He became a regular at games of cards and dominoes at PIRA clubs, pubs and sometimes private homes, mainly in the Falls Road district. Activist priests were regulars at the gatherings. To Maurice's chagrin, they participated keenly in planning killings.

A poker player one night at the Felon's Club, just off the Falls Road, was bespectacled Denis Donaldson. His intelligence and air of authority immediately impressed the big tyre maker. Denis was small and slim, with a warm personality. A good bluffer at poker.

Some players there, when leaving the table with Maurice to get drinks, said they thought Donaldson was important for the future of the Cause – moreso than even Martin McGuinness. Genial little Denny reputedly had a winning way with women; could charm the legs off a chair.

Maurice was a guest at the party that celebrated Denny's 21st birthday. After that, the two met often, sometimes at Denny's home. He and Martin McGuinness were soon Maurice's best friends in the province, the MI6 snoop guiltily felt.

It became pretty clear to Maurice that Denis Donaldson aspired to become a heavyweight in Sinn Fein. Denny dearly wanted to see a united Ireland in his lifetime, and help to achieve that. Ironically, Maurice admitted to himself, he and Denny had vastly different means of trying to get the same result.

Denny had joined the IRA as a youth in the Republic's County Donegal, had helped defend St Matthew's chapel in Short Strand from a Loyalist attack a year beforehand, and was a mate of Provo hunger striker in jail, Bobby Sands. Donaldson and Sands had served time at Long Kesh, also known as Maze Prison, and at the RAF base at Lisbum, south-west of Belfast, for paramilitary offences.

Maurice never heard of Denny being involved in planning bombings or shootings. He did not even own a firearm, he told Maurice over a drink.

However, Maurice felt that engaging Denny's attachment to the Provos, like his own, had absolute limits. Both men were appalled at their fellow freedom fighters' personal revenge killings, robberies and extortion and torturing. The two kept in touch for many months.

August 1971

After another spate of violence, Northern Ireland Prime Minister Brian Faulkner ordered Operation Demetrius, commonly called the Internment. It began on Monday, 9 August.

The British Army, supported by the Royal Ulster Constabulary, swept throughout the province, grabbing all who were, or might be, on a list of four-hundred and fifty alleged militants considered a threat to the community.

The list did not include M. Tansey. It had come from Britain's Special Branch, MI5 and MI6, Maurice reckoned.

The soldiers killed ten civilians and arrested and crammed 342 indefinitely into Long Kesh Internment camp, without trial and mostly with no specific charges being laid. The Internment caused rioting in every community, fuelling widespread and enduring enmity against the British Army.

The Ulster Volunteer Force, along with other Loyalist gangs including the Shankill Defence Association, the recently-formed Tara Loyalist evangelicals, and the Ulster Protestant Volunteers, had lately bombed and killed scores of non-combatant civilians.

Prime Minister Faulkner urged the soldiers to arrest some Protestants but, as author Tim Pat Coogan's book *The Troubles* later confirmed to Maurice, not one member of those fraternities was gathered in the Internment trawl.

Some Provos Maurice had named to London were interned. But most of them he mixed with laid low, stayed away from their usual haunts, and avoided the roundup. Many publicans must have had a lean time.

He also was aware of at least twenty interned Catholics who had no connection with Republican militants. They were caught at the wrong places at the wrong times. He was tempted to write to London about that but he decided that relating those facts would infer a bias in favour of Republicans. He continued reporting to London about once a week. He knew of army responses to about half of his info.

As soon as the Internment began, Maurice spent his time when not at work at home, far enough away from the danger zones. He was again disgusted at his former para colleagues, their flouting of citizens' democratic rights.

He felt the British Government would soon get more involved in the North, trying to curb the province's reckless government, even its own rampaging troops. It soon happened.

In response to public and Parliamentary disquiet, a month after the beginning of the Internment London commissioned a committee of inquiry into the legal and moral aspects of the affair. Its report in March 1972 found that the Internment flagrantly breached the law.

British Prime Minister Edward Heath imposed direct rule on the province from London. But a less-offensive form of Internment was destined to continue until 5 December, 1975. During that time, 1,874 Irish Nationalists and 107 Loyalists were interned. Community anger raged, especially when the brutal nature of interrogations at Long Kesh became public.

A serving officer of the British Royal Marines there declared of the Internment, 'It has, in fact, increased terrorist activity, perhaps boosted IRA recruitment, polarised further the Catholic and Protestant communities and reduced the ranks of the much-needed Catholic moderates.' Tansey agreed with that.

11. Oh, brother…

November 1971

Carol received the telephone call at home when Maurice was at work. The caller was his younger brother Kieran, who told the ex-para's wife that he, too, was now a paratrooper.

'Do you and Maurice mind if I call on you for a visit for a few days?' he asked.

Carol had heard about Kieran from her husband. The Protestant bride, who still had no notion that Maurice was a Provo and spying on them, happily invited Kieran to be their guest for as long as he liked.

'I thought it would be good for you to catch up with him after so long,' she explained when an astonished Maurice returned home that evening. He had not seen Kieran for four years.

He wondered uneasily how his little brother obtained their phone number, which was listed in the directory in Carol's pre-marriage name. Not even his parents had it. On the few occasions he had telephoned them from Belfast, he used a public phone. They thought he lived in the Republic. He could not risk his parents knowing, thus telling the Irish in Birmingham, that their ex-para son was making tyres in Belfast.

Nor did he want Presbyterian Carol taking calls from Birmingham or overhearing his side of conversations with his parents. His sister no longer lived with them at Sparkhill. Maurice had no idea where aloof Maureen was. She was happily married, he hoped.

And, as well as the phone number, Kieran evidently already knew his brother's address. He had not asked Carol for it so he could get there from the ferry by taxi.

Maurice had told his spymasters his new address and phone number in the fruitless hope so far of getting a communication from them. Perhaps even some wages. Would they leak that to the army? Which leaked it to Kieran? The thought of the army knowing he was at

Thirlmere Gardens, and telling a young para private, even though he was Maurice's brother, was frightening.

He reminded himself that the Belfast army top brass would know, from the alerts they had received, that Britain had a spook in the Provos. Gossipy Kieran was likely to tell para and Birmingham Irish mates that Maurice worked at Michelin. The news would spread to paras in Belfast. Some of them might contact Big One Five at the factory.

Kieran might even know or suspect that his big brother was Britain's spy. This was much more alarming. Was Kieran on a crazy assignment to check on his only brother, who loved him?

Kieran even telling their parents that Maurice lived in Belfast would also be disastrous. Skulduggery might be afoot. While he was here, Kieran might spill the beans to him.

Kieran was all smiles when he arrived in a taxi two days later. He told them over coffee he was in Maurice's old platoon and company. He had not brought his uniform. He had joined the army, he said, soon after Maurice left the force, nearly six months ago.

Maurice at first thought it was a lie. How could at-least-once sickly and still skinny little Kieran pass the army's fitness tests? He would be hopeless in single combat. Easy pickings for para thugs!

On the first night with them, Kieran twice mentioned their father Nicholas' continued friendship with Labour Party heavy Roy Hattersley. And the politician's support for the Republican Cause.

Why is he prattling on about Hattersley? Maurice asked himself as he changed the subject. Was Kieran trying to get an inference that Hattersley was a friend of the IRA?

Despite Martin McGuinness' familiarity with but reluctance to talk about Hattersley, Maurice doubted that the politician was any more than a concerned observer of the plight of Northern Ireland's Catholics.

From a public telephone near work, Maurice rang the army barracks at Aldershot. Without giving his name, he asked how he could contact Private Kieran Tansey. After checking a list, a woman said Private Tansey was on leave. So, the lad was a para all right.

Maurice appreciated Kieran's affection for Allen, now nearly six, walking with him to and from school sometimes. The young para was also clearly fond of Carol. The brothers bonded again over a few drinks at a local pub. But Maurice was not enlightened as to how Kieran had found them, or why he was really in Belfast.

They remembered together the days of terror at home at Sparkhill, the time Maurice struck their dad with a broom to stop his again bashing of their mother. Maurice having to run away from enraged Nicholas, sleeping for a week in alleys.

'But I continued going to the English Martyrs primary school,' Maurice said. 'I had to go home when my clothes were stinking too much. At least Dad was a bit quieter after that.'

A bitter memory for the brothers was the Sunday morning after their sister Maureen and Maurice had returned from Mass, when their father slipped on vomit spewed by their lovely old cat, tritely-named Pussy. Something had disagreed with Pussy. Apart from Nicholas's ignoring of her, she was the sole common bond in the rest of the riven family.

Furious Nicholas had stormed to the backyard and returned with a hessian bag and some rope. He grabbed Pussy by the tail and thrust her into the bag, tightly tying the top of it.

He told Maurice, then aged eight, 'It's coming with *me*, you are. You'll be seeing what this friggin little bastard gets.'

Picking up a glass of wine, Kieran said, 'I was near spewing myself over what that meant as you climbed into the truck with him. I was only four then.'

The truck had stopped on a bridge over a canal. The big builder got out and said, 'Watch this.' He threw the Pussy-bearing bag into the water.

'I stood, dumbfounded,' Maurice recalled. 'The bag didn't sink. It floated down the waterway as Pussy shook it.' Maurice had heard desperate wailing. His father wore a mean grin. The non-swimmer boy started to run and jump into the water and rescue Pussy. He was gripped by a firm hand around the back of his neck.

'Let the bastard drown. And it's against the law to go in the canal. It's full a shit, and deep.'

Fighting back tears, Maurice had looked up at his father. 'I'll make my own way home, so you can go to the pub.'

Not a bad idea, it seemed. Nicholas drove off. Maurice scrambled down the embankment in a desperate attempt to retrieve his only-ever pet from the foul current. He clutched a limb from a tree and tried to reach the bag, still partly afloat in the deep and freezing murk. He had lain in tears of loss and frustration as the agitation stopped. The bag sank.

'I'll never forget the horror when you ran home and told us about it,' said Kieran. 'I was stunned. We never had another pet.'

After spending a week with his brother and sister-in-law, Kieran returned to England and the army. He would be back, he had promised. Maurice hoped so. He had enjoyed their times together and wanted to find out what was going on.

Another skirmish with British Army foot patrols took place in November. Maurice and two other Provos were let into a Catholic Church by a priest who was well aware of what they were up to. The church was on the Glen Road, off the Falls Road.

The three gunmen, Tansey aiming above their targets, opened fire from the church at an army patrol passing along the street. A few soldiers were at least injured. The shooters retreated through the church's rear door, which the priest locked behind them before troops ran in through the front.

The three escaped across open parkland as, Maurice learned later, the priest claimed sweet ignorance of the shooting.

The Provos gave him the Armalite AR 18 rifle that he used in the church. They were hard to come by, issued only to elite combatants. Its removable stock importantly made the weapon easy to conceal.

Evidently, none of Tansey's associates was aware that his wife was a Protestant. He had heard of Catholics and Protestants being knee-capped, also tarred and feathered, for being in mixed marriages.

Carol held to her promise never to reveal to friends that her husband was a Catholic. The cruel partisanship of the place, Maurice knew, was fostered by clerics on both sides.

Nearing Christmas, his mind was beset by conflict – his loyalty to Britain versus love for his Irish Catholic heritage, compassion for the downtrodden. There was also unease about his own wellbeing continuing.

The good news was satisfaction that his alerts to London had now prevented events at which perhaps two hundred innocents would have been killed, hundreds more injured. The bad news – his own crimes while spying.

He drove the getaway car after a bomb was set and exploded in Belfast's Callender Street, injuring many civilians. It was the sort of atrocity that had sickened para Tansey when he found that little girl's half foot.

In his first few months of spooking, he had hoped to get a wad of money from MI6. He now assumed that there would never be payment for this bloody assignment.

But, already saving lives, getting at least twenty gunmen imprisoned, he would keep at it. If those brutes were still on the streets, more innocents would have been savaged.

He had now given London the names and whereabouts of most of the members of the Provo Belfast Brigade. He counted twenty eight car bombings he had averted in his ten months of spooking. He had settled the Troubles a bit.

But sometimes arriving Provos had seen security forces waiting at planned bombing sites that London had been alerted to. The terrorists had then bombed less-populated locations, with fewer casualties.

Maurice had tipped off London many days ahead of four expected arrivals of munitions by ship, but three cargoes had arrived at the scheduled drop points without incident. Surely, he reckoned, MI6's apparent strategy of saving Tansey's skin by not acting on some alerts should not have made them ignore *all* of those letters.

After wondering if he should do it, he sent London a week before the event the details of a big Provo birthday celebration he was invited to at McGurk's Bar, North Belfast, on the night of Saturday, 4 December 1971. He had gone to the bar often since shortly before celebrating St. Patrick's Day there. As he posted the letter, he decided that this probably was the last time he would despatch an alert about a Provo do.

He would not attend this one. With the blood-lusting army raiding the bar as part of the Internment, the Provos would have to wonder how the army found out about it. Upcoming celebrations were matters of strict security. He did not want any Provo fingers, or guns, pointed at him.

He was comforted by the knowledge that at least two capable security bouncers at the front door at McGurk's should ensure that Loyalists would not be able to blow up the place.

Maurice returned from his early-morning jog on Sunday to hear on the radio that McGurk's and its Provo celebraters had been blown up by at least one big bomb. The building had collapsed, killing fifteen people. Three of them were women, two were children. Seventeen were seriously injured.

It was the biggest death toll from a single bombing in Belfast since the new outbreak of the Troubles, the beginning of what the newspapers called the dirty war, more than two years back.

At first, Maurice thought a Provo bomb must have self-detonated while young volunteers, as sometimes happened, were being taught bomb-craft in a back room. But that afternoon a radio broadcast said the Ulster Volunteer Force, the most violent of all Loyalist gangs, had victoriously claimed responsibility for the atrocity.

A statement claimed a UVF team had been ordered to plant a bomb in The Glen, another popular Provo pub on North Queen Street. When they arrived there, the bombers had heard that a big affair was under way at McGurk's. So, by means Maurice never knew, the bomb was planted in the McGurk's front porch.

It exploded soon after the planters drove away. It was odd to him that the UVF's statement went into detail about them first going to another pub. They had never related that sort of thing before. It was as if they were hiding the real source of the information, received well in advance, that sent them to McGurk's.

He had an anguishing suspicion that, in this vicious mood of the Internment, his London bosses or army brass in Belfast had leaked the details of the planned celebration to the UVF. Surely not, he hoped. If that was so, the mass killing was his fault.

It was a state secret, but Maurice knew Britain's intelligence-related Government Communication Headquarters, the GCHQ in Cheltenham, could monitor any telephone conversation in the province. Still, he rang the home numbers of three Provo friends who were likely to have been at McGurk's.

The first, Tim, was in shock. He related details of the gore, which he had avoided only because he was in the men's at the time of the explosion. He had climbed out of the place, dragging an injured young boy, climbing over bodies and wreckage.

Tim reported that popular publican Pat McGurk's wife Philomena and their daughter, a sweet kid aged 12 who Maurice had met, had been killed. Pat McGurk himself and his three sons who lived upstairs were in hospital, badly wounded.

Maurice's second call was not answered. The man and wife living there had been killed, he learned later. For a moment on call three, all he heard was a woman crying. 'Oh, Jesus, they've *gone*,' he heard between sobs. 'Those, those vile, bastard Loyalists!'

'*Who's* gone, Mary?' he asked gently.

'Oh, Maurie, it's Fred and our daughter Sally. She was only fifteen. Blown up, they were, the police told me.'

He was offering his condolences when weeping Mary hung up. Fred had been a mate at Michelin. Maurice had dined at Fred's and Mary's home, enjoyed their hospitality. He told Carol, standing nearby, that the victims at McGurk's included a Michelin workmate and his teenage daughter. Plus publican Patrick's wife and daughter.

'What horror!' she said sombrely. 'With Michelin people there, why weren't we invited?'

'We *were*, dear,' he told her. 'But it was a Catholic show. As you're a Presbyterian and we're in a mixed marriage, I said we couldn't make it.'

'Thank the good, bloody Lord,' she said and went to the kitchen.

He now had a surge of guilt and anger about London either not acting on his alert by getting the army to raid the party or perhaps them or the army telling the rampant UFV that the Provos would be celebrating at McGurk's. MI6 must have received his note five days before the bar blew up. The army had not been nearby.

At Michelin the next day, he learned that two members of its Provo cell were among the dead. Three were in hospital.

A week later, publican Patrick McGurk was out of hospital. Maurice knew the genial man well. He saw the publican on television, still distressed about the loss of his wife and daughter. 'However,' McGurk said, 'it doesn't matter who planted the bomb. What's done can't be undone. I've been trying to keep bitterness out of it.' He asked the IRA not to retaliate.

But they did. Maurice was told joyously about a UVF volunteer being executed and another crippled by Provo gunmen. The driver of the UVF getaway car, Robert Campbell, was destined, seven years later, to admit to his role in the McGurk affair. He received fifteen sentences of life in jail but was the sole bomber charged. Perhaps, Maurice concluded, the Provos had killed all the others.

12. Life saver, life loser

December 1971

On his first wedding anniversary, Maurice was drinking with Michelin workmates in a pub in the Falls Road district. He well knew tomorrow would be the first anniversary of Carol's first bridal adultery.

The time in the pub was the prelude to his most evil, his most shameful act.

Provo official we will call Jim Macintosh walked in and told the three of them they had to carry out an assignment immediately. Macintosh had just been informed that a hitherto trusted Provo had revealed that he was about to leave the movement and join the RUC.

The man, whom Maurice knew slightly, had given in to persistent pressure from his family, who wanted him to be a part of the forces of law and order, not the Troubles. His home was in a side street, off the Crumlin Road.

True to Provo form, it was felt necessary to warn the defector in a robust way not ever to think of becoming an informer. Macintosh told them the man had considerable knowledge, gained over many years with the Provos. He had sworn never to tell IRA secrets. 'But,' said Macintosh, 'of course he would say that'.

As soon as it was made clear what punishment the official wanted, Maurice tried his hardest to avoid being involved. 'It's our first wedding anniversary,' he said. 'We've planned a special event, which I'm just about to go to.'

Jim angrily dismissed the excuse. The job would take only about half an hour, he said. Tansey was told he had better get his priorities right or risk Provo disciplinary proceedings. This job was important.

And Maurice, by just the look of his big self, Macintosh said, was intimidating. He was the ideal sort of heavy for this job. Everything was ready and waiting, their Provo senior continued. A stolen and equipped car was outside.

Maurice relented. If he backed out of this now, his spying days would be over. He, too, might become a victim of Provo retribution if he did not get out of the country in a hurry. What a bloody awful sacrifice this was to be for the benefit of the British Crown. Still, if he did not do it someone else would.

Macintosh did not accompany them. The man had simply strolled into the pub and randomly assigned the first Provos he saw there. They drove to their victim's home. Frank took from the car a 9 mm pistol. Maurice carried a paint can holding four litres of petrol.

The third raider waited in the car, their cover with an automatic rifle, as Frank knocked on the front door. When it opened, their man, now described as a deserter, stood there smiling.

He extended his hand to Frank, smiled at his big, tyre-making acquaintance. Feeling a cowardly brute, Maurice wordlessly hurled the petrol over the smiler, as instructed. But he lobbed the petrol low, on the man's waist.

Frank's pistol was in one hand and a cigarette lighter, a Zippo, was in the other. Zippos were commonly used by Provos because they stayed alight when thrown. The lighter landed at the feet of the man as he screamed in horror.

Suddenly, he was a human torch. Flames flared up to his chest.

Horrified Maurice dropped the can. In a flash, he grabbed the top of the doorframe and swung his feet at the flaming body, knocking their victim to the floor. It prevented the flames rising up to the writhing man's head.

Maurice was further distressed when he saw Christmas decorations in the house behind the flames. Their victim's wife burst through a doorway into the hall. Beside her was a girl, aged about five. They shrieked, ran towards their yelling, rolling, flaming husband and father, as Maurice dropped to the ground, picked up the can and ran behind Frank back to the car.

He himself now deserved to be in flames, he felt. The flames of hell. He thought at that moment that he would not mind the wife, who could surely identify them, reporting the immolation to the police. It was not, he sorely hoped, a *murderous* immolation.

As they sped off, his two accomplices silent, Maurice was further chastened by remembering that his instruction was to throw the petrol over the head of whoever opened that door. Hell, it could have been the kid. No way would he toss the petrol on her or her mother. Or at anyone's head, causing death.

He swore to himself that, whatever the circumstances, whatever the risk of IRA retaliation, he would never undertake such a hideous act again. At least his tossing the petrol on the man's lower body had minimised the savagery.

He later learned that the woman had promptly belted out the flames with a Christmas stocking, then tossed a bucket of water over him. Her man survived after several weeks in hospital with burns over half his body. He duly joined the Royal Ulster Constabulary.

Maurice was not aware of any police investigation. He did not even see a report of the attack in the newspapers. And London, he felt, would not want to know about it. Their victim's name is shuttered out of his mind. The shame of it haunts Maurice to this day.

On Christmas Eve Friday, brother Kieran returned to stay with them for a merry weekend. Over drinks after Christmas dinner, he hinted at knowing Maurice was a Provo, in an undercover role. On the Sunday night after his brother had gone, Carol made similar remarks, seeming to be uncharacteristically tense. He did not want her ever to know he was a spy.

He wondered what Kieran had told her but did not dare ask. She knew, of course, that the Armalite was hidden in the bedroom. It was there in case an anti-Internment riot spilled into the place, he had explained.

He was asked in January to make parcel bombs in a Belfast house. He enthusiastically agreed. He and a few others walked into the kitchen, where many bomb-making items were spread over a table. The bombs were almost ready, needing only detonators and timing devices, when all hell seemed to erupt in the street out front. They quickly hid the incriminating material.

Two of his accomplices ran out the back door as Maurice went to a front window. Two British Army Land Rovers were there. One was on fire. Soldiers were running across the street towards him.

As they were not from 2 Para, who would know Big One Five, he rushed out the front door looking confounded, hoping to obviate a search of the house. As he watched, the soldiers ran by and burst into a house two doors along the street. He assumed the attack, evidently from a Molotov cocktail, had come from there.

The soldiers returned to their colleagues, who were quelling the flames on the destroyed vehicle. The culprits must have fled out the back. Soon after, more troops cordoned off the whole street.

Most of the houses were searched, including the one where Maurice was. But the bombs and the gear used to make them, stowed under floorboards, were not found. From remarks the soldiers made, the bomb-makers confirmed that two Molotov cocktails had been hurled from the first house searched.

Maurice and the team later cursed the culprits, who so nearly caused their centre to be closed down and them put in jail.

Two of his collaborators knew the Molotov throwers would be seventeen-nineteen year-old brothers. They were keen Republicans. Maurice's mates found the brothers in hiding that evening. Both pleaded that they were striking back at the Internment.

For an unsanctioned attack that had put the bomb makers at risk, the two were shot in both their kneecaps and left howling. They faced months in hospital but, fearing terminal retribution, they never told the police who had crippled them.

On two occasions when Maurice was travelling in cars in Belfast with Provos, they had to stop at red traffic lights directly behind Land Rovers carrying members of his old platoon in 2 Para. He knew them well.

Once, Maurice was the driver. The other time he was in the front passenger seat as the soldiers stared back at them. Maurice turned away to speak to men in the back seat until the lights changed and the soldiers drove on. He turned his car away from them into the next cross-street before encountering more traffic lights.

It was the closest he had come to having his Provo cover rumbled. If they had recognised Big One Five, those soldiers – except for one – would have tumbled from the Land Rover to shake his hand. After those close shaves, he always took a back seat in cars with Provos.

One of the paras he saw at the traffic lights was named Duncan. Maurice knew Duncan would have run to him only to cause trouble.

That man was one of four soldiers who accompanied Maurice on the overnight train from Newcastle to London in January 1969. The trip followed exercises in Otterburn, Northumberland, near the border with Scotland, the scene of a mighty battle between the Scots and the invading English in 1388.

Before boarding the train, the soldiers had been upset to learn that there would be no bar facilities on the long trip. They bought bottles of whisky and beer and hid them under their uniforms.

They entered a compartment that already had one passenger, a pretty girl, aged about sixteen. She seemed to be shy, gave the impression that she was uncomfortable in their company.

Soon after the ticket inspector came through, the soldiers began drinking the grog. The girl, Helen, told them she was on her way to meet a long-time pen friend. From the looks some of his colleagues were exchanging as they swigged from the bottles, Private Tansey sensed that something was going to happen – to the girl.

He asked the four to move with him to another compartment. He told them they were making a noise and the girl was trying to sleep. But only Peter went with him. Maurice decided he had better get back after a while to see that the vulnerable kid was all right.

He and Peter returned fifteen minutes later. The girl was asleep. 'You leave this kid alone, boys. Okay?'

'Piss off, Big One Five,' Duncan muttered. 'She's okay.'

The five soldiers had assembled on the station platform in London when Maurice saw Helen walk towards another young girl, probably her pen friend. Tears rolled down Helen's face. Her make-up was smeared. Red welts were on her arms.

Duncan smirked and leaned to Maurice's ear. He pointed at the distraught-looking teenager. 'She ain't a virgin no more,' he sniggered. 'I was the first one into her. Then the others had a go. She tried to fight but it was good fun.'

Tansey immediately felt responsible. He should have stayed there with them and stopped what he had feared. Another pack rape by paras. And it seemed that the girl was not going to report them to the policeman there at the station. On the trip on to Aldershot, he resolved to deal with the bastards. One at a time.

A week later, solidly-built Duncan entered the shower cubicle next to Tansey. As he received a severe beating, Duncan the rapist was told before he lost consciousness why he was copping it.

Similar punishment was dished out to the other two. All three yelped that they would never do it again. If they ever *did*, the sceptic told them, he would know. They would be hospital cases.

Confidential conversations about Provo activity still took place in the Michelin canteen. Maurice was now the leader when McGuinness was absent.

One day Martin asked him to attend a planning meeting at eight that night in a unit in the Divis Flats complex in the Lower Falls, near his former army barracks. In order to attend the proceedings, Maurice had to tell his work foreman that he was not well, and had to go home instead of completing the night shift.

Nine men, including McGuinness, were there when he arrived on time. He felt more comfortable that his friend Seamus 'Bumper' Twomey chaired the meeting. They had light refreshments; no alcohol.

Early on, Bumper asked Maurice to suggest where the next car bombs should be exploded, for maximum damage to Internment raiders. It was a good opportunity, Maurice realised, to gain spot-on details sufficiently in advance for London. He suggested two military locations and an RUC station.

But even if London did not get word from him in time to prevent the explosions, they would see that he was still accurate. He knew the three places he named were reasonably well fortified against attacks. Any injured were likely to be security personnel, with medical help nearby. Not innocent civilians. The gathering agreed that the locations were ideal.

He posted a letter for London as soon as the post office opened the next morning. All his notes were still express-mailed, necessitating going to post office counters. He would have much preferred, and also save some money and time, by simply going to street letter boxes with ordinary-rate letters, which should get to London the next day. So that he did not become too familiar to Post Office staff, regularly sending express letters to the same bag in London, he alternated between three post offices.

Four days after the alert was mailed, a bomb exploded outside an army post he had recommended. No-one was killed. A few soldiers were injured. Obviously the army had received no warning. London might not have read his alert until after the bomb went off, Maurice guessed hopefully.

Soon after, however, his information led the army to a little bomb-making centre shortly before explosives were planted in stolen vehicles and taken to the two other targets he had recommended for blowing up.

Injuries, probably lives, were definitely saved that time, he was pleased to know.

He helped make more and more bombs. He drove more escape cars but was never designated as an exploder. Several times his letters got to London in time for the target locations to be saturated in advance by soldiers, who also established road blocks. Attacks were abandoned; sometimes carried out in less-crowded places.

Maurice derived more satisfaction, but not so much when soldiers shot dead a Provo friend driving a getaway car.

Maurice now had his own vehicle, a brown Vauxhall Vector saloon, a cheap one he bought second-hand. When on a Provo job, he kept his Armalite in the spare-tyre compartment, the Taurus revolver in a pocket. Back home, the rifle went back to the bedroom, the revolver to its spot under a roof-insulation batt.

His coterie of Provo associates kept widening. They were a cross-section of Belfast's community – clerks and executives from government departments, a few lawyers and accountants, hospital staff including a doctor, council workers and factory hands. And, enthusing at the fringes, more priests.

But never women, apart from a few girlfriend and wife supporters at bars and cafes. IRA militancy, he had discovered from the outset, was male chauvinist. He recalled getting to know several pro-IRA women when he was cleaning windows but none was an activist.

Maurice was instructed by a Provo heavy to deliver a packet to a prisoner in the Crumlin Road Gaol. He did not know the prisoner, a Provo, nor what was in the packet. His task was just to make the delivery. He muttered to himself on the way that his ranking in the Provos was more senior than that of an errand boy.

He was initially pleased about the job, however, as he was interested to see what it was like in the jail. Inside the prison, instead of being able to leave the packet and go, a warder told him to wait while the contents were inspected. The room he was in was locked.

A warning flashed through his mind. Damn, he should have opened the packet when he was in the car. It was about the size of a shoe box, covered in brown paper and tied with string. It weighted a couple of kilos. Was a hacksaw blade in there? A bomb? Something incriminating enough to straight away put him on the other side of those bars? Was this a set-up? What a damned fool he was, the twenty-four year-old decided.

He sat for ten tense minutes until the officer returned. The packet was okay. He was allowed to leave, not seeing the prisoner. Outside in his car, he wiped sweat from his brow. He hoped he was not getting paranoid. That place looked to be a hell hole.

But the word from those who had been prisoners at both places was that Crumlin Road was the Ritz compared with the crowded Long Kesh Internment centre near Lisburn which, mercifully, he had only driven past. Scores were jailed there as a result of his letters to London.

He knew he should be pleased about it. He was taking militants off the streets. Militants like his bloody self, he realised guiltily.

Inmates at Long Kesh later staged mass hunger strikes for weeks. He heard three warders from there joke about it at a bar. Their prisoners, they said, were better off with none of the piddling amounts of maggoty tucker they got.

Catholic Cardinal O'Fiaich released a statement saying Long Kesh's prisoners lived in inhumane conditions; worse than in the slums of Calcutta.

In accordance with Bernard's stated wishes, Maurice gave London the names of many Loyalist felons. But none of them, it seemed, was arrested. He learned enough from the Provos to alert his mysterious masters well in advance of two attacks by Loyalist groups. But the attacks – the bombing of a pub in Derry and in a busy street again in Belfast's Clonard – went ahead, with resistance from only Provos.

Two civilians were killed in Derry, four in the Clonard. The Secret Service, it seemed to him, was not in the business of interfering with the Loyalists. He was sure the limiting of responses to alerts in the interests of Tansey's life security did not apply to tips about coming Loyalist killings.

Maurice was shopping in the city one afternoon when his parked Vauxhall was stolen. The bombed wreck of it was found two days later. The police had little interest in his complaint. Car stealing was rife. The police had little time for chasing common robbers. Insurance rates in the North were too high for Maurice to bother with it. He bought a used blue Ford Corsair.

January 1972

Martin McGuinness officially became second in command of the Provos' powerful presence in County Derry. The trade union rep spent less time at the Michelin works, where M. Tansey was now the virtual cell boss.

Martin's elevation was reported to London. Also the fact that Gerry O'Hara was Derry's Provo leader. A high-ranking cohort was Paddy

Ward, whom Maurice had a notion was the keen Guinness drinker at his recruitment session with McGuinness. Sean MacStiofain, whom Maurice talked with a few times – at meetings, a public demonstration and a funeral – had gained a high position, either already or soon-to-be Commander in Chief of the PIRA.

MacStiofain was also in charge of Provo secret intelligence and Chief of Staff of the IRA's new Army Council. A man for spy Tansey to be wary of.

Sean was in his mid-forties, as tall as Maurice and well built. Also like him, Sean was born in England to an Irish mother. He had fallen in love with Ireland and adopted the Gaelic name in place of John Stephenson. He told Maurice and others that William Whitelaw, whom he called Willy, Britain's Conservative Government Secretary of State for Northern Ireland, was the only Englishman (sic) who could pronounce his surname correctly.

Some months after Maurice told London of MacStiofain's elevation, Whitelaw attempted to negotiate with him some sort of peace deal. The talks failed. Prime Minister Edward Heath said Whitelaw had found 'talking with Mr. MacStiofain very unpleasant'.

Maurice met IRA Army Council leader Daithi O'Conaill, who was not much older than him, at Dublin Airport after driving Provos Brendan and Jim from Belfast. Maurice's passengers were friends of O'Conaill, who was well dressed and looking like a typical businessman. Brendan and Jim were about to leave on PIRA business in the United States. To arrange to get more weapons, explosives and money, they said.

O'Conaill had been a key organiser of the Provos' split from the mainstream IRA so they could go to war. And he was allegedly the first to push for car bombing.

Maurice later had another session at a pub with Seamus 'Bumper' Twomey, who was in charge of most of the Provos' military action. He was in his 50s. His temper, Maurice felt, had a short fuse, like his dad's. He was from the Falls Road. Maurice nonetheless liked the man, whom he began to meet regularly. Bumper confessed to the ex-para that he had a fear of flying. He travelled only by car, train and ship.

Over drinks, Twomey confided details of several planned assaults and bombings. The news went to London. Army raids prevented one assault and two of the bombings, indicating that MI6 had responded swiftly. But Twomey was not arrested.

Back at a repaired McGurk's bar, Maurice spent more and more time with Gerald McDade. He was another Provo heavy, whom he had met at a Republican dinner. At the bar, Gerald, who liked to be called Gerry, like Adams, introduced Maurice to his Provo brother, James, an immigrant from Birmingham. They swapped stories of their mutual home city and sang a few songs at the bar with its band.

Some of the Provo hierarchy, like Martin McGuiness, drank alcohol sparingly. A few were abstainers. But for most, boozing was their only way of socialising. At times, mostly-young Provos got drunk and so out of control that publicans closed their pubs about 8.30 p.m. to maintain some order later in the streets and avoid brawls in their premises. But the drunks usually staggered off to other bars.

Maurice did his best to drink slowly, but it was impossible to spy on the Provos without being a regular at an assortment of public houses.

He was amazed at times at how quickly things had changed. When he was a Red Devil in Belfast, girls of all religions were encouraged to frequent British army discos and other entertainment centres. Typical was the girl to whose home Tansey had to drive his commander, then nervously wait for Major Jones for an hour in the soft-top Land Rover. The Republicans were content with Catholic girls, who the soldiers called tykes, partying with them at the barracks. But not now!

A Catholic girl who had entered his old barracks in Albert Road was tied to a lamp post and tarred and feathered by IRA thugs. Some girls who went to the barracks, thinking the old days had not changed, later had their hair cut off by Provos.

His former boss, Major Jones, was only one of a heap of soldiers the commander's former driver did not want to confront in the streets of Belfast.

Bloody Sunday

January 1972

By early in the new year, his tyre-making schedule prevented Maurice from attending another mix of drinks and IRA talk in the back room of a pub near Michelin. Two who were there told him the pro-Catholic Northern Ireland Civil Rights Association would protest en masse in Londonderry City against the Internment and Loyalist excesses.

Provo leader in County Derry, Gerry O'Hara, second-in-charge Martin, and Paddy Ward were seeing to it that the protesters were supplied with nail bombs and other offensive weaponry in case they were attacked by Loyalists.

The event was to be on the last Sunday in January, in a couple of weeks. Several Paisleyite targets were listed for harassing, but not subjected to violence. The intending marchers importantly wanted it to be strictly peaceful, Maurice was informed.

'Paddy Ward,' Maurice said to a Provo from Derry, thinking of the man with McGuinness when he was recruited. 'I think I've met him. Does he knock about with Marty, come to Belfast pubs now and then?'

'That's our Paddy,' the man responded. 'There'll be more than a thousand demonstrators on the thirtieth. But they definitely won't be armed. We support the Civil Rights Association but it's not IRA. They're full of anger. They want to vent it, bloody loudly, and hope the politicians take some notice. Nearly every Catholic in Derry has a relative or friend who's been interned or killed. A lot of 'em in Long Kesh aren't even militants. And almost none of them in there's a Loyalist.

'The marchers sure won't be out to kill, but we hope we can supply a few with guns. They would have to strike back if the RUC or Loyalist mobs attack 'em.'

This sounded to Maurice like a potential killing field. The Loyalists would know about the event well in advance. An early presence there of the army ought to prevent violence and allow the protestors to march and make their point in noisy peace. Surely, even during this awful Internment, it was a democratic right to gather and march in protest against measures by the government.

At the meal and drinks break at Michelin the following morning, he was told that the Civil Rights Association had refused the Provos' offer to supply them with munitions. 'They might end up regretting that,' a workmate said. The next morning at Michelin, Martin McGuinness confirmed that to Maurice.

That afternoon he mailed a one-page note to MI6. It said exactly where and when the protest would take place. The note emphasised that the demonstrators would be noisy but not violent. Not with guns or knives or bombs. That the Civil Rights Association, wanting a peaceful airing of their complaints, had rejected a Provo offer to supply them with weapons. That, at the association's request, no Provo militant would be at the scene.

Maurice was comforted that London, then Army Command in Belfast, then soldiers based in Derry, would have nearly two weeks to prepare to supervise the event and prevent clashes with Loyalists.

A few days later, on January 22, about a hundred Catholics marched peacefully to the Magilligan Prison Camp in Derry to yellingly protest against the Internment. Many of the marchers had friends and relatives locked in there.

The march proceeded without incident, Maurice read the next morning, until the protesters were near the prison camp. A patrol of 1 Para soldiers stormed on them from behind sand dunes, waving batons and firing rubber bullets. Scores of marchers were driven into the freezing winter sea.

People wallowing in the water were bashed with batons, some dragged ashore unconscious. The soldiers ignored orders from their NCOs to stop it until the officers batoned several of their own men.

Soon after, the IRA let off two bombs in Belfast's Callender Street, injuring sixty people, mostly women and children.

Maurice had not known either event would take place. He felt bad about that. The bombings must have been assigned at the meeting he had missed while at work at Michelin.

He had told London about the imminent civil rights parade but not the two events in the meantime. Should he write and explain that? He decided against it; hoping, nonetheless, that his phantom masters would not think he had been slack. If he had the phone number, he would have rung MI6 and explained it.

'Cripes,' he told himself, 'they couldn't expect me to know beforehand about *every* damned show… Could they?'

In the wake of army officers curbing violence by soldiers near the Derry prison, Maurice was confident that – knowing via himself and MI6 that it would be a peaceful event – they would prevent assaults by hooligan soldiers at the imminent Civil Rights Association's march nearby.

He was at home with Carol on the evening of Sunday, January 30, when news of the event burst from the radio. He anxiously bought a newspaper next morning on the way to work.

Hardened as he was to the barbarism at times by his former army colleagues, Maurice was mortified to read about armed British paratroopers bolting from personnel carriers like crazed animals. They hailed live bullets at random from SLR rifles at the protesters, who were doing nothing threatening. Apart, that is, from a few marchers who threw stones at them and some Loyalist jeerers, who also threw stones.

Again, the attackers were in the 1 Para Regiment. The same types, they were, as those in Maurice's old 2 Para.

Twenty six unarmed men and women civil rights campaigners, and women and child bystanders, were injured by the soldiers. Two victims had been run down by army vehicles as they scattered from the slaughter. Nearly half of the injured were not expected to live.

Medical reports in the newspapers soon after said the soldiers had killed thirteen civilians. Seven of the dead were teenagers. Five had been shot in the back.

Sickened, Maurice had assumed that – regardless of info from MI6 – the army would have found out about the coming public protest by the Civil Rights Association well in advance. As with the Magilligan Prison affair, basic inquiring would have revealed that a peaceful show was planned.

His letter to London had given the army plenty of time to plan their presence in Derry at the end of the month. But, he wondered, to plan that carnage? No officers, it seemed, had intervened.

Hell, his note should have prevented the killings. Consistently with what he had told London, there were no reports of protesters with guns or the nail bombs the Provos had offered.

Maurice soon learned that the event was widely and prominently reported, shocking the world. Northern Ireland, even many Loyalists, raged with fury. The British Army was censured by the Irish media.

In the next few weeks, the British Government set up the Widgery Tribunal to investigate the circumstances of what was now called Bloody Sunday.

To Maurice, Bloody Sunday was a result of the 'shoot first, ask later' nature of the training in aggression he and his fellow paras, many of them already tough nuts, had received. He sorely wanted to tell the Widgery Tribunal that he had told MI6 well beforehand that the civil rights demonstration would be peaceful. But doing so would terminate his spying. And MI6 might deny getting his alert.

Surely the full story would be revealed one day. His London silvertails surely could not just sit on that one. They should at least tell the tribunal they had informed the army it would be a peaceful and weapon-less event. But had they?

Despite the atrocities by Republicans and Loyalists he experienced in Northern Ireland, Maurice firmly believed that for sheer brutality and uncivilised behaviour, some troopers were worse than either the IRA's or the UDA's combatants. Unlike soldiers, Republican and Loyalist militants had heartfelt generational, territorial and religionist motivations for their barbarism.

As Maurice expected, the sometimes-killers at the canteen table at Michelin fumed with outrage about Bloody Sunday. There would be big-time retaliation. The Michelin men were surprised that Loyalists and the RUC were publicly disgusted with Britain's soldiers.

Scores of young men were already queuing to join the Provos. They and their Catholic families, once hospitable welcomers to British troops whom they saw as peacemakers, now wanted the British Army to leave the province.

Brother Kieran telephoned from England on 15 February, the day after Maurice's twenty-fifth birthday, to say he would arrive there the next morning. He would stay for a few days, on special leave from the paras. He shared Maurice's condemnation of his former and Kieran's current colleagues for Bloody Sunday.

Kieran took Carol out for drinks a few times. The brothers engaged well, despite Kieran again muttering about the diabolical Provisionals. His dark looks inferred again that Maurice was a part of the murderous movement.

Maurice was also uneasy about the near-romantic affection he saw between his wife and brother. Soon after their second holiday in Manorhamilton, Maurice had been mortified to learn, Carol was again philandering at local pubs at night when he was at work. He still agonised about her bedding their best man. But no. Friendly Kieran would not dare screw Carol.

By now Maurice had attended many funerals at Milltown Cemetery. The only enjoyable aspects of them were the traditional Irish wakes that preceded and followed them. A common practice was the firing of volleys of gunshots into the air over the graves, saluting fallen comrades. Sometimes the gunmen wearing balaclavas included Maurice.

March 1972
On the afternoon of Wednesday, 1 March '72, Maurice took part in the session that planned the bombing of a Loyalist celebration to be held in the Abercorn Restaurant in central Belfast.

It was to be the Provisionals' vicious retaliation for the McGurk's explosion.

He rushed home from the meeting at three in the afternoon. Nobody was there. He wrote his warning to London, detailing exactly where and when the bomb would be exploded. He added the names of the five others who planned the bombing, noting that three of them probably would be the exploders.

He drove to the post office in time to catch the day's last despatch of express mail. The letter would reach the British Intelligence bag two clear days before the ominous celebration.

He waited a block away from the Abercorn in his car on Saturday night, March 4, expecting to see alerted soldiers and the police arresting the Provo bombers. Instead, he heard an almighty explosion.

He ran to the gutted restaurant, getting there just ahead of the first fire brigade truck, ambulances and police. No British soldier was there.

Police and medics worked frantically in the smoking wreckage where the planned big bomb had ignited amidst the Loyalists. The restaurant's tables, floor and walls were stained red with blood.

He saw two girls, sisters, who he later learned had been walking by the front of the Abercorn while shopping for wedding dresses. Each girl had lost both her legs. At least two Loyalists were killed and more than one-hundred and thirty, including several passersby, were seriously wounded.

He stood on the footpath, galled, as corpses and the injured were carried to a fleet of ambulances. Victims and watchers screamed and cried.

Maurice resuscitated an unconscious youth with a bloodied chest for a few minutes before medics took the victim, now breathing, to an ambulance. It was a life saved, Maurice the spy hoped.

He again condemned his London SIS masters for not getting the army to prevent the outrage. *Hell*, he fumed, *they knew from me days ago just when and where the bomb would be hidden and ignited. Surely the bombers I named will soon be lumbered.*

But, he later found out, they were not even questioned.

Maurice went home from the Abercorn and vomited in the toilet. A sleepless night followed, writhing in bed, stormed by anguish about the horrid scene, telling himself over and over that he must somehow stop this murderous mayhem. How, he wondered, could he make those spymasters act on more of his info?

Why would they let the Abercorn outrage go ahead? Was it, and other lapses like Bloody Sunday and the McGurk's blowing up, the result of careless inattention? Was the Abercorn a victim of MI6's preoccupation with cloak-and-daggering the Soviet Union's KGB and GRU in their Cold War?

Some letters would have arrived only a few hours before the events he foreshadowed. MI6 might think that was his deliberate doing. They might not know that the Provos usually operated on short-term planning, determining their targets sometimes only hours before the action. It was a clever system. Designed, he was often told, to minimise the risk of leakage of info to the enemies.

To Maurice, the worst instances were the many attacks on weekends planned on Friday nights. There was no way he could alert London to those events, that killed scores, in the absence of a phone number to call.

He would gladly run the perceived risk of regularly phoning London, therefore saving more lives. Contrary to Bernard's claim, he knew the IRA did not have a phone monitoring outfit. He suspected that London's top spooks, waging the Cold War, were more interested in gaining and maintaining political and territorial power than saving lives in Northern Ireland.

He asked himself, should he bypass the clots in London? Begin tipping off the army himself to coming horrors? There was a chance that whoever answered the phone at the barracks would recognise his distinctive, highly-pitched voice. He knew from Provos that British soldiers sometimes leaked secret security info to them and blurted in pubs. His name could get to the Provos. Execution would follow.

He decided to persevere with Bernard's lot. He had hoped the McGurk's horror would jerk them into assiduously acting on his more-important letters. Perhaps, he prayed, the Abercorn disaster would do it.

Maurice wrote a terse note addressed to Private Bag 9, Victoria Street Post Office, 110 Victoria Street, London SW1. 'Why did you or the army not respond to my information, well in advance of the bombings at McGurk's Hotel and the Abercorn Restaurant?

'The army's failure to prevent just those two attacks cost seventeen lives and the injuring of a hundred and fifty more. A lot of the victims were children and innocent non-militants. Why, if you told the army in Belfast or Derry that the Bloody Sunday march would be peaceful – as I told you two weeks ahead of it – did paratroopers kill and wound so many people?

'Do you know why I am not able to alert you to many acts by the Provisionals? So many bombings and attacks are planned, in my presence, only hours ahead. All the information I send you is accurate.

'I am heartened, however, when my alerts result in atrocities being prevented and perpetrators being jailed. I do my best for you, despite not being paid for it. I seriously need a telephone number so I can give you immediate alerts.'

Maurice craved for a response. He again appended his address and phone number at the top of the note and as 'Sender' on the outside of the envelope. After posting it, he considered sometimes contacting a competent Military Intelligence officer whom he knew operated in Northern Ireland. He and others often worked in civilian clothes; tried a bit of spying on the IRA and, possibly, Loyalists.

One of them could readily be advised of his alerts at a dead drop. Like a note behind one of the millions of loose bricks around the city. An empty bottle left in a particular spot in the gutter outside the army barracks would alert his man that an urgent message was waiting.

He was aware from his army days of Special Branch having a hush hush unit called the Fourth Field Survey Troop. They were at Castledillon House, a fine old mansion of stone in a garden in Armagh County, bordering the North's southern boundary with the Republic.

But, as he reflected, Maurice decided not visit the Troop. He recalled that it worked closely with the RUC's Special Branch.

A sometimes-undercover operative there was a Lieutenant (later Captain) Robert Niarac, on assignment from the Grenadier Guards and connected somehow to the SAS. Maurice, however, had not met him.

Not even the likes of Niarac knew Tansey was a spy, it seemed. Also still sleuthing from Armagh, he felt sure, was Julian Ball. He had met Julian, commonly called Tony, at the Hereford SAS barracks.

Provo lore said Fourth Field Survey Troop agents like Niarac and Ball collaborated with militant Loyalists, sometimes supplying them with bombs and weapons. Maurice hoped that was not true. He hoped it was not British forces, acting on his information, who set up the UVF's bombing of McGurk's bar. And failed to stop the bomb at the Abercorn.

Julian Ball was killed in a car crash in Oman in 1988. Niarac was widely accused of murdering, by his own hand, an acquaintance of Maurice's and an influential IRA leader, John Francis Green, in 1975. Niarac was on a mission to infiltrate the Provisionals in Armagh County on 17 May, 1977, when the men he was spying on saw through his cover.

Niarac was tortured for information about Special Branch's and British Intelligence's activities in the North and then killed. His body has not been found.

Maurice felt alienated for two weeks. London had not responded to that questioning, explanatory and pleading note. Was MI6 reprehensibly slack? Or... or, he wondered darkly, did they now not give a damn about the Troubles?

With the Cold War on, were they too busy spooking on Soviet Russia? Trying to out-fox the KGB? Were KGB moles in British Intelligence? If so, and if a mole was opening Tansey's letters, that rat would not give a stuff about Northern Ireland.

To break the strain and also for Maurice to try to warm his relationship with Carol, the couple took a week off work. They spent two days and a night with a jubilant Allen back at their favourite hotel in old Manorhamilton. They enjoyed marvellous Saturday-night craic there. On the Sunday, with Allen and his wife cheering him on, Maurice caught another fighting salmon.

He drove them north through the province to County Antrim to marvel at Ballymoney's Neolithic tombs of Irish clan leaders who had died some 5,000 years ago. The family had a picnic of roast chicken and chocolate cake in rare bright sunshine, no wind, on the grass beside the carved slabs of rock.

The three then went to the massive Broad Stone burial sites at nearby Finvoy. At Dooey's Cairn, another ancient funereal monument at Dunloy, Allen and Maurice spent an hour kicking a soccer ball, taking turns as goalie.

Maurice engaged well in cafes and pubs with the locals, including a chatty old woman who swore she had played hide-and-seek last night with leprechauns at the bottom of her garden.

A woman at the bar chuckled. 'Ya musta been drunk, Doris!'

'No, no!' Doris declared. 'But them happy little goblins – *they* was drunk.'

The holidaying spy marvelled at the friendliness of the people of this part of Protestant-predominant Antrim; so unlike Belfast, so relatively free, if seemed then, of religious rivalry. Like most people south in the Republic, the Irish here were among the most engaging folk on earth.

Carol had a great time. Allen, nearly seven years old, was tickled pink to be in the countryside. The child's fascination and joy at seeing a few wild animals reminded Maurice of his holidays as a kid in County Galway.

The couple's bonding became viable, nearly romantic. But, because of that first morning of the marriage, he could never truly love or trust her. He, by the way, did not philander with other women. Maurice returned to work at Michelin refreshed, determined to continue minimising the North's bloodshed.

Abercorn bombing co-planner (aka) Mervin clearly trusted implicitly the capable recruit, now a regular strategist and activist, sometimes considered a top leader in the Provos.

After all, from a Provo point of view, the Abercorn bombing had happened as planned. Two weeks after the holiday, Mervin gave him the details of a plan to detonate a large car bomb in Belfast's Lower Donegal Street five days later. He also mentioned that The Four Steps, a Protestant pub on the Shankill Road, would cop a bomb in a couple of days. Maurice informed London. The bombs went off as planned, without army involvement. Some were injured but no lives were lost in the two explosions.

14. 'You're blown, brother.'

May 1972

Kieran returned to the Tansey home a week later, with a bottle of Pernod for Carol. Maurice, home from a day shift at Michelin, was weeding in the back garden when Kieran came to his side.

'Bruv, there's something we have to talk about. Something important, that'll take a while. How about we go to a pub after dinner?'

Ah, he's finally going to confess to how he knew where I live in Belfast, reveal the real reason for coming here, Maurice decided. 'Sure. As soon as I've put Allen to bed and kept my promise to read him a bit from a storybook.'

The brothers sat with a beer each at a table in a quiet corner at the local hotel.

'I know you're bloody curious about why I keep coming here,' said skinny Kieran. 'Please don't ask how, but I know absolutely that you're a leading light in the Provisionals, Maurice.

'You're a planner, a bomb-maker, a bomber and a gunman. You do that because you're a very important spy for Britain's Secret Intelligence Service. Their main man in the North. Their *only* real spy.'

Kieran swigged at his drink and stared studiously at his intense-looking big brother, who forced an amused curling of his lips.

'And I have a message,' Kieran said. 'One you'd better take seriously, for Carol and Allen's sake as well as your own.'

Kieran paused again, as if collecting his thoughts. 'There are good grounds for believing that certain elements in the IRA suspect, strongly suspect, that you're spying on them. And, as you'd know, they don't need much evidence to torture and kill a suspect.'

'Dammit, what's the basis for such a crazy claim?' Maurice asked stridently.

Was this a ploy to get him to admit to spying? If there was any truth to this, surely MI6 could find a messenger he would *really* believe. Why, he asked himself, couldn't Bernard himself make contact?

'I told you,' the young man said, 'I can't reveal that. But the suspicion comes out of Michelin. The advice is that you leave Michelin right away. Move into another house. Arrangements are being made for you to easily get a decent job with Imperial Chemical Industries. Its factory is up north, near the sea at Carrickfergus, isn't it?'

'It is,' Maurice said flatly. 'I have to know the basis for this garbage, Kieran.'

'Hell, I can't tell you! But you can guess that I'm here at the secret direction of high officials. They want you to know that they highly value your work. But they've got information that the Provos are not far off busting your cover. There's a definite rumble. You have to clear out of Michelin quick smart.'

'Bullshit,' said Maurice, remembering that Kieran was a regular fibber as a kid. 'What on earth makes them or you think I'm a spy in the bloody Provos? Anyway, I know ICI is a stronghold of Protestants. It probably has a cell of militant Loyalists.'

'Oh? That might be why they want you to go there. To sort of change sides. Perhaps spy on the bomb-crazy Loyalists, who kill so many poor Catholics and battle with the army. Please, bruv, do as I recommend. As *they* recommend. Your house could be attacked any damned moment. A Provo or two are snooping around, suspicious that you work for British Intelligence. Please, do it.'

Maurice was not about to admit to anything. If he was their sole spy in the Provos, how could London have information about how the Provos regarded him?

'Michelin's not an IRA front! And the money's pretty good there.'

Kieran laughed. 'You're a good spy, all right. And I know that when you were in the paras you did time in the MRF.'

Maurice remembered the name from his SAS days. 'What's that?'

'The Military Reconnaissance Force, of course. Undercover specialists.'

How does Kieran know that? 'Sure, but even ordinary soldiers need to be capable in the ancient art of deception.'

Kieran looked at him doubtfully. 'That training would set you up for what you're doing now. My info is that there's an important cell of the Provisionals at Michelin. It's why you went there in the first place.'

He realised grimly that Kieran might be right. His little brother could get that notion of why former paratrooper Tansey went to the tyre factory only from the Brits who assigned him to go spooking back in August, 1970. Damn, he might as well admit to it. 'Okay, your information might be right. But, Kieran, who the hell told you that?'

'Fuck, I really can't tell you. You know what it's like to be sworn to secrecy.'

Kieran smiled. He took two empty glasses to the bar for refilling. Maurice figured that the SIS might be smarting about that note he sent a month ago. If they *were*, why not ring him?

He slept little that night. Surely, if the Provos suspected him, he would feel it, recognise any changes from the close brotherhood. A key indicator would be his relationship with Marty McGuinness. And that, he was positive, was iron-clad.

The Loyalists, as much as any of the warring sides, would want him dead. He considered writing to London again. Asking about his brother's claims. But, again, they would not respond to their unpaid life risker.

With the Taurus under the pillow while Carol slept, he decided grimly that Kieran was not lying. Was MI6 sending him on a new mission? Simply manufacturing a reason for him to leave Michelin? Hell, he had done pretty well there, despite London's callousness.

Even at his briefing and assigning, Bernard had not indicated any interest in infiltrating Loyalist cells. But staying on at Michelin was now a risk he should not take. For Carol and the kid's sake, their safety, he decided to resign. And, to continue minimising the violence in this scenic land, perhaps nail some extremist Loyalists, he would have a go at working for ICI.

After a quiet breakfast, the piece worker told Carol he would be on a double shift. A day's work followed by a night shift. He expected to be back after dawn tomorrow.

Kieran followed him to the front gate. 'Please, do as I recommend,' he said. Maurice said nothing. He felt, at least, that if Provos were going to attack his home, it would be when they knew he was there. So, for now, Carol and Allen were safe. Carol would go off to work at the hospital soon. Allen to school.

The Provos at the table in the Michelin canteen were as chummy as ever. Two of them, as usual, talked of a planned car bombing Maurice already knew about and had alerted London to. If an element in the Provos suspected him, the element was not present.

Still, he confirmed to himself back at his tyre-making machine, he had better leave the factory. And find another home, the location of which he would try to keep secret. Maybe it should be in a Protestant suburb near the ICI works. Then he would seldom have to go through Belfast suburbs, being seen by Provos on his way to and from work with a mob of Loyalists.

Claiming that he had aching limbs from the rigours of his job and that a doctor had advised him to take on a less strenuous occupation, Maurice gave Michelin's personnel office a day's notice of his departure. They offered him easier work in another part of the factory.

'Thanks,' he said, 'but I've already lined up a job elsewhere.'

He went to a street phone box and called the personnel manager at ICI. It would be madness to admit to working at Michelin, well known for its Catholic staff. He told the manager he had lately been a foreman at Jones' motor body works in Antrim.

Only a few minutes into his spiel, the officer interrupted. 'What religion are you, Mr. Tansey?'

'I'm a proud Presbyterian.'

'Come in here tomorrow, fill in an application form and you can be confident that something you will like can be arranged, Mr. Tansey.'

As he hung up, he felt like kicking himself. Heck, he had not asked what the pay would be. Just as he had failed to ask about wages when being assigned by Bernard and the brass. He knew though that some outside influence was in play at ICI. Normally, it would not be easy to get a job there. The province still had high unemployment. It seemed that ICI was not going to check with Jones's motor works. The personnel manager had not even sought a reference.

Now his tracks had to be covered with the Provos. No way could they know he was going to ICI. They would not buy it if he said he was going there to spy on the Loyalists. Such a thing was alien to IRA thinking. Associating with the enemy surely signalled coming torture, death. Like the setting alight of that poor Provo bastard who confided that he was joining the RUC. Going to work with Loyalists would be seen as far worse than that.

The Taurus was in his pocket. If the Provos really thought he was a spy, they might want to finish him before he left Michelin. He'd be ready, and do them in.

He was pleased to know that McGuinness was going to join the gang in the canteen for the afternoon break. Maurice and the others at the table always were in working clothes, sometimes T-shirts. But Martin the union rep, not a Michelin employee, dressed smartly, often in a suit with a tie. He had an office at the trade union headquarters and was simply a visitor for union stuff and running the cell of the surviving twenty militants.

'I've got some important news,' Maurice announced to Martin and twelve others at the table, hoping they did not suspect that the bulge in his pocket was a gun. 'On my doctor's advice, I'm leaving the strenuous work upstairs for something that's more relaxing. And I want to spend more nights at home. I've just given my notice. I finish here in the morning.'

He was relieved to hear a rumble of protests. They did not want him to go.

'My friend, you'll be missed big-time,' said McGuinness. 'But I can understand. You set a cracking pace on your machine. But don't let the move interfere with your Provo work.'

'I won't.' Maurice lowered his voice, causing them to lean closer to him. 'There's no way I'll abandon the Cause. I told you long ago, Marty, that I planned to go back to Birmingham some time with my wife and her son. But now I want to stay here. In particular, help knock out those lunatic Paisleyites. So, I'll rest up for a bit, then look for another job. I'll keep in touch with you guys, of course.'

'Good man, Maurice,' said McGuinness. 'You'll have a break before the night shift. Let's talk about it then. Up the street.'

He knew he should never trust anyone. It could be a trap. He kept his hand on the gun in his pocket as he walked to the pub. But a genial Martin was there waiting. The two spent half an hour at a small bar. Martin said he would inform the Belfast Brigade leaders that his friend had to leave Michelin on medical advice but would still be a front-line planner and militant.

'After you have that spell, let me know if I can help,' said Derry's 2IC. 'What about getting a good job in Derry?'

'My wife and I have thought about that, but she says it gets too cold up there in the winter. Thanks, anyway. You spend more of your time up north now, I gather.'

'I do. On Provo stuff, of course. But there's still Provo planning and liaison, and a trade union role, for me in Belfast.'

Walking back in the dark to the tyre machine, Maurice wondered with wry amusement what his status would be if he became a spy for the Brits on the Loyalists as well the Provos.

Leaking to the Provos anything he happened to learn at ICI about Loyalist plans would make him more than a double spy. And what about telling Loyalists about the Provos? A quadruple spy? No, sleuthing for the Loyalists was not on.

If being at ICI did not work out, if he sensed real danger now in Belfast from either side, he would take Carol and Allen to England, pronto. He could turn up with them at that Secret Service safe house on Kings Road, West London, if it still functioned.

In the meantime, he had better find a new home. Preoccupied with thoughts about the future, he left Michelin quietly at two thirty in the morning, more than two hours early.

He entered his home quietly in the dark so he would not wake anyone. He opened the door to the bedroom and stood still. Kieran was there, pumping on top of Carol.

What he had feared was confirmed. His first urge was to charge in and decorate the wall with his brother's blood. First, it was his best man and bride, sixteen hours into the marriage. Now, it was his wife and brother damned treacherously betraying him. And not for the first time, he suspected. They had probably got drunk on Pernod.

But no. He had vowed as a kid, devastated by his father's raging violence, never ever to assault a member of his own family. He could never even smack Allen when the lad was naughty.

He crept outside and sat in the car, parked a short distance down the road, as usual. He was beset with devastation. Should he simply go back in there, throw Kieran out of the bed, pack some of his own belongings and leave? For good? Would divorce cost him his work permit?

No wonder husband No. 1 had divorced her, he thought. That man maybe wrongly thought he was Allen's father. More likely, the lad was sired by a drunk at a pub. Carol's first husband was in Belfast but had never made contact.

Maurice wondered how many men Carol had bedded since she married him. The word nymphomaniac lurched into his mind. Going back and making Kieran a hospital case, even letting them know he had seen them rooting, would terminate the marriage and Maurice's last real connection with his family. And probably wreck his real role in Belfast; saving lives. Young Allen would be a pretty neglected kid at times, living with his sometimes-boozed mother.

He went back inside at dawn, when he would be expected to arrive there. Still stunned, he went to bed quietly beside evidently-sleeping Carol.

Maurice left the bed to join Carol, Allen and Kieran for breakfast. His brother was unusually subdued in the face of Maurice's attempts at chatter. Did he think Maurice had seen them? Would Kieran tell Carol?

Kieran would be returning to England in a couple of hours. As Maurice left the table to return to bed, his brother embraced him. Over Kieran's shoulder, he saw Carol's lips purse as the little man gave thanks for Maurice's hospitality. He hoped the two of them were not in love.

As on the first morning of their marriage, he would have to try to dampen his pain and fury. To forgive. But he would never forget.

Still at home mid morning, Kieran on his way to England, Maurice phoned Carol at the hospital. He told her he had finished his days at Michelin, for reasons he would explain when he saw her. There was another matter, an urgent one, they should discuss and attend to. Could she take the afternoon off from work?

He drove to ICI and filled in the form. The question was not on it, but a personnel executive bluntly asked, as had his superior on the phone, what his religion was. Presbyterian, he repeated firmly. The exec. ticked a printed piece of paper on his desk. He told the applicant he could begin work there in three weeks.

When Carol arrived home, he sat her at the kitchen table and said he had discovered the existence of a cell of the IRA at Michelin. It made this house a target for an attack from Loyalists, so last night he had resigned. A job was waiting for him at ICI.

'Heavens, I've been worried about that IRA gang,' she said. 'Kieran mentioned it a few times.'

He wanted to keep in touch with some friends at Michelin, Maurice told her, but in case his sudden departure from there caused alarm from IRA thugs, they should find another home.

'We ought to get one today,' he added. 'A place with an extra bedroom, and close to ICI, which is a Loyalist place.' Protestant Carol excitedly agreed.

By late afternoon they had found, and arranged to buy on a deposit through an agent, a comfortable home in Ballyhenry Avenue, Newtownabbey, close to Glengormley. An open public space, where social sport was played, was over the back fence. The Ballyhenry Primary School, for Allen, was close by. The house was about only fifteen minutes' drive from ICI at Carrickfergus.

With himself and Carol on pretty good salaries, there was no shortage of cash. The house, not quite completed, was in a new estate with a mix of religions, mostly Protestant. It was also near the B90 Manse Road by the quarry where the Loyalist alleged murderer was murdered.

He buried in the new back garden the holy silver medal his mother had given him when she spotted her son skulking out of the house with his bag, on his way to the army recruiting office. He had worn it on a chain around his neck lately, shown it to the Provos at Michelin. If Loyalists ever found it on him or in the home of the new ICI employee, if they saw him wearing green, if they saw him with the true flag of Ireland… execution.

Settling in happily at their new home, Maurice assessed the state of the Troubles in 1972.

Few on either side of the conflict now knew whom they could absolutely trust. The Official IRA and the Provisionals feuded nearly all the time, as did the UVF and the UDA. And now the British Army was making more arrests. That seemed odd, with the Internment subdued. The flaring of arrests had ignited more hatred of British forces in the wake of Bloody Sunday, even from peaceful Catholic non-members of the IRA.

No peaceful march could proceed without a real likelihood of crazed soldiers swooping on them. If not firing real bullets, they would wield batons and kick people to the ground. Arrest anyone who resisted. And who would not resist that?

Regular targets for bombings and snipering by Provos were army posts in the Crumlin Road, Grosvenor Road, Hastings Street and Springfield Road. Provos also raided RUC stations. Several soldiers and police had been injured lately. Sometimes attacking Provos were caught and jailed, but Maurice had always got away clean. Nearly all the attacks had been pre-warned to London.

He was pleased that British Intelligence had responded to some of his letters lately. Many atrocities were averted by raiding soldiers, who could have learned of imminent attacks only from him via the SIS. A few more Provos were arrested.

Maurice still had to be present at some of the violence he had warned London of. Otherwise, he might draw Provo suspicion on himself. He was playing potentially-deadly roulette. It was thanks to pure luck and his alertness that bomber etc Tansey was not killed or arrested by the army or the RUC. He was now not so sure the SIS would prevent his jailing. He had lost faith in Bernard's promises.

Waiting for his first day at ICI and fuelled by flared contempt for his old regiment, Maurice agreed, when asked by Martin McGuinness, to help lead an ambush of a British Army patrol in the Divis Street district. The soldiers carried out random street-by-street house searches there, behind their barracks, leaving behind wrecked homes of innocent Catholics.

Maurice and his companions waited from before dawn in partly-derelict properties. They also had snipers on rooftops. At 10.30, a two-vehicle army patrol approached. The Provos opened fire.

Maurice shot many rounds above the soldiers with his Armalite. The crack shot could have easily killed six or more of them. The conflict continued for half an hour, evidently with some soldiers dead and injured. At least one Provo was killed, about six wounded.

The ex-para knew army reinforcements would be coming. Probably with a Saracen armoured vehicle from the barracks. He knew the vehicle's deadly capabilities. With a few of his comrades, he made a fast escape out the back of a ramshackle building.

He was not so much concerned about being killed. The risk of going to the over-crowded and barbaric Internment jail worried him more. He knew Long Kesh warders gossiped to influential prisoners, who would be told about it if prisoner Tansey claimed he was an ex-soldier, a spy for Britain. The inmates would know that the phony Provo's despatches to London had put many of them in Long Kesh. Vengeance from both IRA and the camp's few Loyalist prisoners would be swift and terminal.

Provos suffered several more casualties that day after leader Maurice and some grateful mates retreated. Many more were arrested and interned. He had not had enough notice of the ambush to warn London.

15. Tansey the Loyalist

June 1972

The big Imperial Chemical Industries factory, mostly making fibres, was on the coast at northern Carrickfergus, past a village named Eden, near where the old A2 Belfast Road became the Marine Highway. The rest of the thoroughfare was Larne Road, joining Belfast to the northern port town of Larne.

Maurice worked day and night, sometimes on weekends, in a huge warehouse on product-quality restriction and customer returns. His salary was good. Commuting to and from work was easy in his new, dark blue Morris coupe.

He posted a note to London from the Glengormley Post Office, a short walk from home. He told them he had scored the job he understood they wanted him to get. The note included his new address and phone number.

He waited hopefully, but did not get a response. Getting a note from them, direct word of the value of his information after a year and a half of unpaid spying, getting a request for a lead on something, would have been stimulating.

Sure, Bernard had said their first spy's personal safety was paramount. Not all IRA attacks Maurice foreshadowed would be acted on. But act on fewer than half lately? Ridiculous.

Perhaps their continued failure to contact him was a sort of Secret Service way of showing approval of him becoming a double spy, the devious buggers. Perhaps they would contact him only if they had something to bitch about.

Normally, he soon learned, applicants deemed suitable to work at ICI waited for months before signing on. His prompt start there indicated to him that the Secret Service had dropped a word in his favour to the company's British boss.

In his first week at ICI, in the canteen, a fellow worker casually wondered to him how, as a Protestant, Maurice had got employment at Catholic-dominated Michelin.

'What makes you think I bloody worked *there*?' the new employee asked, looking astounded, which he was. And fearful.

The worker, as Maurice recalls, was named John Elles. He said, 'A Protestant who works there, who makes out he's Catholic, mentioned to a friend of mine that you suddenly left Michelin.'

'Sure, I worked with that Roman Catholic lot,' Maurice admitted. He knew only non-Catholics used the word Roman.

'Quite a few other Protestants, like your friend's friend, worked at Michelin. All of them kept their religion a secret. But some bloody how, Catholics there found out that I'm a Presbyterian. They might have spotted me going to church. But at least they wouldn't know that I'm a Loyalist. One born in Hampshire.

'A fellow Prottie at Michelin warned me that it's the base of a cell of the IRA. The rotten Provisional lot that's done so much damage.'

'Yeah, I know that,' said questioner Elles. 'So?'

'So, I got out of the bloody place quick smart. Those thugs could have arranged an industrial accident at my expense, if they didn't want the drama of shooting me.'

Elles' nonchalance vanished. 'Well, we've done some checking. You're on the list the Ulster Volunteer Force has of IRA men, Tansey.'

Maurice buried a stampede of alarm about those rampant bombers of McGurk's. He doubled over in loud laughter, then placed a hand on Elles' shoulder. This man was surely a member of the UVF or the Ulster Defence Association.

'How fucken amazing!' Maurice chortled. 'What would it mean being on a silly list like that? And just because I worked at Michelin.'

'It ain't funny. It's a death list.'

Tansey's show of humour vanished. 'Well, they're awfully wrong,' he declared, staring hard at his questioner. 'Thank God you told me, John. Maybe the UVF saw me knocking around with IRA bastards who I didn't know were part of that gang of Popist lunatics. They'd be blokes I worked with at Michelin.'

He was tempted to mention McGurk's. 'I drank with all sorts of Michelin men at pubs around Mallusk. John, surely you know I'm no damned Provisional, or whatever.'

It seemed that Elles bought the lies. Over the next few days, coolness from fellow employees Maurice had encountered at ICI evaporated. He hoped his name had been erased from the wish list of death. He had never contributed to the Provos' list of Loyalists marked for execution.

More smiling faces around him indicated that what he told Elles continued to bubble about at the factory. His mentioning that his wife was a Protestant helped. He even made a point of being seen at two services at the local Presbyterian church.

That raised the memory of the only other time he had been in a Protestant church, claimed to him then to be the house of the devil. Wedding guests had taken the protesting Catholic altar boy in there and washed his bleeding head with Protestant holy water after he had been hit by a car. He had been running from the groom after, with some other kids, he had thrown at the bride confetti the boys had collected from earlier ceremonies. Maurice's handful had accidently included two cigarette butts, which hit the bride's face.

Although his overwhelming desire was to minimise the bloodshed of all Northern Irish innocents, he leaned on the side of the Catholics. England's Protestants were definitely the invaders of the North, its controllers through generations of brutal force. Much worse invaders they were than were the Vikings, who had eventually settled peacefully, under Irish rule.

He wanted to see all the island run by the true Irish. With absolute tolerance of Protestantism.

The only solution he could think of was for a British Government to undertake the disruptive measure of returning the North to the Republic. In some cases forcefully relocating the province's ardent Loyalists to comfortable and productive lifestyles in England, Scotland and even America, Canada, Australia, New Zealand…

He knew it would take a gusty government to take that on, probably amid mass opposition from much of its electorate. The province obviously was important to the British economy and the nation's self-esteem. Many would be killed, but that was happening here anyway, with no real settlement in distant sight.

Hell, he half-heartedly figured, he now might be asked to join ICI's cell of militants. That would be what the SIS wanted, but why on earth had they not said so directly? Their priority, he felt sure, was the IRA. Was Kieran, screwer of Carol, really their messenger?

He had not heard from his brother in three months. He decided to check on his whereabouts. He rang Aldershot, posing as a friend who wanted to speak to Private Tansey. The soldier was on an exercise in another country, he was told.

Carol now seemed to be tensely withdrawn from him, probably resentful that he was now not interested in having sex with her. She seemed ill at times in the morning.

One evening a few months after Maurice went to ICI, Carol announced that, with a doctor's confirmation, she was three months' pregnant.

He knew he should act joyously, but was stunned. Devastated by his proof of her affair with Kieran, her philandering with all sorts of characters at night when he was at work, he had not made love to her for longer than three months. Nor to anyone else. He fought to hide his consuming woe.

She saw what he was thinking. 'Okay, it can't be yours,' she admitted. 'But can you treat it as if it is?'

'So, who's the father? Kieran?'

'How on earth could it be Kieran's?' Guilt was written all over her face.

'The night before he went back to England, three months ago, I came home early and saw you two in bed together.'

He repressed the urge to tell her what a disgusting betrayal that was. 'Count him and yourself lucky that I turned around at the door of the bedroom and went back outside for a couple of hours. He would have copped a big bashing.'

She swallowed hard, stared at the table.

'Maurice, I'm sorry. It was a damn crazy act by two drunks.' Her eyes had moistened, but it sounded like the apology on the first morning of their marriage. 'It's *you* I love, Maurice,' she added quietly.

'So, okay,' she continued. 'I'm sure it's Kieran's. Can you accept the baby as if it's *yours*, please darling?'

He soon agreed, preferring to think what was growing in Carol's belly was sired by Kieran rather than a drunk from a pub. For all of that, Carol had been a good mother lately; a good cook, who did most of the housework.

'I sensed over breakfast that morning that Kieran knew I had seen you two in bed,' he said gently. 'Did he mention that when I went back to bed?'

'Heavens no! I'd have gone straight up to you and confessed. I *am* sorry. It won't happen again.'

He felt it was going to be interesting when and if Kieran returned. Perhaps his knowledge of being sprung in bed was why they had not heard from his brother.

At ICI, he heard about a planned major Loyalist counter-attack on the Official IRA and the Provisionals. He was pleased to have less contact with Provos, for at least a while, but told a few of them at a pub of the Loyalists' plan – he overheard, he claimed, at another pub.

The IRA event was cancelled. Rippling gratitude from Provos was heartening after the venue they were to meet at was blown up, empty. If any Provo had suspected big Tansey was spying on them, surely that had now gone.

No letters went to London for weeks. His days at Belfast, he felt, might be concluding.

He was alarmed when told by a Michelin mate in a restaurant that a few former paras, now civilians in Belfast, were now training Provos in gunmanship and combat skills.

He hoped the story was wrong. Perhaps the soldiers had got out of the army in disgust about Bloody Sunday. Or they were part of that Derry massacre, and feared prosecution. Perhaps, with Tansey gone from the Michelin works, the Brits were trying to plant another spy or two in the Provos. In any case, he did not want to make contact with those ex paras, who probably knew him.

He spent most work breaks in the ICI Social Club rooms, which had two full-size snooker tables. He was at a dining table with computer-room supervisor Rob Doran when John Elles strolled up to them and sat down.

Within minutes, Elles made it clear that he was a boss of the UDA. The three of them, Elles announced, were to work together on a special and important assignment.

They were in the right places at ICI to run a scheme smuggling into the province small arms and, more importantly, military-grade explosives including anti-personnel mines that UDA-related teams, especially the Ulster Volunteer Force, needed more of urgently.

Before Maurice could be involved, Elles told him, Maurice had to gain better warehouse skills. He had to be able to handle various fork-lift vehicles so he could personally stack and deliver the secret goods. He also had to master ICI's storage system.

With management ignorant of the trade, of course, Elles told them, Maurice and Rob had to doctor the official records and always know where the guns and explosives were concealed in the big complex, ready to despatch to the UVF and others.

Maurice felt he had no option. He and Rob keenly agreed to be smugglers. London was going to know all about this.

At times, concerns arose at ICI about the quality of batches of product. When that happened, a product-restriction order was placed on them, with identifying cards. Maurice stacked the rejects at the far end of the warehouse, where they were held for further inspection and probable dumping. Some of the reject terylene and crimplene intended for clothing was diverted for making the likes of car seat belts and fibre ropes for ships. Sometimes, when most of its contents were faulty, a full container load went to Tansey's stack at the back.

UDA staffers, ensuring that ample stock boxes were kept aside for their illicit trade, regularly rejected products that were in good order. These were marked with an orange tick for the attention of Tansey, who gave each a number and readied the whole lot for shipment.

When the container or a batch of big boxes was at sea on the way to a customer in a country where arms dealers waited, ICI's Loyalists and warehouseman Tansey urgently recalled the numbered boxes by telephone and telex messages because, it was claimed, it was belatedly discovered that the cargo contained faulty product.

Dodgy dealers at the port of destination emptied the ICI boxes and filled them with explosives and armaments. They ensured that the returning containers of contraband weighed the same as when they arrived, averting attention from Customs inspectors. Those inspectors, in any case, would give only cursory inspections to consignments to and from reputable ICI. Perhaps, Maurice surmised, dodgy Loyalist Customs inspectors were involved.

Each carton contained twenty-twenty three kilos of weaponry. Maurice added them to his stack of duds due officially for dumping.

He was told when it was time for sneaking the weaponry to Loyalists in the province. In the dead of night and alone, he loaded the secret cargoes onto a fork-lift and took them to a scrape hole under ICI's back fence. Men waiting there carried the boxes across the railway line to a small boat at the beach, about wo hundred metres away.

The boat took the boxes to pick-up points around the coast. Computer boss Doran meantime listed the boxes as dumped. The ICI smugglers never risked sending their munitions by road.

Maurice was dismayed at the thought of the mass destruction enabled by his sly work. Every time he heard about a UDA, UVF or Orange Order shooting or bombing, he knew he was the likely supplier of the means of the outrage. His only alternative was for him and Carol and Allen to leave the province in a hurry. But the deadly trade would continue.

Among the first lots he handled were several boxes of explosives and rifles and hand guns from dealers in Yugoslavia. Grenades and compact bombs came from Argentina, one of a few South American countries that supplied most of the weaponry. Some weapons he inspected, that were shipped from Germany, were made in Russia. Maurice noted that nothing came from Republican supplier, Libya.

Over several months, he delivered about twelve loads to the men at the fence. He was promoted to be the boss of the restricted-products division.

He avoided socialising for a while with anyone in Belfast he knew was a member of the UDA other than ICI employees. Members he best remembers, apart from Rob and John, were Tommy Herron and a girl, Marie McGuire. She was the sole female activist Maurice met in Belfast.

He wrote to London twice, giving them the likely arrival dates and ports of nine loads of arms. London also got the addresses on eight deliveries by boat to Loyalist activists up the coast. Four were shipments from Germany and Venezuela.

For his own safety in case of an internal witch hunt, he insisted in the letters that the cargoes be intercepted well away from ICI. He recommended that Customs in the North be alerted to check all ICI's incoming freight.

The messages went to London in ample time for the cargoes to be stopped. But, to his knowledge, they were not. He wanted to tell the Provos about the trade. They, at least, would act. But giving an invented explanation of how he knew about the shipments would be dicey.

He loved Larne, the freight and passenger-ferry port north of ICI, used for some of the province's trade with England. It was a forty-five minute drive from home. Calm and peaceful, it was, with an extraordinary lack of open bitterness between its Catholics and Protestants.

He went fishing for cod off Larne a few times with UDA men from ICI. Regulars were John Elles and Tommy Herron. He hoped they would not encounter that amateur fisherman from nearby Derry, Marty McGuinness.

They went to sea in a twenty-foot open boat with a powerful inboard diesel motor. A shallow draft and no superstructure. The craft easily handled rough seas they encountered at times, well off the coast. Maurice always came home with a bag of fish.

On the third trip in the boat, Tansey said he was pleased it had such a shallow draft, enabling them to run it onto beaches.

'Sure,' said Tommy Herron. 'Don't you know that's why we use this one to go right to the beach near ICI for all your loads of armaments? With fishing gear on show, she can sneak in just about anywhere on the coast.'

Maurice sent London a description of the boat, repeating what he had written about its smuggling along the coast. The shrinks, he hoped, would alert the Royal Navy's elite warriors of the Special Boat Service. He knew it operated covertly off the Irish coast. His SAS special trainer Geordie Tasker, although typically derisive of another armed service, had told him the SBS was there to counter arms smuggling by Republicans and Loyalists.

Newspapers and the radio news later informed him that British troops and the RUC had found weapons and explosives at UDA and UVF strongholds in Belfast and Derry – at addresses he had given to London. Descriptions of the weaponry told him it had come from ICI.

His letters to London finally were getting results again. He had prevented more bloodshed.

Soon after, Customs found weapons and explosives in an ICI container shipped into Larne. But the fishing boat continued its guns and explosives runs.

He was still wary of being seen with UDA types by Provos and with Provos by UDAs.

He grew a full beard, a droopy moustache and let his hair grow to his shoulders. It was often pulled back into a ponytail. In company, a briar pipe, which he seldom lit, often hung from his mouth. As far as the Provos knew, he was still unemployed, in no hurry to find work. He joked to them about living on his wife's income from the hospital. They did not know he now lived farther north of the city.

A common social meeting place for his ICI colleagues was the Central Bar in Carrickfergus, opposite an old stone castle. Rob Doran introduced Maurice in there to Charles Harding-Smith, leader of the UDA, and Harding-Smith's friend John White, whom Maurice thought was another mean-looking bastard. Charles was from the Shankill district where, Rob said, most of the UDA's activities were planned.

Soon after the meeting, Maurice had drinks with Loyalist Association of Workers boss Billy Hull and the head of the Orange Order, the Rev. Martin Smyth. Maurice joined them when they talked with unionist politician Bill Craig, arranging their support for Craig's planned formation soon of a shadowy movement of Paisleyite militants called the Vanguard. All the names, with details of the plans, went to London. Evident action – nil.

Maurice drank regularly at the social club and played with ICI's cricket team. Long-haired Tansey, fast bowler and No. 5 batsman, helped them win a few trophies. He also played soccer with an amateur club made up mostly of ex-members of the Boys Brigade, an all-Protestant fraternity. During one match he broke an ankle.

A hospital doctor wanted to apply a plaster cast up to his knee. That would have made it difficult to relocate cartons in the warehouse. Maurice insisted on getting instead a small plaster covering of his foot and ankle, with a heel fitted, so he was able to move around at work easily enough.

The plaster was still in place a few weeks later, causing him to limp, when he was provoked in a bar, jealously told by a fellow worker from the warehouse that he was Tansey the Pansy, a gutless soccer player. The man had never made it into the team but fancied himself as a tough. He was glad Maurice was injured.

'Pansy' Tansey was told he had better come outside and get a hiding. The foul-mouth shaped up in the street. He was on his back, his nose broken, a rib fractured, in a minute.

The next day, pregnant Carol complained that a builder's labourer working on the nearby Ballyhenry Primary School which Allen attended was regularly exposing his dick at her. Maurice went to the worksite and loudly told the big and muscled offender to keep his dick to his stupid self.

The next day, the couple were in front of their home, getting into the Morris, when the builder, aged in his twenties, charged up to them. 'I'll flash any fucken where I want to!' he yelled menacingly. The builder was about the same size as resident Tansey.

'You yell out at me like that again in front of my workmates,' the abuser threatened, 'and you'll get a belting, you weak cunt.'

He spat at Maurice and swung a round-arm punch, which the ex-para easily ducked under. A kick, a right hook and left uppercut sent the builder flying over the low wall in front of their home. He was still on the ground, barely conscious, when the couple drove away.

Two days later, both of Maurice's assaults were common knowledge at ICI. He had not only put his fellow warehouse worker in hospital, but broken the jaw of the builder and cracked his left leg in two places. The ICI men were embarrassingly awed. That builder, he was told, was a prominent militant in the UDA and an all-Ireland heavyweight boxing champion.

Maurice felt that it was only a matter of time before someone in the UDA or the IRA found out about his real reason for being in Northern Ireland. But he was going to hang in. The police, army and Customs raiding of UVF weapons consignments had resurged his determination to minimise the Troubles.

By then he had agreed, when on day shifts, to drive to and from work a girl employed in ICI's main administration building. She lived near the Tanseys' home. The shortest route to and from ICI was on the B90 Mance Road. Every time he drove on it brought memories of shooting dead in the quarry the nameless alleged assassin.

It was a winding and at times dangerous route, particularly early on some mornings when it had patches of black ice. He was cautiously driving the Morris to work around a bend, the girl beside him, when he hit the footbrake. It did not respond. As he reached for the hand brake, the car slid across the icy road and crashed into a big crag of basalt.

The front of the car was smashed in, the front screen shattered. The vehicle was a write-off. The girl screamed, bleeding from her head and shoulder, then lost consciousness. It was a quiet location, with no buildings nearby. Nor was there other early-morning traffic.

Maurice, still with his foot in plaster and bleeding a little at the top of his head, used all his strength to force open his door and hurry to her side of the smoking car. Petrol might be leaking. Flames could be imminent. The passenger door was badly bent. It took him several minutes, with a steel tyre lever from the boot, to prize it open enough to get her out.

He dragged the girl well away from the wreck. She was breathing weakly, had not opened her eyes under his resuscitating some fifteen minutes later, when another car arrived and the driver ran to them.

'Thank you,' he said to this rare Good Samaritan in a land where so many ignored a scene of violence. 'There's a phone box three kilometres away, in the direction you're going. Please, get there quickly and ring 999. This girl might die. It was an accident. The brakes failed.'

Maurice kept resuscitating for what seemed an age before the arrival an ambulance, its siren blaring. The girl survived but had a month in hospital with severe internal injuries. She was left with facial scars which, for such a pretty lass, was devastating.

An accident investigation team found that the brake's master cylinder had been tampered with. It was no accident. Some bastard had tried to kill him. He hoped it was that damned boxing builder he had knocked over the front wall. Not the UDA or IRA.

A friend named Ricky lent him a car for a couple of weeks until he bought another new, blue Morris coupe.

ICI men mentioned to him that the UVF planned to bomb a forthcoming Provo gathering in a Belfast pub. Although it put in jeopardy his safe standing at ICI, he warned the Provos. Like his claim of how he found out about the previous planned Loyalist bombing, Maurice said he had heard about it from men sitting near him in a restaurant.

The event was quietly relocated. A bomb exploded in the pub the night the gathering was to have been held. But the pub was nearly empty. Only two drinkers were injured. This second saving of lives enabled him to maintain his cautious contact with the grateful Provos.

16. The bomber priest

July 1972

In mid-month, a group of friends from Michelin asked him to join them for a celebration in their favourite pub, then a quiet yarn in a back room.

He thought it might be connected to the Sinn Fein and IRA delegation that had gone to London in an RAF aircraft on July 7 for an historic meeting to try to negotiate a peace settlement with the British Government. Members were Gerry Adams, Martin McGuinness, Seamus Twomey, Sean MacStiofain, Ivor Bell and Daithi O'Conaill.

Secretary of State for Northern Ireland, William Whitelaw, had led the Government side. As the Republicans were about to leave the meeting, McGuinness had delivered an emotional condemnation of the paratroopers on Bloody Sunday, killing and wounding some of Martin's former schoolmates.

Martin was the sole Provo who had Maurice's home phone number – not, though, his new address. Martin had phoned his buddy Maurice to tell him about the London meeting. A cease-fire was introduced but soon ended.

Maurice was dressing for the Provo gathering on a Friday evening when he realised what it would be about. It was July 14, Bastille Day. Some there wore green hats, ribbons and jackets, as if it was St Patrick's Day.

These men likened themselves to the rebels against the monarchy who brought on the French Revolution in the late 1700s. They expected that the Provos' campaign of Troubles would get a similar win, joining Northern Ireland to the Republic.

There was bitter amusement, beery jeering at the government across the Irish Sea, about the general English-speaking world's fastening on old England's mockery of the Republic of Ireland by using the term 'beyond the Pale' to describe something stupid and repulsive. The Pale, Maurice knew, was territory around Dublin once ruled by England.

Few in the pub had much notion of the words when, with a scraggy old fiddler, they stumbled through *La Marseillaise*. Catholic France, after all, was an historical supporter of the Cause. The common enemy was England.

A few there again thanked Maurice for alerting them to the two UVF bombs. They urged the bearded long-hair to keep dining and drinking at Loyalist hangouts, where he might find out more about the UDA. This was bloody marvellous; giving him in their eyes a good reason to fraternise with the enemy. He agreed to the request. They quietly cheered and a pint was presented to him.

'Them fooken animal paratroopers,' young Provo Tommy McMahon declared angrily, downing a draught of beer. 'The way they mowed down all them kids and women and innocent men on Bloody Sunday. Mark my bloody word, Maurice mate, we're gonna make 'em pay.'

'Them soldiers, the thugs, are gonna get a bullet or a bomb for every single person they killed.'

That would require a lot of ammo, the former tyre maker decided as he sucked on his empty pipe. He knew these people had no notion of the extent of para thuggery.

His mind flashed back to episodes in five countries. 'Yeah, they're brutes,' he said, turning to sober Martin McGuinness, who had also applauded his star recruit's preparedness to mix with some Loyalists.

Maurice nearly choked on his Guinness when Marty said, 'So, mate. You'll be our sort of spy!'

'Sure,' said Britain's spy. 'I sure hope it works.'

But triple-spy Tansey had a job to do for London. 'So, what's planned?' he asked the group in general. 'How're you going to deal with those paratroopers? I want to be part of it.'

'Later, pal,' said Joe from Derry.

Well into the night, when many of the celebraters had left, most there were tipsy. Joe looked at McGuinness for his approval. 'We're going out the back.'

Nine Provos carried their Guinness and whiskies to a small room behind the bar. It was an old parlour for group parties. Even now in high summer, a peat fire glowed near their table.

Something significant was afoot. Maurice was pleased he had again drunk sparingly. He made out he was as inebriated as most of the rest of them.

'This is between us,' said Tom McMahon as they sat there. 'More revenge is coming for Bloody Sunday. For the whole crazy Internment. There's a priest I know up in County Derry. As some of you know, he's one of us.'

McMahon looked to Martin, Provo 2IC in Derry, who nodded and said, 'He's Father Jim Chesney, the parish priest in Cullion, a bit west of Claudy. He lost some dear friends on Bloody Sunday.'

Maurice's mind went to the maps he had studied. Claudy, yes. A smallish town, an old one. A short drive south-east of Derry city. Just south of the A6 highway to Belfast. There was nothing new to him now about a priest being an IRA activist.

'Daithi O'Conaill has agreed to us taking bombs to Father Chesney,' said Joe. 'As Martin, Billy, Jack and Kerry here know, we've delivered three of them. They'll need only fusing before they go off nicely in cars. Father Ches is going to explode them about the end of the month, in a fortnight, in a street in Claudy when it's busy, with Loyalists about. And plenty of troopers, if he's lucky.'

'*Three* bombs?' said Maurice.

'To be sure. That priest means business. He's done things for us in the past.'

'Bejasus,' said Tansey, looking excited. He had to prevent this. Find out all he could. 'I want to be part of that.' Others clearly shared his stated enthusiasm.

'I know the place well,' said young Marty. 'So many friends of mine were killed on Bloody Sunday...

'The curious thing is,' the red-haired leader continued, 'Father Ches wants to do it with only two or three locals, who are probably also priests. One hell of a job that will be, for just a few men. Three bombs. Three vehicles to be stolen. And dangerous. For a priest, that is. Well, I rang Father Jim today.

'Told him a gang of us wanted to go there, get hold of the vehicles, plant the bombs and park them where he wants us to. *When* he wants us to. Jim Chesney can set the timing for the explosions, all at about the same time.'

Maurice wondered if Britain's GCHQ in Cheltenham had heard the phone conversation. It would require only the using of a key-word to alert their electronic devices.

'About the end of the month, you said?' a drinker interjected and hiccupped.

'That's what he told me today,' said McGuinness. 'He's going to get back to me soon about that. So, if it's on, are you all in?'

'Too fooken right! Good one... I want to kill them soldiers... count me in,' they chorused.

'Right,' said McGuinness, picking up his glass of the black stuff. 'I'll let you boys know at Michelin, you at home Maurice, when Father Ches calls back. I'll be back in Derry by then, but you boys can get back in here to sort out the details. Decide who does what. You'll be in charge, Maurie.

'Then report to me or Gerry O'Hara. We've got plenty of men in Derry keen to help Jim Chesney. But it might be safer if it's done by a team from Belfast. You'd have to be on the way back to the city when those bombs go off. It'll be after the blitz here, of course.'

'What sort of bloke is Father Chesney?' Maurice asked.

'He's a true Provo. I know Jim pretty well. Dark, with clumpy sideburns, mutton chops really, that go down below his chin. A solid build. He's thirty eight. And a pretty good priest.'

Maurice wondered what sort of priest would plan mass murders. He had to wait until Monday morning before he sat in his car alone and penned a note to London, giving the location, likely date and naming Father Chesney, the priest's parish, the names of the men who had been at the planning meeting.

Again cursing the absence of phone contact with London, he wondered if that was because the SIS did not want its GCHQ electronics-listening allies to hear information Maurice phoned them.

Was there inter-departmental rivalry between the spook bosses? Like the evident relationship between the FBI and the CIA? Like the regular slinging off by his former army mates at the navy and air force. Their enthusiasm for picking fights with American and other servicemen.

For the first time, he took the risk of appending his real name and address to the back of the envelope containing his Claudy warning to MI6's Private Bag 9. That should ensure that it was opened promptly. If the Secret Service was not acting on his alerts because they had changed the address and not notified him, the letter would be returned to their troubled spook in the Troubles.

He drove to the Glengormley Post Office and paid to send his missive by express mail, as always. They would get it on Tuesday, a couple of weeks before the bombing in Claudy. As he left the post office, he uneasily remembered his note of an assurance of a peaceful event that turned out to be Bloody Sunday.

This one, though, could not be ignored. It was a specific alerting to a plot of mass killings and destruction by the IRA in a country town. He was pleased to be preventing it.

A charge of criminal intent on Chesney ought to come soon, sending him to jail and disgracing him out of the church. Maurice hoped that would assuage his guilt over perhaps causing the paras to be there for Bloody Sunday, and the UVF at McGurk's.

17. Bloody Friday, Bloody Monday

July 1972

On Saturday, 22 July, Maurice rushed from home to a Provo pub in the city after hearing more radio news about bombings the day before all over Belfast's Protestant districts. News flashes had first told him about it after his late night delivery of smuggled munitions to the back fence at ICI.

The radio had said the swathe of bombing was the work of Provos. He bought two newspapers on the way to the pub and learned more. The Shankill in particular had received a nasty plastering. Eleven citizens had been killed. Seriously injured were fifty-three men and boys, seventy-seven women and girls.

The front pages of the newspapers near-screamed with outrage at the worst-ever day of terrorist assault in Belfast. Bombs in vehicles and suitcases had been exploded between 2.10pm and 3.15pm at nineteen places. The first was at the Smithfield bus station, also damaging houses in nearby Samuel Street. Six minutes later, a bomb set by three men with a sub-machine gun blew up the Brookvale Hotel and houses in Brookvale Avenue and Antrim Road.

The last of the nineteen horrors was an explosion in a stolen vehicle at the busy Cavehill Road Shopping Centre. Shops were wrecked. The three killed there included a mother of seven and a boy aged fourteen.

The *Belfast Telegraph* said the city had not experienced such a day of destruction since the German blitz of 1941. The *Irish Times* said, '... Irish men and women should ponder how a virulent Nazi-style disregard for life can lodge in the hearts of our fellow countrymen; all the more virulent in that once again the innocent have been the main sufferers'.

Photographs graphically showed the devastation, the dead and the mutilated. The Provisionals had claimed contentedly that it was their doing. Maurice was shocked that it had happened without him getting prior word.

He was near shaking with fury at the Provos and grief for the dead and injured as he stormed into the pub, trying to act calmly. Provos drinking in a corner there were quietly and happily abuzz about it. Despite, he soon learned, none from Michelin being involved.

'I didn't know that was on,' he said, showing astonishment.

Billy said, 'What a massive, bloody victory! We don't see so much of you now, mate. You'd normally be one of the planners. You'da planted a bomb or two yourself yesterday if you'd wanted to. Don't you remember Marty mentioning it when we talked about the Claudy job in the pub on

Bastille Day? I suppose the rest of us thought you knew about it. The blitz.'

With a mental thud, Maurice remembered it. McGuinness had mentioned 'the blitz' in passing before describing Father Chesney to him. Damn, he was so fired up then about Claudy. It had not registered. Passing references to coming operations – onslaughts, slayings, revenge jobs – were so damned commonplace.

Waiting for a beer, repulsed at being part of this celebration, he was uneasy about what they were thinking in non-alerted London. Five days ago he had told them about a planned bombing in Derry about the end of the month.

They probably reckoned he should have warned them about nineteen bombings in Belfast yesterday. Like he should have alerted them to the protest march near the Magilligan Prison Camp in Derry a week before Bloody Sunday.

With all the secrets he had given them, surely they could not reckon he was now pro-Provo or getting negligent. If they were curious about this, they should bloody well ask him. He hoped again that London understood, at least from his letter of complaint, that he could not know beforehand about every damned thing.

If in fact Kieran was right and it was the Secret Service that got him to leave Michelin, his ignorance of yesterday's mayhem was their fault. Still at Michelin, he would have known all about yesterday and alerted them. It was one they would have *had* to act on. Should he write and explain? Have another go at the silvertail clots?

No, like how he felt after the Magilligan Prison Camp protest, it would achieve nothing. He would simply continue giving them accurate info that came his way.

He managed to contain his anger for fifteen more minutes with the celebraters.

The awful day was soon called Bloody Friday. Tansey's only relief came from the news over the weekend that the death toll had been reduced from eleven to nine. He was not aware of any of the perpetrators being arrested.

He had doubts about Adams' being involved. But on his way to work on Monday morning he sent London a note of two sentences and a post script. It told them he had not known in advance about Bloody Friday. However, three Provisionals had just claimed to him that a main organiser of the blitz was Gerry Adams, now an active but undercover Provo. His PS said, 'I hope action is proceeding to prevent the bombing at Claudy at the end of the month'.

His London bosses must have received his warning about Claudy. His first alert to it, with the sender's address on the envelope, was not returned to him.

A year later, Maurice wondered if the note about Gerry Adams had influenced the man's arrest and his jailing at Long Kesh. The charge related to Bloody Friday. After an IRA-organised escape attempt, Adams was released in 1976. He was re-arrested two years later for alleged IRA membership, which he hotly denied. The charges were dismissed and he became joint vice-president of Sinn Fein. In 1983 he was elected as the party's president and, representing Belfast West, became the first Sinn Fein Member of Britain's House of Commons since the mid 1950s. In line with party policy, he refused to take his seat in the Commons, despite Britain lifting its ban on him travelling there.

Most of Maurice's fellow workers at ICI on Monday blazed with shock and anger about Bloody Friday. There was stormy talk in the social club about retaliation. But he heard nothing sufficiently specific to interest London. Anyway, he concluded, telling the Brits now about planned Loyalist revenge might sharpen any suspicion of him being a real Provo.

He could have gone to the Loyalist social club that evening and learned more, but the whole drama was nauseating. His fevered mind settled as he drove home, where Carol told him a man who did not give his name had telephoned.

She said, 'He had a bit of an accent from the north. He wants you to ask the Michelin boys tomorrow about what he called Project C.'

It was Marty, Maurice assumed to himself. *C for Chesney and Claudy.* 'Did you say I was at ICI?'

'No. Just that you were out. I know you don't want people to know where you work.'

That earned a hug for Carol, prominently pregnant.

At a pub near Michelin after work the next day, intended Claudy team leader Tansey was told that Father Chesney had declined the offer of help from Belfast. The cleric still insisted on blowing up Main Street, Claudy, with a few friends.

One or two of the fellow bombers would be other Provo priests, one said. Chesney did not want others, from Belfast, to risk being caught. Maurice figured that Cullion's parish priest also wanted to minimise the number of witnesses to his bastardry.

He waited to read or learn from the Michelin boys that Chesney had been arrested or that the presbytery had been searched for bombs.

On the evening of Monday, July 31, the news from Claudy broke on the radio. A bomb had exploded in a stolen Ford Cortina at 10.15 in the morning in front of McElhinney's bar and store on Main Street. Six people killed there included a girl aged eight.

A policeman had spotted a second bomb in a stolen Morris Mini Traveller outside the Main Street post office.

At 10.30am a third bomb, in a stolen Mini Van, went off outside the Beaufort Hotel on Church Street, killing three shoppers. The second bomb had blasted into the post office at nearly the same time, but the street and premises there had been cleared.

So, nine dead, including the little girl. An unknown number were injured. Many shops were shattered.

A news report said two men had tried to ring 999 on public phones at places near Claudy to alert the police half an hour before the first explosion. But an earlier blast of some sort had cut off the phone lines. Triggered by the bombers, Maurice suspected.

In desperation, the two men had rushed into a shop and reported that the phones were not working. They had asked staff in a shop to rush to the local police station and report that three bombs were about to explode in vehicles parked in Main and Church streets, Claudy. By the time the police could react, the first bomb had gone off. One of the first officers there had spotted the second bomb and cleared the street, saving lives.

Jeez, Maurice muttered. *In Church Street. Exploded by one or more priests!*

The newspapers said the bombs might have targetted British Army troops who, the night before, had begun Operation Motorman, a campaign to regain control of Catholic enclaves in Derry and other places that were 'no go' to the army and the RUC. Other reports said it was in also a response to Bloody Sunday, perhaps also Bloody Friday.

Maurice shook with fury, aimed at the Secret Service. He had gone to Ireland to save lives. His main impediment was MI6, his assigner.

And Bloody Sunday, the Internment and now Operation Motorman demonstrated to him that the army did little more than terminate lives.

Unlike their open boasting after Bloody Friday, the Provisional IRA publicly denied involvement in the Claudy genocide. A Provo 'internal court of inquiry' promptly reported that its local unit did not carry out the attack, now called Bloody Monday.

A man who police believed owned one of the cars blown up in Main Street was arrested as a bomber suspect. However, Maurice read, a Father James Chesney and another person confirmed the man's alibi –

that he was at the priest's home in Bellaghy well before and when the bombs were ignited. The suspect was released.

In September Chesney himself was stopped at a police roadblock. A sniffer dog alerted them to an odour of explosives in the car, but it evidently the matter went no further.

A UDA man at ICI's social club swore to Maurice and others that the IRA and Chesney were the Claudy perpetrators, that the Catholic Church and other authorities were covering for them.

Secretary of State William Whitelaw was said to have participated in secret talks about it soon after the explosions. There seemed to be more public intrigue about Bloody Monday – Claudy – than about Bloody Sunday or Bloody Friday.

Maurice, biting his tongue to prevent an outburst of what he knew, had another moment of fury. He thought particularly of that eight-year-old girl who had been blown up. He would never forget the sight of those two young sisters whose legs were blasted off at the Abercorn restaurant.

He considered going to a public telephone and anonymously telling the RUC that Chesney was their man. But perhaps they knew that. Perhaps the Secret Service had an agenda. Were they blackmailing the priest into spying on the IRA for them? Maurice would gladly go to Derry and deal with the murdering reverend himself. It was impossible, the still-inactive Catholic knew, to be a real priest and also a mass murderer.

He fumed again about not being able to phone London and protest at their failure to prevent the horror. He read in a newspaper that investigating police thought the culprits for Bloody Monday, in a largely Catholic community, could be either Republicans or Loyalists.

'Hell, London *knows*,' he told himself. 'Is Bernard's outfit happy to let the Derry cops waste all that time?'

It was possible, he conceded, that MI6 had been so alarmed at the public rage following the excesses of the paras in Derry on Bloody Sunday that they had decided not to send the army's thugs to Claudy.

He wrote a note to London with the names of three more Provo volunteers he had met. They included a clever young bomb maker called Patrick Magee. A postscript said: *A reminder. The main bomber at Claudy, armed by the Provisionals, was Father James Chesney, parish priest at Cullion.*

In a few weeks the Claudy bombing was just another old atrocity of the North. Father Chesney, Maurice learned, continued as a priest. He would be hearing confessions and imposing penances on penitents like young Tansey had been, telling God's claimed representative that he had pinched fruit from an orchard. He wondered how many clergymen Chesney had enlisted and confided in.

And how in God's name did Chesney, upset about friends being killed on Bloody Sunday, think that the bombing of more innocents, including people of his home parish, would avenge that? His incredulous anger grew when he read that five of the nine killed at Claudy were Catholics.

November 1972

When she developed labour pains, Maurice drove Carol to hospital. He was waiting in a corridor when a smiling nurse told him he had a healthy baby son. He went to Carol, in bed and holding the silent babe.

He still hoped the father was Kieran. He held the blue-eyed boy, thinking he recognised a Tansey look about him.

Excited Carol told him it had been a smooth birth. 'I've been thinking, darling,' she said. 'I've never met him, of course. But it'd be good to name him after your father, Nicholas. Okay?'

The real father's father too, Maurice reflected grimly. The idea sounded repugnant. But it would be a bit much calling the boy Kieran, he decided. Carol had no notion of what a violent drunk was the babe's grandfather.

'Fine,' he said, taking the gurgling pinky in his arms again. 'Hello Nicholas Tansey.' He would see to it that the child did not grow up to be like Nicholas senior. That night he went to a public phone to inform his parents in Birmingham. His mother Ellen expressed no surprise or joy at Maurice having a son. She promptly put Nicholas on the line.

'Carol gave birth today to a terrific baby boy, Dad,' he announced. 'And we're naming him Nicholas, after you. He's your first grandson.'

He heard a grunt, a slur as his father said, 'A good name. I'll have a pint on it.'

At first Maurice thought the line had gone, then he realised that his father had hung up. He had anticipated them wanting to see baby Nicholas. If so, Maurice would have had to make some quick changes; rent a place in the Republic so he would seem to be living there. And he would not impose on Carol, Allen and the baby a visit to Sparkhill, Birmingham.

Maurice knew 1972 was the worst year in the grisly history of Northern Ireland's Troubles. At year's end, Bloody Sunday was still the catalyst for months of almost daily killings. In the first half, before he left Michelin, he was involved in more jobs for the Provos than he could recall in detail.

He checked and confirmed the accuracy of a report that in 1972 nearly two thousand bombs had been ignited in public places. There were 10,600 shootings. A total of four hundred and sixty-seven people had been killed. Proper action by London would have more than halved those terrible statistics.

January 1973

By the end of the month, on the anniversary of Bloody Sunday, British Army GOC and Director of Ops in Northern Ireland, war hero Lt. General Harry Tuzo, had had his fill of the stresses of his post. After less than two years at the job, he elected to leave the province.

The army in the North, Maurice calculated, had now had four commanders in less than three years. He felt that Tuzo would have likened his time in the province to his time as a prisoner of war, regularly tortured, in North Korea.

He and Carol had not heard from Kieran for a year when the young para telephoned in March to say he would return for a two-day visit.

'We've been concerned about you, bruv,' said Maurice. 'You thought you'd be away for only a month or two when you left last time. After three months, I rang Aldershot, asking to speak to you. I was told you were on an exercise out of the country.'

'Yeah, I got back a week ago with the rest of the company. It'll be good to see you again. Thanks for the note you sent months back, giving your new phone number. You've changed jobs, I hope?'

'I have. I'm now at ICI and it's going well.' He gave his brother their new address. He wondered how Kieran would take the news that he was baby Nicholas' father.

Kieran arrived, poking fun at his brother's beard, mo and long hair. This time he had two bottles of Pernod for Carol. 'Like last time,' he said, 'I nicked them from a bar in Birmingham. I work there part-time.'

Maurice did not like the aniseedy stuff. Kieran and Carol were into the second bottle of it when Maurice left for a night shift, including gun smuggling, at ICI. He dared not return home early that night. But surely they would be damned careful. He supposed Carol would tell her brother-in-law that Maurice knew he had sired the baby, now four months old.

Maurice left his bed the moment he heard Kieran on the move soon after dawn. He confronted his little brother at the front door. He was carrying his suitcase.

Kieran turned and faced him, looking grim. 'So you want to bash me up, do you?' he accused loudly from outside the door. 'I know you came to the door and saw us screwing in your bed. I got back to my own room. And you didn't do a damn thing, you big, weak shit. You know I'm Nicky's father. You're not accepting the damn message I gave you, either, you weak shit of a brother. You're still dealing with the IRA.'

So, Carol had told him. Maurice advanced and grabbed him with one hand by the throat. Firmly, but not hard enough to choke him or lift him off the ground. 'You sneaky little bugger! And not even an apology. What sort of brother are *you*?' He delivered a firm backhander to Kieran's face, causing him to drop his case and fall to the ground.

The youngster said, 'I'm the sort of brother who's going to make sure the bloody IRA really knows about you!' He picked up the case and hurried to a taxi waiting in the street, that he must have booked. He yelled from an open window as the taxi left, 'I'm going to tell them myself. Right bloody now!'

Maurice slowly returned to the bedroom. No way would Kieran the para go ratting about his own brother to the IRA. Anyway, he would not have any idea of where to go, who to see. Kieran surely was heading for an aircraft or the ferry across the Irish Sea.

Over breakfast, Maurice told Carol and Allen he had seen Kieran briefly as he was leaving. He understood there had been an urgent call to get back to his barracks. Kieran, he lied, had not wanted to wake them to say goodbye.

Carol looked at him a little uneasily but was soon cheerful again. Allen left for school. She admitted that she had told Kieran he was baby Nicholas' father. 'He was pleased, but he was awful scared of what you might do to him,' she added.

bbb

A month later, Maurice learned while drinking at the Brown Bear in Mountjoy Street that the UDA was going to murder influential Republican Senator Paddy Wilson, a founding member of the North's Social Democratic and Labour Party.

The party had a fine program of civil rights, wealth redistribution, cross-border co-operation with the Republic, friendly contact between Catholics and Protestants. Maurice promptly mailed an alert to London, asking them urgently to urge Wilson to leave the island immediately, for at least a while, and why.

Eleven days later, on 26 June '73, his secretary found the bodies of Wilson and his friend Irene Andrews, knifed dead. Wilson's throat was cut and he had been stabbed many times.

A police spokesman said the UDA had claimed responsibility for the murders. The killers were members of a mob of UDA henchmen called the Ulster Freedom Fighters. Maurice soon had a good idea, correctly as it turned out, of the names of those who had ordered and carried out the executions. They were men he had met through ICI.

He hoped London had at least warned Wilson, who might not have taken them seriously. But it seemed that the politician had not been warned. Surely, if he *had* been warned, someone close to Wilson would know about it. Maurice cursed himself for not telephoning Senator Paddy.

Drinking with ICI men at Campbell's Pub in the High Street in Larne, Maurice was introduced to Andy Tyrie, who had lately deposed Charles Harding-Smith as leader of the UDA. He stayed with Tyrie for an hour, relating well with the man, in his late twenties.

When they met again at the Windsor Bar by the Shankill Road, Tyrie was with a man called here Lenny O'Mara, a rough-neck character who bragged about his skill with knives. Also there was Unionist official Glenn Barr. The other two seemed to be cool and cautious towards O'Mara. Andy Tyrie told Maurice in the men's that O'Mara was a notorious brute with a quick temper. He had delivered several murders for the Ulster Freedom Fighters. Victims of his, Tyre claimed, were Senator Paddy Wilson and his girlfriend.

Maurice named O'Mara and two others in a letter to London. There were no arrests.

A few days later, Maurice played golf with the three UDA heavies at Port Rush, on the way to Londonderry. Andy and Len O'Mara held a private meeting in the clubhouse with militants who ran UDA operations in the northern city while Maurice and Glenn enjoyed a meal nearby. The four returned to Belfast together the next morning.

During the trip, UDA boss Andy Tyrie praised Tansey's covert and reliable despatching of weapons and explosives from ICI.

The following Saturday night, ICI computer boss Rob Doran and Tansey were guests of honour at a 'thank you' party of about fifty people at a private home in Lancasterian Street, Carrickfergus.

Maurice felt like a devious interloper as the gathering drank to and flattered their two ICI smugglers. The Union Jack had a big presence in there. Not in sight was the tricolour flag of Ireland. That was the case, the former paratrooper noted, at Loyalist clubs he had visited.

A day later in the company of some Provos, Maurice considered himself a professional hypocrite for smuggling weapons intended to kill Provos.

Early in 1974, driving to work at Carrickfergus along the notorious Mance Road, Maurice had gone about a third of the way on a dark winter's night when he was forced to stop by a group of people flashing torches at him. The road was blocked by two cars. He was alarmed, but could not crash through.

As he slowed down, unwinding the window, he was sure they were not RUC or the army. He pulled off the road, conscious of the Taurus revolver beside him. Seven men stood there. One was studying under his torch what looked to be a catalogue of photographs. Another reached in and removed the car keys from the ignition.

He told them who he was; lied about where he lived. They opened the boot as Maurice left the car for questioning.

'You might as well also have a look under the bonnet,' he said helpfully. He reached through the open window on the driver's side for, they thought, the lever that unlocked the hood. He had made from lead strapping at ICI a holder for the revolver. It was on his near side of the wheel arch, beside the bonnet lever. In a flash, he whipped out the gun and aimed it at the head of the closest interrogator. 'Who are you lot?' he demanded.

They all seemed to talk as one. 'We're Provisionals!'

The man with the gun at his head shivered. 'Who the fuck are you, carrying a gun?'

'Look, I don't want any trouble here. Now you've got my name, you ask around later and you'll find that I'm one of *you*. A senior one. You ought to know me. I can't be sure you're really IRA.

'Chuck your weapons over the hedge-row over there and move one of the cars aside. Take the ignition keys from the cars and throw them where the weapons are. Do that and I'll continue my journey. For all you know, I might have armed men on the way to here in a back-up van.'

He held the man as, to his surprise, the rest of them quietly tossed away their weapons and cleared a car from the road. The man who moved the car threw a set of keys after the weapons. He went to the second vehicle. Instead of keys, he produced a handgun. He fired it twice at Maurice. The bullets narrowly missed him and his hostage.

Maurice aimed carefully and quickly. A single shot hit the gunman's shoulder. He grabbed his own keys from the bewildered man at his side. He ran to the moaning gunman and took his pistol and the keys to the second car.

The offender grasped at Maurice's legs. A bullet went into his thigh. The road blockers yelled in protest as Maurice hurried to his Morris and raced away. A kilometre on, he tossed the keys and pistol out the window.

He reflected at ICI that the gunman had got what he deserved. Maurice's shots were deliberately aimed not to kill. They were in self defence.

At lunch time he went to a pub where he knew Provos would be drinking. He told them about the roadside shooting. Concerned men undertook to investigate. They would report back to him at the pub the following day.

With them when Maurice returned was the very man he had held at gunpoint. The man apologised profusely. The stupid ass who Maurice had shot, he reported, was recovering in hospital. The fool had just missed killing one or both of them. The shooter also owned the car, the only keys to which Maurice had thrown out beside the road, along with the offender's gun. The car was still beside the road.

Maurice told him where to look for the keys and gun and bought him a pint of Guinness.

After that, Maurice always left home early, still in daylight, for night shifts. That gave him hours to play snooker and cards in the factory's social club. Similarly, he did not leave for home until dawn. He was not challenged again on the Manse Road.

Three months after Kieran had taken off, angry at Maurice's slap on his face and revealing his belief that his brother was still spying for the Provos, Maurice had not heard from the little trooper.

Kieran surely had a responsibility to keep in touch, learn how his son was faring. He should know that Maurice would not take seriously that threat to dob him in to the IRA. That, with all this time for tempers to settle, Nicky's dad would be welcomed back. At least Kieran could phone and test the climate.

Maurice phoned his mother. 'No, not a damn word from Butcher's Block in more than a bloody year,' she told him.

'Mum, he's your son. Kieran. If you still call him Butcher's Block to his face, it's no wonder he doesn't keep in touch.' Mother Ellen hung up. She had cruelly given him that sobriquet, pointing at baby Kieran's big head, soon after her younger son was born.

The next call was to Aldershot. A sergeant he knew took the call, so Maurice said who he was. After a brief chat, Maurice claimed he was living in the Republic, near the North. 'I haven't heard from my brother Kieran, one of your privates, in months,' he said. 'Can you get him to the phone?'

'Sorry, Big One Five old mate, but Kieran's AWOL. It's months since he went on a week's leave. We've had not a word. MPs have checked around Hampshire and Birmingham, with no joy. Do you have any idea where the little bastard's gone to?'

'No, not a clue. I've just checked with our mother. She hasn't seen or heard of him in ages. You can understand me being worried, Claude.'

'Okay, look I'll let you know if he turns up, or we get a lead on where he is.'

'Thanks. We're all pretty anxious here. Kieran left our place months ago. To return to the barracks, I supposed.' Maurice risked giving his former colleague his home phone number.

He and Carol wondered over dinner where Kieran might be. 'Look, I didn't tell you,' he said, 'but that morning he left early, he knew I'd sprung you two in bed. He sounded scared about being Nicky's dad. I hadn't known then that you'd told him.'

'Yes. I had to. And over more bloody Pernod. But we didn't have sex again, Maurice. I'm trying hard to be faithful to you.'

'I figured that, you hot-blooded little thing. But Kieran still had a notion that I'm spying on the bloody IRA. I slapped his face, but not hard, after he failed to apologise for bedding you. As he took off in a taxi, he yelled out that he was going to tell the IRA I was a spy. But, hell, Kieran wouldn't do that. He wouldn't even know how to.'

'Why would he say that?' she pondered gravely.

'It was just a silly blurting, with his face stinging. He was on his way to the airport or the ferry.'

As they washed the dishes, Maurice was preoccupied by a thought that Kieran might be dead. If he had ratted to the Provos or even the Loyalists, surely it would have to be at the behest of Military Intelligence. 'No, impossible, you idiot,' he told himself.

The next day he reported to the police in Belfast, Hampshire and Birmingham that Kieran had been missing for many months. The officers told him they had also received inquiries from 2 Para at Aldershot. The army had sent them photographs of Kieran. He was on their missing persons' lists.

Remembering the name of the taxi's company and its plate number, and after spending a lot of time at taxi ranks, Maurice found the driver Kieran had left with. The young Englishman, the cabbie said, had ended the ride somewhere in the centre of the city. No, he recalled, he did not think it was near buses to the airport or ferry.

Maurice went to the Belfast morgue several times to see if his brother's body was among its unidentified and bloodied victims of violence. He met many others there, also looking for the cadavers of probably-murdered relatives and friends.

He grieved, more afraid by the day that Kieran had met a sudden death. Had he in fact angrily gone to see someone to whom he thought he could say his big brother is a British spy? Kieran's possible motive for doing that was the source of fruitless speculation.

Had that cost his little brother his life? If so, who could have killed him? Republicans or Loyalists? It would have been easy for those Kieran contacted to fill him with grog. The little youngster was a cheap drunk. Could he have blurted, drunk or under torture, that he was a message boy for the Secret Service?

When with Maurice at the local pub, Kieran had seemed to think the Loyalists were friends of the army. Kieran, he recalled, had ignored Maurice's advice not to wear his army dog tag in Belfast.

Even Loyalists hated the paras for Bloody Sunday. If either Loyalists or Provos found the tags, they – not believing his tale – could have slain him. His body could have joined the scores of corpses in the North never to be found.

If he ever found out who had killed Kieran, they would pay for it.

18. Which side is my enemy?

From March 1974

Maurice spent an evening drinking with three acquaintances from ICI in a cubicle in a pub in the Protestant town of Ballyclare. The main topic of discussion was the implications of the tied Parliament after the British general election of 28 February 1974. Considerable confusion had prevailed before Labour's Harold Wilson regained the Prime Ministership, replacing Conservative Edward Heath.

Former First Secretary of State for Northern Ireland, William Whitelaw, was the new Deputy Leader of the Opposition. Maurice's dad's mate Roy Hattersley was the Minister of State for Foreign and Commonwealth Affairs.

Maurice knew the IRA would be cheering Labour's precarious win. The UDA men with him were angry with Britain's voters. They saw the Conservatives as allies, Labour as pro-Republican.

In March, a week before St Patrick's Day, UDA gunmen he knew from the Windsor Bar, who we will call here Bobby Bates and William Moore, arrived out of the blue at Maurice's home on a Sunday afternoon. They wanted Maurice to go with them for drinks at a Loyalist pub in Antrim, about thirty minutes' drive away.

Maurice was immediately suspicious. In all the time he had lived in Belfast, not one militant on either side had visited his home. They had got his address from his personal file at ICI, he supposed. He did not want to invite them inside, as Carol was home with baby Nicholas and Allen. But he could not tell the visitors to piss off.

He re-lived for a moment his attempts to avoid the job for the Provos of turning that poor man at his front door into a ball of flames. Much as he hated yielding to UDA brutes, he might also put Carol and the kids at risk if he refused to go with them.

'Good,' he replied. 'I'll grab a jacket and join you in a moment.' He also grabbed his revolver. He was glad he had when he saw that at least the front number plate was blotted over. At the driver's seat in the car, parked a few doors along in the street, sat the notorious thug we will name Lenny O'Mara. Maurice's heart pounded. Had they found him out? Was this an execution squad?

If he ran, they could so easily shoot him in the street, and maybe then slay his family.

His only choice was to take a seat in the back with Bobby Bates and play it by ear. He might be able to escape later, or shoot the rats if they showed an intention of murder. His alarm heightened as the car turned towards the city. Away from Antrim.

'What's the problem, Maurice?' asked Bobby. 'You look worried.'

'Nah, I'm fine. I just remembered I should have told my wife where I was going.'

'Well,' said Billy Moore from the front passenger seat, 'we decided to show you first-hand just how good those shooters you get for us are.'

Maurice said, 'Thanks boys, but I already know how good those guns are. Let's go for a pint of the black stuff, eh?'

'First things first,' said Bobby. 'We want to show off some guns.'

Assassin O'Mara was ominously silent. As they travelled along Old Park Road, then right into Alliance Road, Bobby produced a tommy gun from under his legs. Len at the wheel held up a revolver.

'Get ready, Maurie,' said Billy. 'You might need to duck soon.'

Maurice had his revolver ready for action as he car turned a sharp left into Berwick Road in West Belfast's Ardoyne, a Catholic enclave. O'Mara and Bates, with their windows down, opened fire on houses as they slowly passed them. A man out mowing a small lawn, a girl skipping with a rope, fell to the ground. Others might have been shot through windows.

After their weapons were emptied, the car sped down the Crumlin Road and into Upper Shankill, where they led Maurice into the bar at the Brown Bear. 'Here's to us knocking off some Popists,' said O'Mara as he attacked his pint. 'We've gotta even things up for Bloody Friday.'

Maurice had to drink along with them. At least two of these men claimed to have some sort of Protestant religion. What nature of God did they worship, he wondered, who would bless such reckless slaughtering? Ditto the Provos on Bloody Friday. The paras on Bloody Sunday. That priest on Bloody Monday. He had to stay with them for an hour, forcing himself to be amiable.

O'Mara twice asked him if, when Maurice was at Michelin, he ever got any info about planned raids by the goddam Provisional IRA. Casual as the thug tried to sound, the other two keenly watched Maurice's snickering denial. They exchanged quick glances. To Maurice, it was portentous. He was sure that something grim had prompted the pointed questions.

Smilingly declining a ride with a drunken and maybe murderous driver, he took a taxi home. Perhaps, he thought on the way, he should have got angry instead of laughing. Did they have a sniff of his real role in Belfast?

ICI was a splendid company for him to work for, apart from his receiving and despatching explosives and guns. The pay and conditions were better than at Michelin and the work was not arduous or dirty. There was no such thing as clocking in or out. Senior management, unaware of the smuggling, was lenient if he happened to arrive at work a bit late.

Apart from the smuggling, ICI was a good enough place to ease his tenseness if he did not get out of the country damned soon.

But he could not settle the constant and draining conflict tearing at his mind – his determination to save lives, his sense of hollowness because of MI6's evident slackness and failure to communicate, his ingrained compassion for this conquered corner of Ireland, his disgust at the murderous excesses of both the IRA and Loyalists.

A premonition of looming personal disaster grew stronger nearly every day. Kieran's likely murder, also the youngster's affair with Carol, had aggravated the gloom. He felt alienated from his family here and in Birmingham. It seemed, though, that Carol no longer philandered at pubs.

His mind sank into deep and dark depression during a night shift after delivering another load of guns and grenades to the boatmen at the back fence. He went back to the quiet far end of the warehouse, where more boxes of ammo and bombs were ready for despatching. More deliverers of death and destruction.

He still had no idea how seriously the suits in London regarded his now-rare letters. About half of them got army responses. And which side, he wondered, was his enemy? Which side was maybe planning to slay him? Provos or the UDA? Both of them? Was it the lot to whom Kieran had ratted on his brother before the lot killed Kieran?

Deep down, he felt strongly now that all of Ireland should be run by the Irish. So many elements of the society he was part of were repugnant. The precarious nature of his life in Belfast and his chagrin at London's spook masters had shaken his mental control.

He would never overcome his shame from taking part in bombings, shootings, torture, setting that poor family man alight, making bombs for the Provos and now smuggling a lot of more-deadly weapons for the Loyalists. He felt responsible for those two sisters losing their legs when the Abercorn exploded, the eight-year-old girl being blown up in Claudy.

For a moment, Maurice thought about using the smuggled stuff to blow up himself and the factory. Then he slashed his wrists with a rusted razor blade.

He was unconscious, in a pool of blood, when by sheer luck a warehouse cleaner found him. He was rushed to hospital where, he learned later, his life was touch and go for a while.

Recovering in a hospital bed after a second blood transfusion, he knew that if he had been found an hour later he would have been a cadaver. He felt ashamed of what he had done. Weak. A chicken, he declared to himself, as he saw semi-accusing looks from nurses.

At home, his remorse was lightened by Carol's compassion, her stated understanding of his dilemma and grief when he confessed that he was a spy for Britain.

Hey, sulking here's not going to solve anything. Get positive! He snapped out of it. He calculated that he had saved the lives of well over two hundred non-combatants, and spared at least a thousand men, women and children from injuries and grief. He really had not been the direct cause of any death.

Back at work, gossip had reigned about him trying to commit suicide. Maurice knew they would not believe it if he claimed it was an accident. He cheerfully told his workmates he had been overcome with depression because of a family drama, now settled.

They accepted it but he was going to get the hell out of this province of madness, with his family. If not now, Carol and the boys could follow him later. (Scars on his wrists are reminders today of his 'silly depression'.)

Carol, now knowing her husband was a spook, was alarmed about the thuggish-looking men who had come to the front door recently. The couple decided that, for the safety of the children, they should go to another country. They discussed the options. America? Canada? They favoured an English-speaking democracy farther from Ireland.

As Maurice would be on night shift at ICI that week, Carol took the Monday off work at the hospital. They went to the Immigration Office for Australia – land of warm sunshine and peace, with no religious violence, and well-populated by Irish and their descendants.

They filled in a stack of forms. After a call from the office soon after, they went back for an interview with a woman immigration officer. They were asked about things they had stated in the forms. Why they wanted to go to Australia, what their work skills were, it they had any ailments, details about their children, if they planned to have more of them.

The officer liked knowing Maurice was a former paratrooper. She would check, he knew, on whether either of the Tanseys had a criminal record. Again, he was taking a risk. What if someone in the immigration office who saw the notation of ex-paratrooper Tansey was an IRA of Loyalist informer?

The officer they applied to, an Australian, also seemed to like their prospects of settling happily in the new land. She detailed work and lifestyle options in various states. She hoped they would elect to become Australian citizens, which they would. They were offered subsidised fares of only £25 each. The two boys could fly with them for nothing.

Maurice was not able to name a date when they could go. They first had to sell their home, he explained.

He was amused to read at home in a brochure promoting the place that, 'There are no dangerous animals in Australia'. He already knew about its crocodiles, sharks, poisonous spiders, jellyfish, octopuses, dingoes. And the snakes! Horrid things to his wife, native of the land with none of those silent killers. Even Presbyterian Carol thought the absence of snakes in Ireland was Saint Patrick's doing.

In moonless darkness on a Friday two nights later, she was walking home from work along a quiet road when a car pulled up beside her. A man shoved her onto the back seat and held a gun at her head.

'We're the Provos,' another man told her. 'We know all about your bastard husband and what he does. He's a spy. An ex-British soldier. He's got seven days to get out of our country or the four of you will be dead. We know where you live and where your son Allen goes to school.'

She was still up, shivering with fear, the lights out, when Maurice arrived from work many hours later. They concluded that perhaps a Provo had seen the form at the Australian immigration office.

'Yes, dear,' he promised, fuming again, 'we can leave in less than a week. Go to at least England for a while before flying to Australia. I'll see a property agent on Monday about selling the house, cheaply and quickly. Meantime, we've got a safe house of retreat.'

He wanted to go to find Marty McGuinness and tell him about alleged Provo gunmen grabbing his wife; their wicked threat. But was doing that really safe? Surely such an event would not take place without a Provo heavy sanctioning it. He decided to remain at home; not risk driving to and from ICI. He rang the factory and said he would be off sick for a week.

It was cruelly common in the North, he was well aware, for both the IRA and Loyalists to kill the families as well as their primary targets.

On the afternoon of the next day, a Saturday, he saw a van parked in the sports field and close to their back fence. Vehicles had not parked there before. A bomb might be ticking in it.

He grabbed Carol and the children and ran out the front door towards his car. The moment they reached the pavement, the back half of the house exploded. The bastards had set a car bomb.

Carol and Allen burst into tears of fear and bafflement as they took off in the car. The boy and Maurice had developed a close father-and-son-like bond. He often took Allen for walks, still regularly kicked a soccer ball about with him, played cricket, read him bedtime stories. And he liked nursing and feeding gurgling, sometimes giggling, baby Nicky.

On the drive, Maurice kept a close eye out to be sure they were not followed. He stopped the car around a corner for five minutes. He dropped off Carol and the boys at Carol's mother's home in a quiet street in Glengormley.

Furious Maurice decided to sneak back home. The bombers would be watching the result of their handiwork from nearby, looking for evidence of deaths. He would slaughter them if he could get hold of the Armalite. It was in the main bedroom, which he hoped had not been destroyed. A good weapon, it was, for giving them a spray.

Maurice parked the car a block away from his home. He crept through the front door, appalled at the damage. The back half of the place was shattered. If baby Nicholas had been in the bassinette in his room near the back, Allen in his adjoining room, they would have been killed.

He ran to the main bedroom and grabbed the Armalite. He crawled and ducked through debris to the back yard. Those swines were about to find out what a top-shot para, SAS-trained, could do, he hoped.

He heard movement, raised the rifle and peered around a smashed door. At a beagle nosing about in the wreckage.

The van was a pile of smouldering rubble. The little vegetable and flower garden was hidden under fractured trash. Maurice watched through the remains of the fence for several minutes, hoping to see bombers on the move. A cautious circuit of the field followed. The bastards had gone.

Surprisingly, the RUC was not there. Surely Belfast was about the only city in the world, he figured, where neighbours would not report such a murderous blast. And, good God, what about that seven-day deadline delivered at gunpoint to Carol? There had been no point in reporting that to the police or to the lax Londoners.

He dug his fingers in the dirt under a battered rose bush and collected the silver and sacred medallion he buried when he bought the house. It would have to be hidden at his mother-in-law's. He gathered some clothes for the others and himself. With the electricity gone, he emptied the refrigerator of most of its contents and went back to his family.

The women were distraught. They wanted to tell the police about the bombing.

'I'm afraid we can't do that,' Maurice ruled gently, realising that Carol had told her mother about the threat from the Provos, his spying. 'In this community, telling the police would, at best, be a waste of time. It would definitely generate RUC interest in me, in us.'

He thought again about the safe house in London. Would the buggers let him in there now?

He telephoned his trusted friend, ICI computer man Rob Doran and told him what the IRA had done. 'They must have found out about the stuff we're smuggling,' he said.

Could he meet up with Rob, who might be able to lend some assistance? Rob had a holiday home north near the coast, he recalled. It would be a good hideout until he and his family left the country.

Rob hesitated for a moment. 'That's damned terrifying,' he said. 'Maybe I'm next on their list. Sure, mate, you, your family too, can go stay at my place in the country.'

Maurice oozed his gratitude.

'So,' said Doran, 'we ought to meet straight away. How about going to the Carrick Rangers Footy Club social bar tonight, about seven?'

'Good. I'll be there.' Maurice knew it as a Protestant hangout, a popular drinking hole, near the railway line, off Taylors Avenue, Carrickfergus.

Why, he wondered after hanging up, could they not meet at Rob's home? Was this, even from buddy Rob, suspicious? Could the bombers of the house be UDA? Was it really the Provos who bailed up Carol? He dared not seek more help from either side. Nevertheless, the Taurus loaded and in his pocket, he went to the club in a taxi.

He walked in, deliberately fifteen minutes late, after watching the entrance to the club for half an hour as a few men walked in and out. Rob was not there. At the bar, he got a message that Mr. Doran was running late and would be there shortly. Gawd, Rob was twenty minutes late already. The place looked ready to close.

Few customers were there. Three men at a table, men he did not know, were watching him closely. Gunmen could be outside, waiting for him to leave. He went to the gents' toilet to see if it gave a means of escape from the premises. But it did not. As he walked from the gents', four toughs were at the table, glaring at him. He dashed for the exit.

'Come back here, you Fenian bastard,' one of them yelled.

He heard them in pursuit. They would be armed, shoot him in the street. He told himself to use his SAS training. He was supposed to be the whiz of martial arts. Those brutes, he felt, were probably the ones who blew up the house, tried to kill the four Tanseys.

He turned and waited on the footpath, down the steps beside the front door. The gun was ready if he needed it. Damned Rob Doran, his one good mate at ICI – he thought – had betrayed him.

He chopped karate-style at the back of the neck of the first man out, who crashed face-down on the footpath. The second pursuer fell over Maurice's first victim in the darkness at the base of the steps. He copped a Tansey boot under his nose and collapsed, senseless, on his back.

The other two lunged at him. They were competent combatants. It took the ex-soldier a few minutes to hammer one of them senseless. The other engaged him along the footpath and got out a pistol.

Maurice knocked it from his hand. He delivered a blow that toppled the thug backwards and over the edge of the railway bridge they were on. The pugilist screamed as he fell to the rails. Maurice looked down at the inert body, used his handkerchief to wipe his own prints from the thug's pistol and tossed it down there. He hoped a train was not coming.

He was about to go and drag the man away from the rails when he turned and saw the first man he had flattened stagger back into the club. From where he would phone for more UDA fighters.

Maurice ran towards the main road. He stopped, wiped his prints from the Taurus and hurled it on a roof. He saw a grey police Land Rover coming slowly. He waved at the police urgently, causing the vehicle to halt beside this man with a bloodied face.

'Take me and lock me in a cell,' he said loudly from beside the car's front window. 'My life is in danger. No damned kidding. There are two militants of some sort unconscious outside the Rangers Club. They tried to kill me. Another one fell from the bridge near there onto the railway line. A fourth one is in the club phoning for reinforcements. Three of them probably need medical assistance.'

Two curious RUC officers invited him in through the vehicle's back door, asking for his name and address. On the way to the club, they called an ambulance. 'So, you out-fought four of them, did you?' the police driver asked. 'Getting only a few scratches?'

'Well, yes, with some lucky punches. Tripping a couple of them as they ran down the front steps after me.'

'Why were they after you?'

'I don't know. I'd been in the club only a few minutes, didn't even get a drink, when they came at me. It's something to do with the UDA, I think.' He obviously was now back and high on at least the UVF death list.

Three of Maurice's combatants were carried into an ambulance. They were too incapacitated to be questioned by the police. The attacker who had run back into the club could not be found. The club staff were not helpful.

Maurice was driven to the Carrickfergus police station, from where he was allowed to ring Carol. He cryptically told her what had happened, that he would be jailed for the night. He was politely put into a cell alone. The UVF or UDA would be out looking for him, he was sure. He hoped to God that they did not know where Carol and the kids were.

In the morning, he was photographed and finger printed, surprised to be charged before a magistrate with common assault, causing injuries to three men. He was relieved to be released on bail, pending a hearing on August 29. He was ordered not to leave the province before that hearing, in three months. If he did, a cop told him later, he would be found and jailed.

Damn, he realised, no Australia for at least three months. Never, if he was convicted and jailed. Even if he survived jail, Australia did not accept immigrants with criminal records.

The police informed him that three of last night's attackers were still in hospital. One was in a bad way but was not likely to die. Maurice described to an officer the assailant who had gone back in the club.

A policeman said the three in hospital, the fourth one if the RUC found him, would be charged. In that context – four attackers versus a defender – Maurice felt that surely he should be found not guilty. But it would be a pro-Protestant court.

He went directly to a post office and wrote to London, reporting that he had been charged in court for fighting with Loyalist thugs who tried to kill him. Who probably had blown up the Tansey home. The note gave the court list number of his case and when he would face the charges, which could land him in jail, well populated with more militants wanting to kill him.

'When briefed at Aldershot, I was guaranteed that criminal convictions would be prevented,' the note added. 'I'm a soldier at war.' He gave them Carol's mother's address and telephone number, asking for their urgent advice that the charge was, or would be, dropped.

He waited, staying quietly with Carol and the kids, not contacting ICI. After that fight, Loyalists would want his scalp in a big way.

On the Monday morning, Carol called the hospital, saying she was too ill to go to work. Allen was happy to miss school.

Long-haired and bearded Maurice went to the building company that was still working on the new housing estate where his wrecked home was. He arranged for them to repair the house as a priority. Quick work from them would earn a bonus.

Since the car brakes had failed, nearly killing the girl secretary from ICI, he had looked there for that fighting flasher, the likely saboteur, wanting to throttle and accuse him. But he had not seen the UDA lout since he punched him over the front wall.

The foreman informed Maurice that the man had left the firm. They gladly took on the repair job, no doubt knowing what had happened. Customer Tansey payed in cash up-front half of the amount they estimated it would cost. He and his family were migrating to another country, he explained. He needed the property to be in reasonable order so he could sell it.

A local real estate agent was keen to handle the sale. He would keep in contact with the builder and put the place on the market as soon as the job was done. The arrangement was that if the agent received an offer that exceeded the outstanding mortgage and met the cost of the repairs, he would settle, allowing for the extra value of fixtures and furniture.

The builder repaired the house and it was sold in a few weeks. The price he got was a little less than the cost of the repairs and the amount owing on the mortgage. If the place was not booby-trapped, someone had got a bargain, complete with the fittings and furnishing the Tanseys were not able to get out of there and sell. Going to the place was too risky.

Hiding with Carol's mother, they seldom ventured outside. Allen remained away from school. Maurice and the two women kept alert for any vehicles parking near the house.

No word came from London about the charge being dropped, nor even the provision of a lawyer. Smooth-tongue Bernard had definitely promised immunity, guaranteed that Private Tansey had a licence to commit crimes. And, being in the Reserve, he was still a soldier. The bastards must have abandoned their experimental snoop, he decided fearfully.

19. The attic

From June 1974

Maurice had no one he could trust who might offer him a hiding place until he left the province or went to jail. And it was too dangerous for those young lads, for Carol and her mum, for him to remain at the house in Glengormley.

He remembered Bob Rossan, his best mate in the paras, with whom he had holidayed so often in the Shankill. Maurice had met Carol, former friend of Bob's wife, soon after being best man at Bob and Toni's wedding. Maybe, just maybe, good old Bob was back here on leave. Hoping to find a hideout, he rang Bob's old Shankill number.

'Hello?' It was Bob.

'Bejasus, old mate. I didn't expect you to be in Belfast.'

'Big One Five! Terrific. Where are you?'

'In Belfast. Been here for four years. And you?'

'I left the paras months ago. Dishonourable discharge, I'm afraid. I'm glad to be away from the bastards, especially after that Bloody Sunday massacre.'

This was good. Could he tell his friend the whole damned story? 'Bob, it's great that you're here. I'm not far away, up at Glengormley. I need urgent help. Can I go to your place?'

'Of course. Hell, I thought you were still in England. I've looked for you in phone books there, even in the Republic and Belfast. You wanted to marry that old friend of my wife Toni, I remember. Carol.'

'Yep, we got hitched three and a half years ago. She's got two sons from other, ah, relationships.'

'That's good. And I'm still with Toni. But, being a tyke, you'd better stay out of the Shankill in these bloody awful times. You name it and I'm there, Maurice.'

They met half an hour later in a pub south of Newtownabbey. It was a Saturday, 1 June '74, the first day of summer.

Bob was surprised to be embraced by the big, still muscular man with a beard and hair in a ponytail. 'There's a good reason for it,' Maurice explained. 'You'll know it soon. My young brother Kieran's now a para at Aldershot but he's AWOL. Did you meet him?'

'No. He must have enlisted after I left.'

'Well, he's apparently been a para for more than a couple of years. He was on foreign duty for a long time before he got back to England and came to Belfast to see us for the fourth time more than a year ago. I haven't heard from him since then. Nor has the army.

'I think it's tied up with the trouble I'm in, in this bloody land of the Troubles. I've got a nasty feeling Kieran was killed as he was leaving Belfast, probably because he was a soldier. I've hunted around, but there's no trace of him.'

Rossan looked troubled himself. 'Hell, this is serious business, then,' he said quietly.

Maurice could not tell his friend the whole awful tale of achievement, and the woe, that had brought on today's predicament. For all their shared good and bad times together in the army – Maurice's rescuing Rob from a near-death beating by (alias) George the razor slasher, and Driscoll the snake biter of Singapore – Bob was a Protestant.

He would despise anyone who participated in the IRA's militancy. And he probably retained a loyalty to the British Crown, washed into his brain by 2 Para sergeants and officers. Even though he had spied on the Provisionals, Maurice could not confess to being one.

His story to Bob implied that nearly all his years in Belfast had been at ICI, smuggling weapons and explosives for the UDA and UVF while spying on the Loyalists for Britain.

He outlined his briefing at Aldershot by Army Intelligence officers and the spy master, his scores of reports by letter to London. He related much of his current predicament, centering on the UDA busting his cover lately, threatening Carol, blowing up his home and attacking him outside the Rangers Club.

He told his friend of their arrangements to migrate and that he faced charges in court for defending himself. He was very much on the run from the UDA. Also from the IRA, who he thought had found out he was a Loyalist smuggler of weapons and explosives. He could not leave the province before the court hearing, three months away. Carol and the kids should be safe at her mother's home, but his presence there risked the lives of the four of them, plus his mother-in-law.

He needed somewhere to hide from the hunters. If he was still alive at the end of August, it would be jail or Australia. He could not bring himself to admit to his stupid attempt at suicide.

Bob Rossan had sat stilled over his Guinness, looking pained and astonished. He was anxious to speak. 'I now know why you went from 2 Para to the SAS. It's terrifying. And, being a Catholic, doubly risky at ICI.'

'Yeah, I made out I'm Presbyterian. Like Carol is.'

'Still risky. You were probably a silly mug to take it on. Silly, but damned gutsy and noble, Big One Five. For England and the lives you've saved. Deadlier stuff than being in the paras or the SAS.

'But why not go now to the Secret Service or Military Intelligence? They'd get your charged dropped, sneak you out of the province and put you all in a safe house with new identities. And pay for it all. Christ, it's the least they can do after what you've done for them.

'I thought of that.' Maurice marshalled his thoughts. 'This is going to be hard for you to believe, Bob, but the Brits have repeatedly failed me. Through the army, they acted on a lot of my alerts to coming atrocities, shipments of weapons and all that.

'But, in all my years at that, I never got a response of any sort from my spymasters.'

'*What?*' Rossan exclaimed. 'Fucken incredible!'

'And worrying,' said Tansey. 'My letters asked the London spivs to get in touch with me several times, at least to give me a Belfast contact-man or drop-off point for leaving urgent messages. But it was like flogging a wet mattress.

'I fear now that the Secret Service has wiped me. I don't even have their telephone number! Just a post office box number in London.'

'The ungrateful idiots. So, how, and how much, did they pay you?'

'They didn't.'

'*What?* You did all that valuable spying for them, put your life on the line every day, for no pay, no expenses?'

'Not a cracker.' Maurice managed a wry grin. 'My motive was to save lives. Honest. I'm afraid I can't trust them now to keep my family safe.'

Bob took a slow and thoughtful swig at his drink. 'Those bastards in London would live in luxury. It makes me ashamed to be British.

'As you'd know better than me, we were trained to think our intelligence services are brilliant operators, the first line of British security. The providers of information leading to the army's actions. Spies planted in the guts of the enemy surely are the intelligence service's most important assets. To hell with 'em, I say now.'

Bob found a smile. 'My friend, I've got just the place for you. But just for one. Somewhere out of the city that only I'll know about. You can go there right now. You won't need your car there, so follow me in it to the Shankill and leave it there. I'll sell it for you.

'There's a do with Toni in an hour that I just can't get out of, sorry. So, can you take a train? You can lock yourself in a little bed and living room in the attic at my parents' old home that's now a b. & b. It's at Carrickfergus, by the Belfast Road, beside the Belfast Lough.'

Maurice was elated. He grasped his friend's hand. 'You're a true friend, Bob. And, bejasus, I need one.'

However, he contemplated, the hideout was on the same shoreline and dangerously close to ICI. It would be only half an hour's drive north-east of Michelin at Mallusk. He telephoned Carol from the bar. For his and their safety, she urged him to go with Bob straight away, to wherever. Every time he could be seen entering or leaving her mother's home presented a danger from UDA or IRA spotters. She, her mum and the kids would be fine. She had enough cash. 'What about clothes and things for three months?'

He would not have gone against the wishes of his apparently now-faithful wife. Cheered by her reaction, he told Carol that Bob was selling the car for him. The cash from that would buy his food and clothes later. He did not want to be seen at her mum's place again. They wished one another well, not sure if they should look forward to his day in court. She accepted her man's instruction not to take the risk of going to the court, where there would be assassins from both mobs after their blood.

Bob, he told her, would keep in touch and take messages to and from him. She could phone Bob or the RUC in an emergency. No one but Bob would know where he was. Carol assured him she did not want to know.

At the Shankill, Rossan gave him a key to the front of the house in Carrickfergus. 'I've got a spare one. The attic is at the top of the stairs, over the first floor, and it won't be locked,' he said.

'There's a bolt only on the inside. I'll go there tomorrow with a bag of food. And you'll have plenty of money for more of it once I've sold this good-looking Morris.' He smiled as he touched his mate's beard. 'At least, Big One Five, you won't be needing a razor.'

Bob cautioned him earnestly never to leave his hideout. Any guest downstairs, people on the street, could be UDA or IRA, which had probably put out alerts to look for him.

'I'll ring my mother when I go into my house here, tell her I'll be in Carrickfergus for a spell. I'll say I'll be going back regularly for a few months and I won't want to be disturbed. Mum doesn't go there much. She can tell the old duck who does the cooking and cleaning.

'Then, if there's any wondering about who's moving about up there, there'll be a quick answer. The attic's pretty basic, but it's been my little holiday retreat for years.'

So near to ICI, he would not go out on the streets. Maurice gathered that his old pal went to the attic when he had fallings out with Toni.

When he left the train in Carrickfergus after skulking under his hat, he bought a pile of fish and chips and let himself into a gracious-looking residence. He saw nobody. He quietly climbed the staircase to the first floor, then up a narrow set of steps to the attic. As Bob had said, it was not locked. He bolted the door behind him and looked about at his funk-hole for the next three months.

It was a quarter of the size of his bedroom at home. One single bed took up a third of the floor space. It had a hard, kapok mattress. One blanket, no sheets. One tap and a metal basin were under a little wall mirror. No towel or wash cloth. No soap.

He hustled around the room. Hell, no lavatory! No bath or shower. No radio or television. Not even a power point. No chair. No stove or oven! No bloody utensils or dishes.

A solitary globe hung from the ceiling, which followed the pitched line of the roof. No roof insulation. No heater. The only good thing was a small window overlooking Belfast Lough and about twenty metres of grassland behind the house.

A freighter was heading for the Irish Sea. He wished he was on it. Skipping bail was not such a bad thought. He could not face, however, being on the police's wanted list for the rest of his life on top of being on a couple of other lists. Denied access to Australia, America, Canada.

ICI was just up the coast, to his left. But the window, facing the water, did not show it.

He sat on the bed and contemplated the months ahead. He could leave, but what were his options for three months? Not a damned one was really safe, he decided. He would stick it out, make sure he never despaired, did not go nuts in this little place.

He did not fancy having a crap and disposing of his faeces. He had the urge now. And the lavatory would be downstairs, where house guests were. Maurice dropped his trousers and backed onto the basin. He was pleased to have the fish-and-chips wrappings for toilet paper. He had to put the used paper out the window. A breeze, thank heaven, took it to the sea.

Most of the evening was spent gazing at the mostly-empty lough under a grey sky. A highlight was two spaniels that sniffed about at the shoreline for a while. A sense of safety now was his over-riding comfort when he went to bed. Hell, he didn't even have a gun, he reflected as he drifted to a good night's sleep under the one blanket. Most of his clothes were on to keep out the cold. It was good that Carol had the Taurus and the Armalite.

He was not a regular reader of books but as he sat on the bed in the morning he wanted a stack of them here. And a pack of cards for playing solitaire. There was no table, bench or wardrobe. This was his own damned impulsive fault. He should have done a check-list with Bob, who was so meticulous with his own gear in the army. He grabbed a piece of surviving wrapping and used his ballpoint pen to make a shopping list.

Bob called quietly from the door about mid morning. Almost shaking with fear, he placed two plastic bags of mostly-tinned goods, bread, some bananas, on the bed. He now looked mortified. 'Hell, Maurice, I've got two big suitcases full of stuff I bring here. Should have brought them, but the clothes would be too little for Big One Five.

'I've got to say, I took a hell of risk coming here today, to a man on both the UDA and IRA death lists. And they'd kill anyone who helped you. They have watchers all over the place, of course. There's got to be a chance that I was seen with you yesterday and I was followed here. Especially from the Shankill.

'Anyone there would dob me in if they got a whiff of me helping you, a Catholic ex-soldier who spied on the UDA. I lost a lot of sleep about it last night. For your safety and mine, Maurice, it's too dangerous for me to be here often.

'I hope you can get by with me coming, and just for a short while, once every few weeks. Besides, I'm about to start a new job driving a delivery truck.'

Maurice desperately needed many things. 'Yeah,' he said, 'it's best to be on the safe side. I'm enjoying the safety here, thank you. But is there a chance of getting a knife and fork and spoon, a can opener, a plate or two, from downstairs?

'Don't suppose there's a spare lavatory and a stove, is there? A garbage bin? Oh, and a roll of lavatory paper and some soap?'

'Dammit,' said Rossan. 'I'm sorry, mate. There's a toilet on the ground floor that I use. And I can help myself in the kitchen. But it really wouldn't be safe for you to go down there or for me to take gear up here.

'I passed six people on the way in. Guests come and go all the time. Anyone could be a militant or an informer. Can you make do?'

'Yeah. I have already.' His friend through rough times in the paras was so damned scared. Perhaps he himself should be. Pressing Bob to deliver stuff here could make him abandon desperate Tansey. And it was odd that Bob could not bring up things from the kitchen.

Bob glanced out the window. 'I've got to go in a moment. Is there a message for Carol? But, you know, even being on the phone with her, let alone calling at where she is, has dangers I don't want. Sorry.'

Maurice grinned uncomfortably as he handed over his shopping list and £20. At the top of the scraggy list were toilet paper, soap and a can opener. A tin of instant coffee, which he would have to drink cold.

'I'll be back with them in two or three weeks,' Bob promised. 'Oh, and your Morris is with a car dealer, who was pleased the rego papers and things were in the glove box. I bought my own car from him, so it was okay when I told him I was selling it for a mate who's in Dublin. He reckons he can get five hundred for it.'

After a struggle, the new hermit opened a can of baked beans with his pocket knife. He ate them cold on bread, also sloppily sliced with the little knife. He cursed himself for not listing butter, jam and salt, a toothbrush and paste. Next time. There was no phone for ringing Bob.

The man of regular activity, morning runs, had to settle into a routine of nothingness. His only entertainment was doing push-ups on the floor and looking for life out the little window, which opened from the bottom only about twenty centimetres. If he had to exit this place, with thugs at the door, he would have to smash the glass, squeeze out and leap.

Seagulls provided most of his entertainment. He would be glad to swap the money from selling the car for a battery-powered radio. But he did not want to hear any more news about the Troubles.

Bob would bring any interesting info, perhaps messages from Carol. But she would have to ring him. Bob was not likely to call or visit her. He settled for months of indolent ignorance. At least in prison the food would be regular and warm.

Nearly three weeks later, Bob's purchases did not include toilet paper or a can opener. He would have them when he returned in a few weeks, he said, hurrying to get out of the place. Maurice luxuriated with a bar of soap and a tooth brush, but no paste. Several floor boards squeaked. He avoided them. He could not advertise his presence to people he heard sometimes in the rooms below. The aroma of cooking food sometimes entered his den. He hungrily envied those buggers down there eating bacon and eggs, apple pie, fish, with tea and coffee; all of it hot.

He could not blot from his mind memories of the past four years in the North, nor sober speculation about the future. The possibility of going to jail, mixing with IRA and UDA prisoners – some of them thinking he had put them in there – haunted him when awake and asleep.

He hoped Carol and the kids were okay. He began to miss their company, despite his lingering disillusion with Carol. She, too, would be feeling randy by now.

After a month, he felt like a hibernating bear, seeming to sleep half the time. He exercised on the floor every day to stay fit and minimise cabin fever. He lost track of the days, had no idea of the date. Bob eventually responded to his request for a calendar, on which he marked off every day.

The light globe failed, leaving him in the dark at night for the rest of his hibernation. At least, being summer, he had sunlight through the window until nearly 10 p.m.

Late in July, Bob brought £460 from the sale of the Morris but still no can opener. Maurice became expert with the pocket knife, which he sharpened on the sandstone ledge under the window. Bob also uneasily brought from Carol, from her own initiative, his spare pistol, a silver Smith & Wesson and a box of .22 bullets.

'Unless you hear my voice, never answer a knock on the door,' Bob warned. 'On the way here, I thought for a while that I was being followed, so I turned back south and did a circuit of a few blocks. Your hunters will be everywhere.'

The pistol was an old one left by her dead father. He was pleased Carol had kept the Taurus. His clothes stank until he washed them in the sink using his precious bar of soap. He lived naked, mostly in bed and using the blanket as a cloak, for three days while the clothes dried on the floor by the window. He did not sponge his body until he had dry clothes ready. The privations, the absence of a bathtub or shower, reminded him at times of home in Birmingham.

Bob called with canned food in mid August, this time waving a can opener but still no toilet paper. Maurice would have to continue wiping his arse with the wash cloth.

He asked Bob to be sure to visit the local RUC station on the 27th, two days before the court hearing. He must impress on them please the need for defendant Tansey to have a police car arrive at the house at nine in the morning of Thursday the 29th, an hour before court.

Bob could tell them that the altercation Tansey was charged with had been against four UDAs. That he was on the UDA death list. That the UDA and IRA would be well aware of the date of the hearing. That Tansey probably would not make it into the court alive without police protection. The Carrickfergus police, he added, could readily confirm that.

But first, could Bob please buy him underpants, a singlet, white shirt, a plain tie and a grey suit to wear in front of the man who would determine his fate? And a damned comb and toilet paper? He could not go to court in these clothes, stinking again. Bob wrote down the sizes and took £100.

Since he had acquired a family of sorts, Maurice had shed the reckless, Red Devil fatalism that had put so little value on his life. He dreaded a threatening knock on the door. His nights were populated by scenes of violent doom at the hands of silvertail spy masters and crazed Irish fanatics.

Trying to keep positive, he dwelt on the rare good days of his youth. His holidays when a kid in the Republic, his arrival as soldier at Hong Kong, the holidays with Carol and Allen at Manorhamilton and in Antrim. But his father's drunken brutality, his mother flashing The Rod, the sack-drowning of Pussy, polluted the memories.

He compelled himself to re-live his happy times when he was 12, getting away from home on Saturdays and Sundays, riding his pushbike in the Cotswalds, only thirty kilometres away from Birmingham. Exploring magnificent old villages such as Stow-in-the-Wold, Moreton-in-the-Marsh and The Slaughters, visiting Blenheim Palace and Warwick Castle.

The boy from the dirty, often polluted city marvelled in the mood of rural Olde England at Stratford-upon-Avon. He often strolled along the banks of the River Avon, past a huge waterwheel.

The attic dweller's mind saw again two huge, white swans as they slowly paddled across the stream towards the young man in shorts silently sitting in warm sunshine on the grass at the river's edge. The swans stopped, making small swirls ten metres from the shore, as the boy stood and stepped quietly into the water among some lilies. He held out a crust of bread in each hand, just above the water.

The swans studied him and the bread for several minutes, then looked at one another. Discussing, chuckling young Maurice was sure, if it was worth the risk. 'Come on. I won't hurt you two beauties.'

They honked and surged to him. Two big beaks snatched the crusts. They paddled away, wagging their necks and gurgling with pleasure that hunger had overcome wariness. They stopped and looked back at the boy, showing him his gifts had been consumed.

'You're welcome,' he told them. 'I'll be back sometime.'

Maurice saw himself crossing a bridge to the other side of the river and the Royal Shakespeare Theatre, where for the first time he learned about a famous playwright.

Riding home on his bike as the sun set, he was thrilled about making the day for those swans, having such close contact with the marvellous and timid creatures. The citified lad had envied the children who lived around there.

Maurice still smiled at the memory as his mind turned to contemplating his uncertain future. If he was found guilty and went to jail, with no help from Bernard's lot, death would follow. If he beat that charge in court and could leave the province, he would definitely take Carol and the boys with him, despite his wife's slutty lapses. No way could the collective targets stay on in the province.

The safety and bright futures for those two terrific boys were down to him. It was his undercover work that had put their lives at risk. He would sure sacrifice his life to protect them.

As Thursday approached, he had even given names to the two orangey spaniels that regularly patrolled the shoreline out through his window. Pity they're not green, he smirked. This was the first period since he left the army that the spooks in London did not know his whereabouts. But if they had belatedly tried to make contact for the first time, had got the charge dropped, Carol would get word to Bob.

He was galled to realise that he could not now see his court-appointed lawyer, whoever it was. No way could he go out now to meet him or her. Anyway, how could the lawyer be found? Whoever was appointed should be there waiting on Thursday morning. Maurice began rehearsing how he would brief his defender in less than half an hour. Dicey stuff, it was.

He hoped his rep in court was not a militant, like some IRA legal eagles he had met. The charge of attacking Protestants would be heard here in Carrickfergus, a heavy Protestant domain. Fortunately, no jury.

His defender and the court prosecutor would know already that he was a Catholic, from the police charge sheet.

Feeling smart in the suit, wearing a tie for the first time since his wedding, he realised he was skinny, at least a couple of stones (twelve kilos) lighter than when he entered this funk-hole. The tie Bob had bought was striped green and gold. What sort of silly political statement was that? The tie was just like the one he got on leaving hospital, aged four, after throwing those cigarette butts on a bride outside a Protestant church and being clobbered by a car. It was a rare moment of generosity from his father; the reward for upsetting English Protties.

He left the pistol and bullets for Bob, who was too fearful to be there to be thanked for his kindness. Bob was his saviour, even though his attitude was pretty gutless for a former paratrooper. Maurice hoped events would not necessitate his going back for the gun.

Entering the street on Thursday, seeing traffic, people walking about, was like venturing into a noisy new world.

He must look like a dodgy felon with this scraggly beard and hair to his shoulders, he suddenly knew. He should have got hold of a razor and scissors, cleaned himself up for the court. And, dammit, he was bearded when UDA and IRA men last saw him.

***

Maurice hopes sincerely today that the reporting of the help he received from Bob Rossan does not offend the IRA or Loyalists. He emphasises that Bob was never a civilian militant and did not know his friend had spied on the Provisionals.

***

Two uniformed and armed officers stood outside a marked police car as he strode to them. He got in the back seat and sat low for the short drive with a minimum of conversation, which was surprisingly friendly.

'They tell me you walked up to a police wagon and asked them to take you to a cell!' one of them remarked as Maurice pressed his hair into a pigtail. 'The easiest arrest I've ever heard of.'

The officers stood on the footpath as he bolted between them from the car and into the foyer of the courthouse. A small and suited man with greying hair walked up to him. 'Good morning, Mr. Tansey.'

Several hard-looking men stood about, staring at him. He recognised two of them. UDA bastards. This little bloke couldn't be an assassin, could he? 'Er, yes. How did ...?'

'I've seen your police mug shot,' he smiled. 'I'm appointed to defend you, Mr. Tansey. We've got forty minutes. Let's go in through this door.'

Maurice was led into a small office and locked the door behind him. His mind spun, grabbing at his hours of rehearsals for this moment, about how he could quickly brief this man enough. And did his lawyer really want him to be freed?

The man, Mr. Cunningham, clarified the nature of the charge and began firing questions. Maurice had decided to be frank, apart from steering clear of the subject of spying.

Within fifteen minutes, Cunningham seemed to warm to him. He was really on his side, Maurice hoped. Cunningham liked his client's line of defence, especially that he had no criminal record and had made arrangements to migrate with his family to the safety of Australia.

All four UDA men he was charged with attacking were now also on bail, facing assault charges, Cunningham advised. But, with their own court case pending, they had declined to be witnesses against him. They had made statements to the prosecution, though. Statements claiming Tansey had launched an unprovoked attack on them.

Maurice raised a slight laugh at that.

Cunningham understood that, because of the charges against them, the court would not require the four to be in court to confirm their version.

'I'd prefer to have them in there for cross-examination,' Cunningham said soberly.

The sole witness would be one of the arresting officers to whom Maurice had run. One man against four, two of whom were known UDA crooks with criminal records, said Cunningham. A finding of guilty would get him, despite his clean record, six months to two years behind bars. 'Definitely plead not guilty.'

'So, what are my chances?' he asked.

'Not bad. Your magistrate is a fair man, but I'm not in the business of predicting the outcome of proceedings. Why do you think they chased you out of the club and wanted to bash or kill you?'

'Because they knew I was once a British paratrooper, I suppose.' That admission alone, dropped in court, would surely spell death if he went to prison.

Cunningham took more notes. 'That's really good news.' He recorded details of his client's time in the army. 'There's no need for you to give evidence,' he added. 'Not unless circumstances require it.'

Maurice was pleased to hear that, but, he told Cunningham, if need be he was ready to tell the court what happened at the Rangers Club.

As the lawyer led him to the courtroom, two men stood in their way. 'Spying bastard!' said one, running a finger across his own throat.

'Gentlemen!' Cunningham objected. 'Step aside, please.'

The thugs glared at Maurice as he passed them, grimly showing them two clenched fists.

Most of the seats in the little courtroom were occupied. Carol was absent, as he had required. Her noted presence might help with the magistrate, but also put her in danger. She would be followed home.

At one side of the central walkway he recognised five from the UDA, including two ICI employees. At the other side, two of several scowling men in suits had drunk with him at Provo pubs, had wanted to help bomb Claudy. He sat beside his lawyer, who leaned to his ear. '*Spying?*'

'That's utter rot.'

All stood as a balding man in his fifties walked in from a side door and sat high behind a big bench.

The arresting officer testified briefly that the accused had admitted to fighting with four men, who also faced charges. But that Mr. Tansey, bleeding from his face, had run to their police vehicle and said that, unprovoked, the four had attacked him. Defendant Mr. Tansey had recommended that they call an ambulance for three of the four.

Mr. Tansey had asked to be jailed for the night, saying he feared another attack from the UDA. The three taken to hospital, now out on bail, were in sound health, the officer understood.

Cunningham eloquently told the magistrate his client was the attacked, not the attacker. He had struck back in self-defence, with skills learned when he was a paratrooper with the British Army. The fact that he was a former soldier had probably motivated the unprovoked assault. Maurice heard muttering from behind him.

His client, his lawyer emphasised, had never been charged with criminal misconduct. He had no criminal record. He was a family man, with two young children.

Maurice was heartened to see the prosecutor nodding. He hoped the magistrate saw that. Anyway, anything that the prosecution disagreed with would, of course, be challenged.

The prosecutor said defendant Tansey was believed to be a big man of violence, who had lain in wait as the four left the club after a social gathering. He asserted that the defendant had murderously hurled one man over a bridge to a railway line, where he could easily have been run over. The defendant, clearly a militant, should not be let back on the streets to harm more innocents.

Cunningham related the events from when his client entered the Rangers Club and outlined his army record, including his time as a peace-making para in Belfast, his honourable discharge.

He summed up by telling the inscrutable master of proceedings that no party guilty of assault would run directly to the police, ask to be jailed for his own protection, then ask for an ambulance to help the men who attacked him.

He added that Mr. Tansey and his family feared more violence from activists because his client was a former British soldier. The family had been accepted as migrants to another country. If Mr. Tansey was cleared of this charge, they would leave Northern Ireland immediately for the safety of a new land.

Maurice hoped to himself he would not have to hang around in Belfast to testify in court against his four attackers.

The magistrate terminated proceedings after a little more an hour. 'I have concluded that indeed the accused, Mr. Tansey, was the victim of an unprovoked attack,' he said.

Maurice mused that that opinion ought to slam those four thugs in jail.

The magistrate continued, 'His attorney's statement that the four pursued Mr. Tansey from the club was not disputed with any firm evidence. And there is no evidence that the accused is a danger to the community. On the contrary.

'Further, I am aware that the four others involved in the altercation have declined the opportunity to appear before this court to dispute statements by the defence. In view also of the fact that you have a record free of criminal misconduct, Mr. Tansey, and that the prosecution's silence on the matter indicates that you were honourably discharged from the British Army...'

He looked at the accused with a flicker of a smile. Maurice began to beam as the magistrate wrote something.

'It is the verdict of this court that the accused, Maurice James Tansey, is *not* guilty of the charge of criminal assault. You are free to go, Mr. Tansey.'

As thrilled Maurice turned to shake his lawyer's hand, ignoring more mutterings of discontent behind him, Cunningham jumped to his feet, as he had been asked to.

The magistrate looked at him. 'Mr. Cunningham?'

'Your Worship, I thank you. I have a confidential note I would appreciate you reading before leaving the court.'

He handed to a court attendant a note he had written at Maurice's optimistic request in the event that he won. The attendant passed it to the curious-looking man on high. In a minute, he put down the piece of paper.

'Very well, Mr. Cunningham.' All stood as he left.

No way was Maurice going to go out there and mingle with that mob behind him. Maybe with more of them waiting out in the street. Murderous spite directed at him was the only thing he could think of that the UDA and the IRA had in common.

He and Cunningham remained in the room as it was cleared of spectators. Cunningham led him out the door that the magistrate had exited by.

'Good day, Mr. Tansey,' said the jurist from behind his desk, surrounded by walls of books of law.

'It's now a *very* good day, thank you, sir.'

'I have no doubt of your innocence. So, I gather from your note, Jack, that Mr. Tansey is in danger?'

'He is, Henry. A police escort brought him here this morning. There's little doubt that some militant group has him marked down for at least violence, probably murder. They would all know the date of your hearing. In fact, we were menaced by two of them on the way into court.'

The magistrate looked startled.

Maurice was suddenly pleased about that confrontation. And heck, Jack and Henry! Are these two mates? If only he had known that. He wondered if, but felt sure the sly sleuths in London had not covertly influenced the magistrate's verdict.

Cunningham said, 'So, Henry, I'm asking you to require the police to take Mr. Tansey from the court precinct and provide an escort. To let him leave by the back door and have a police car waiting in the parking lot.'

'Certainly.' The magistrate called a court officer, who left to find the police.

The officer returned in four minutes. 'A police van for Mr. Tansey to sit in the back of will be out the back in five minutes.'

Maurice shook the magistrate's hand and embraced Cunningham as he left him at the back door. He ran, wanting to dance, to an officer waiting at the back of a paddy wagon. This was the biggest break of his life. Heck, sometimes justice prevailed in the North!

He asked them to drop him off when they stopped at a traffic light in the central city. He would merge into the crowd and he wanted to do some shopping. On the way, he saw a police car some thirty metres behind. It was there to discourage followers, no doubt.

He leapt from the van, went to a public phone and told Carol and Bob Rossan the good news. He bought an overcoat and hat to disguise himself and had a barber shave off his beard and moustache, and cut his hair short. In a restaurant, he luxuriated over his first hot meal in three months. Steak, apple pie and three cups of creamy, hot espresso. Then a pint glass of the black stuff, magnificent Guinness.

He waited until dark to take a taxi to Glengormley, unfortunately just a bit east of the Michelin factory. He walked a few blocks until he could slip through the back fence and into the home of his mother-in-law.

Allen, Carol and her mum leaped from their chairs as he walked into the living room. As they hugged, his tears of joy and relief blended with theirs.

20. To the land down under

August 1974

They had to get out of Northern Ireland. The next morning, he telephoned their contact officer at the Australian Immigration Office. He told her they would be ready to take a plane from Heathrow any time after a few days. Using phony names would be good, he knew, but impossible.

The Loyalists and IRA, with so many public servants and clerks in their ranks, could easily be aware of bookings on aircraft and ferries from the province. He felt all the more now that a stooge in the Australian immigration office had revealed his para background to the UDA or the Provos. That had brought on the threat to Carol, the bombing of their home, the murder attempt at the Rangers Club.

The migration officer called back half an hour later with the details of a Qantas flight from Heathrow in two weeks, September 13, which Maurice saw was a Black Friday. By late afternoon they had packed three bags of possessions, had a teary farewell with Carol's mother and taken a taxi to the city.

Maurice booked, in their correct names, a flight for the next day from Belfast's Aldergrove Airport to London. They went to a second travel agent and, still using their real names, bought tickets for the same day on the ferry from Belfast to Liverpool. A third booking was made to take a bus to Dublin.

The four of them, Nicky in his pusher happily sucking a dummy, took a train up to Larne, his old fishing spot well north of ICI and the attic in Carrickfergus. They stayed under another surname in a hotel there for four tense days until they could make the next leg of the trip.

He hoped assassins had gone to Belfast's ferry terminal and airport and bus depot. Perhaps their watch now centred on Dublin. They were not likely to think people fleeing to Australia would go on the little Larne ferry to Stranraer, Scotland.

As the boat ploughed into a choppy Irish Sea, Maurice, alias Gerald McGuinness, went alone to the stern and gazed at the receding coastline in chilled, autumnal weather. His raised palms pushed the land away. *Farewell, Northern Ireland.* For good, after four gory years.

Goodbye, you damned Troubles. An amazingly-bland name, that, he told himself. A more fitting title for province's bloody mayhem would be the Horrors.

And what a naive young soldier he had been, he reflected, at the session in Aldershot in front of that silvertail, maybe-MI6 Director, Bernard, when they assigned him to be Britain's first snoop in the IRA.

So damned brain-washed by army discipline, he was, that he had not dared to demand a salary or even expenses money for putting his life in daily jeopardy. And his requests there for better lines of communication with London had been pathetic. He put it down to a mere private, keen anyway to save lives, not daring to hassle that parade of brass.

As he returned from the deck to Carol and the boys in their cabin, he sang to himself an old Irish favourite. *'Far away in Australia… now has come the time… Far away in Australia, I will be happy there.'*

In the morning Allen, thrilled with his first experience at sea, clung to Maurice's arm. After admiring the coastline along Scotland's Loch Ryan, they disembarked and hired a car which Maurice drove to Birmingham.

He had to have a final farewell with his parents, patch over that grief of the past. With his family beside him, he knocked on the door that evening at his childhood home – later the Ajmal Khan real estate agency.

His mother opened the door and stood there, po-faced.

'Mum, meet my family!'

She backed away silently as he went to hug her. He wheeled Nicky's pusher in ahead of him. Carol and Allen, who had been so keen to meet Maurice's folks, followed warily into the dining room. Father Nicholas did not move from his chair at the table. Maurice smelt the familiar old odour of booze and fags.

'Dad, Mum,' he said, lifting wide-eyed Nicholas from the pusher. 'Meet my wife, Carol. This clever young man is Allen. And *here*, Dad, is your grandson, your namesake, Nicholas Tansey junior. He's nearly two.' He walked towards the table with the babe in his arms and stopped. His father stayed in his chair and snorted.

'Maurice, you're a disgrace to this family,' mother Ellen ranted from over his shoulder. 'You've been up to no good in Northern Ireland. It's *your* fault that Butcher's Block's missing.'

His father's stare was now a glare. 'You lot, get outta here!' he instructed. 'Now! We've disowned you, you filthy English spy.'

Maurice was appalled. God, had the IRA been in touch with them from Belfast? He itched to put down Nicky and punch this man who did not even want to meet his grandson. He saw that his dad had a similar urge but remained seated. He would know that Maurice now could make short work of him.

The four left. Carol, who had not said a word in there, angrily slammed the door behind her. 'Butcher's Block?' she wondered.

'Yeah. She named Kieran that when he was a baby. He had a big, round head like a butcher's wooden chopping block, she reckoned. Kieran hates it. As I do.'

'So you think he's alive?'

'Let's hope, dammit.'

Using a third false surname, they stayed at a motel on the fringe of the city. On the evening of what he thought would be his last night in England, Maurice was still tormented by that ugly scene with his parents. Damn, he would have one last try at his father. He drove to Sparkhill. At the third pub his father had favoured, Maurice spotted him at a table.

With him, Maurice was pleased to see, were Uncle Matt and dear old Eddie McCabe, a building contractor mate of Nicholas' since Maurice was a kid. He recalled wishing long ago that friendly Mr. McCabe was his father. As Maurice came to them, Matt and Eddie jumped to their feet and took turns at embracing him.

'Maurice, what an amazing surprise,' said Matt. 'Here, take a seat.' Clearly, the two did not know of the young man's visit to his old home in Sparkhill.

Maurice had a bigger surprise when his father walked around the table and put an arm over his shoulder. Maurice stood. The two looked hard at one another, smiled and shook hands.

As Matt delivered a pint of Guinness to him, Maurice felt that this place was familiar. Yes, it used to be called the Mermaid. It was the same pub his father had taken him to, aged four, after the boy's confetti and cigarette-butt throwing, the fright in the Protestant Church and time in hospital. Nicholas had spent ages bragging about Maurice's intrusion on a Protestant wedding.

It was then that the boy had to battle to down his first glass of the black stuff. He had thrown it up in the lavatory. Dad and his gang of Irishmen had been at this same table!

He spent an hour with them, chatting contentedly, delivering a selective version of his days in Belfast. He spied for Britain on the UDA, he confided. Prevented many bombings, had some Loyalists arrested. Father Nicholas looked bewildered.

Maurice checked his watch. He had to get back to the family, he declared. They had to be at New Street Station by ten in the morning for the train to London, to catch their flight to Australia.

'We're in fear of retaliation from the UDA,' he added. 'I'm on their death list. I had to bash up four of them who tried to kill me a few months ago. So please tell no one we're going to Australia. That includes the Provos, who think I was a UDA activist.' The impressed threesome so promised.

He returned the hire car on the way to the station the next morning. Standing there as they alighted from a taxi was Nicholas Tansey. Tears coursed down the old man's cheeks. He opened his arms and the three of them embraced.

'I'm sorry, son.' He turned to his daughter-in-law. 'That time at home was bloody awful, Carol. I was a mad goat. I didn't know what Maurice was really doing in Belfast. Can I pick up little Nicholas, please?'

As they waited on the train platform, his father chokingly confessed that he had been a crazy drunk of a father. 'Forget that Belfast stuff,' he admonished. 'I'm proud of you, Maurice. I know Kieran's disappearance – his death, I fear – had nothing to do with you.'

Maurice Tansey will never forget the sight of his father standing on the platform, one arm raised, the other wiping away tears, as the train pulled away.

This family had to be intact when they left the country on Black Friday, 13 September 1974. Possible watchers were not likely to recognise Carol, so Maurice waited with the kids nearby at Heathrow while she checked in their luggage and collected the tickets.

On the flight, he reflected that Australia was home to some three million Catholic descendants of Irish free settlers and convicts Britain had transported from the late 1700s to the mid 1800s. Of the 163,000 convicts sent to the then colony, 36,000 wretches went from oppressed Ireland.

Since then, more than half a million Irish, like the Tanseys now, had fled to the lucky country.

From Melbourne airport, they were taken to modest quarters in the government's migrant hostel in suburban Springvale. They joined a crowded community of immigrants mostly from Europe, predominantly Italians and Greeks, a few black Africans, some South Americans, Asians who probably escaped from the Vietnam war, and Indians. Few residents spoke English.

The public toilets were stinking centres of filth, he and Carol found. Some hostel residents thought the lavatories were for washing their hair. Some defecating was done in the children's sandpit.

On their first afternoon there, Allen was leaving a delicatessen with a carton of milk when a brawl broke out in the street. A young man was stabbed. He collapsed, dripping blood, on top of screaming Nicky in the push-cart.

The boys came home traumatised, causing Maurice and Carol to decide to leave this camp as soon as they could afford other accommodation. The kids had not experienced that sort of thing even in Belfast.

The brawl was between Serbian and Croatian immigrants. The Australians were crazy to house those two traditional enemies in the same place, Maurice felt, bringing national feuds to this new land. But what about Catholics and Protestants from Northern Ireland? He well knew that the IRA had a lot of sympathisers, money senders, in Australia.

A veteran police sergeant who patrolled the hostel told the Irish immigrant that Croats and Serbs brawled often, in several states. But, no. He had never heard of violent religious rivalry by the Irish.

Allen enrolled at a local school, where he felt welcome. Despite his absence from school for more than three months, he handled his lessons well. Maurice soon found a job at the Motor Producers assembly plant in the suburb of Westall, opposite a railway station and near the hostel. His factory later became the Nissan Motor Works. There was a busy production line of reassembled imported vehicles.

He became a stock chaser, responsible for ensuring that the correct components were in place as vehicles came on the line. His incredible memory soon had the locations and catalogue numbers of hundreds of parts, down to small screws, many of them looking identical, imprinted in his mind.

In three months, he was promoted to be a leading-hand, a human encyclopedia of component numbers to keep the production line moving.

In nine more months he was a foreman, renting a comfortable flat in the suburb of Carnegie, near Caulfield Racecourse. That Serbian-Croatian conflict was an imported aberration in this land of sunny peace and opportunity, Maurice soon knew. Carol was happily employed as a secretary at a college of technology.

A manager at Nissan told him he should have a business card to give to clients, perhaps attracting more of them. 'We'll print a few hundred,' he said with a smile. 'And you give them out whenever you can. It's also good PR.

'But the name Maurice sounds a bit too formal. How about us naming you Maurie instead? That's the Aussie way.'

New foreman Tansey was impressed. He had never had his very own business card. 'Sure,' he said. 'Maurie's better.' From that day, nearly everyone called him Maurie.

Late in 1975, he was at home when he answered his ringing telephone. 'Tansey,' he said. Stupidly, he soon realised.

'You're a fooken dead man, Tansey,' said a male voice with a muffled accent of West Belfast. 'Were you thinking you could run away from us, you spying rat? We know where you live. And your damned family. Have you checked under your bloody car today? We know you take different routes to work...'

Maurice was gripped by alarm. Visions of past horrors crowded into his mind. 'What's your bloody problem?'

'You spied on us, you English shit.'

'That's rubbish. You've got the wrong person. I lived and worked in Belfast, trying to keep the peace. Anyway, what side are *you* on?'

'You'll find out when we blow you up or put a bullet in you.'

'I saved many more than two hundred lives, Catholics and Protestants.'

'Rubbish,' said the caller. 'You had a lot of us jailed and killed. We're coming for you, fucken Tansey.'

Calling Maurice an English shit branded the caller IRA. The new Aussie resident said, 'Are you trying to bring the damned Troubles to Australia? Who the hell do you represent? You ought to be grateful to me. Tell me who you are and what side you're on.'

The caller hesitated. 'We're gunna kill you, Tansey. Bloody soon. You put a lot of good men in jail.'

'Come on then, you gutless idiot. I'm well armed, ready for battle – .' The caller hung up.

Carol walked up to him, looking nervous. He did not realise she had stood at the doorway, hearing at least some of his side of the exchange.

'Who was that?' she asked. 'Was it a threat?'

There was no way she would believe a claim that the caller was an angry customer from work. 'Ah, a silly idiot making out he's IRA. He's just trying to scare me, talking about a bashing up, reckoning he's going to go public with claims I was a berserk soldier on Bloody Sunday, the fool.

'Don't worry about it, love. If he *really* wanted to do harm, he wouldn't be making silly phone threats.'

Carol turned and walked away, not looking convinced. Maurice waited for half an hour and warily checked the undercarriage of his car in the driveway. No bomb. No tracking device.

Three similar calls came in the next two weeks, each seemingly from different men. One had the brogue of the south of the Republic, perhaps County Cork. Another sounded like a Derry man. That confirmed Maurice's thinking that the swines were Republicans.

He did not tell his wife about them but knew they would have to find another residence. And soon.

Another caller a week later shouted, accusing him of betraying the loyal supporters of British rule. He called Maurice a Popist bastard, soon to cop a painful death. That one had to be a Loyalist.

He walked into the living room from work on a Tuesday evening to see Carol sitting crouched in a chair, looking drunk, with a half-empty bottle of whisky. Maurice had not seen her in that state since Belfast.

'That bastard who rang you the other week has called back,' she said with a slur. 'You bloody lied about that call. They're going to chuck a bomb into this house, for God's sake! Kill all of us.'

Her debilitating fear did not wane. She did not go to work the next day; spent at a hotel. She staggered home and went to bed, howling with dread of an explosion. It was left to Maurice to cook for the children, keep the house tidy and, with a rifle nearby, watch out for a bomber.

On his way home three days later, a pistol in his pocket, he opened the letterbox by the front gate to see a 9 mm bullet on a piece of paper. He grabbed the bullet and the paper and dropped to the ground.

A red scrawl said, 'The next slugs for your head, Popist shit.'

Maurice brought out his gun and looked up and down the street for the culprit. He saw only local residents.

Popist again. He would like to tell the Loyalists he had spied on the Provos for them. Smuggled in tons of weaponry. He could tell the IRA callers that he stitched up the Loyalists. He would love the two sides to strike here at the same time and do in one another.

There was no point in reporting it to the police, he decided. The sight of men on guard here would only please the threateners; not deter them if they were serious.

Keeping the bullet and note a secret from Carol, he took two days off work and moved his family to another apartment. He got their new phone number in the unlisted category. It was also in a false name.

The threateners would know where he worked, so he gave two weeks' notice of his departure, refusing to give a reason to his confused boss and friend, who did not want to lose his talented foreman. Maurice drove wary and circuitous routes to and from his new home.

He was on the run again. The first callers from each gang obviously wanted to confirm that they had the right target. Why had they rung again and again? Was this just a campaign of bluff to intimidate him? Serious killers would strike without warning.

But he could not be complacent. He spent a few nights outside with the gun, lurking near his front and back doors. After the Rangers Club fight, aware after the court hearing that he was ex-SAS, raiders would know they faced a battle.

The relocation to a new home, however, did not help Carol, obsessed with the terror she had thought they left behind in Belfast. She became a regular at three pubs, often coming home drunk and so disarrayed that she had obviously been fornicating. Just like in that first year and more of their marriage.

She laughed at his exhortations, then accusations. 'I'm going to get drunk where and with who I bloody like,' she yelled. Allen grimly looked on.

Carol became addicted to alcohol again and began stealing money from the college to buy booze and wager on horse races. Under suspicion, she was spotted taking a colleague's handbag and leaving the college. She was followed to a betting shop. College staff pounced as she took from the bag several banknotes which had been marked for identification.

Maurice went to the college and pleaded with the principal not to take legal action. He promised to refund the money she was accused of stealing over many weeks. The headmaster settled for simply dismissing her. She was back at a pub at the time.

Maurice returned home in the evening from a farewell event on his last day at work shortly before Christmas '75, looking forward to decorating the tree and wrapping the kids' presents. Carol was not there. She would be with one of her boozy boyfriends. He had had enough of it.

The IRA or UDA bastards would inevitably track him down here some time, despite his taking those complicated routes to here. They might be crazily vicious enough to strike for Christmas, killing the boys as well. If the car was not there, they would reckon he was not at home.

He wished the children a merry Christmas and packed a bag. Carol was still absent. He left her a short note, saying he was divorcing her. He drove to Brighton Beach, where he lived in the car for three days. During that stay, he went to the Carols by Candlelight at the Myer Music Bowl. He had attended the event with the kids last year. They would watch it on television. He arrived early to get a seat in front. They might sort of share the event and see that he was okay. While there, he realised that the Irish thugs might also spot him.

He walked into Carol's and the boys' home on a Saturday afternoon, worried about them. After getting no response at the front door, he walked inside after going through the unlocked back entrance. Fumes of gas permeated the place. He ran to the unlit gas stove in the kitchen and turned off all the taps, which were on full blast. Opening windows and the front door on the way, he hurried to the lounge room. If a match was lit, the place would blow up.

Young Nicky was asleep on the floor near the television set, showing a kids' program. Carol was flat on a sofa, unconscious. An empty vodka bottle was beside her. *Was this her doing? Or was the gas turned on by Irish thugs?*

He opened more windows and yelled at and shook his wife and the child, generating groggy wakefulness. Allen, a responsible young man, aged twelve, walked into the room wearing the jumper of his football team, with whom he had just played. The boy assured Maurie, whom he never called Dad, that all would be fine, so long as Maurie left the house before Carol recovered.

She now hated him, the perplexed stepfather was told. Surely, Maurice figured, this smart boy often wondered who his real father was. Allen said he would not leave Nicky alone with her again. Maurice reluctantly left, promising to phone regularly.

A few days later he rang and gave Allen the number at a home unit he had rented, paying the bond from his generous payout from Nissan. He had made sure he was paid in cash, as his wages had been deposited in a bank account in Carol's name, and heavily plundered.

At the age of 30, Maurice had never had his own bank account. Carol, he learned, had incurred enormous debts in his name.

He went into voluntary bankruptcy, sold the car to pay some creditors, and had to surrender his passport. Divorce followed, on 25

October, 1978. He was anguished at not gaining custody of the boys. Carol had told the Family Court judge that Maurice was not their father.

He was naturalised as an Australian. He found a job as a sales rep, which included getting a car.

A little more than two years later, he happened to meet Carol with Leon, a fine fellow, a lifeguard at a swimming pool, whom she had recently married in a Catholic church. Carol proudly told Maurice that she was now a Catholic. The couple later had two children. Maurice knew she would never return to Ireland. He sincerely wished them well.

On a downer, he felt there must be some sort of absolution available through the Catholic Church from his sins for Britain, despite his long disillusionment with his religion. He went to a suburban church one evening, was praying awkwardly in there alone, when a priest walked in.

'Father, I'm a lapsed Catholic,' he announced. 'I want to make a confession, please.' He had violated many times most of those Ten Commandments. He, at least, had not committed murder or adultery.

The astonished and kindly cleric gave him God's absolution. Trying to bury his many doubts, Maurice felt that his life had been given a new start. The mindset materialised into heartening advancement in his new working career.

He was soon running his own business producing and selling machines vending hot and cold food and beverages. The work included travelling around Victoria, New South Wales, Queensland and the nation's southern island state, Tasmania. He had recognised a massive potential for the business. He knew the days of office tea ladies with trolleys were coming to an end.

The date 11 July '79 marked the termination of Maurice's nine years in the Army Reserve. He sent his Record of Service to Exeter and received it back updated and officially stamped. It was proof that throughout his days of spying he had still been in the British army.

21. The new romance

August 1979

On 27 August 1979, Maurice was sickened to learn that the Provisional IRA had blown up a boat at sea off the fishing village of Mullaghmore, in County Sligo, south of Donegal. The explosion had killed Lord Louis Mountbatten and three others – his young grandson, a local teenage boat boy, and Baroness Brabourne, the 79-year-old mother-in-law of Mountbatten's eldest daughter. Others on board were badly injured.

Lord Louis, also aged 79, was Britain's First Sea Lord, the last Viceroy and first Governor-General of India. He was a much-loved hero in Britain, notwithstanding raging claims after his death that he was a pedophile and a homosexual. The receiver of a KG, GCB, OM, GSIE, GCVO, DSO, PC and FRC was a close friend of the Queen and the uncle of Prince Philip. He was an admired mentor to Prince Charles.

He had gone out to set lobster pots and fish for tuna from his holiday castle in Mullaghmore. It was dangerously close to the town of Bundoran. Maurice knew from his times holidaying in nearby Manorhamilton that Bundoran was a popular retreat for IRA militants.

A Provo had planted a radio-controlled bomb of 23 kilos in Mountbatten's wooden fishing boat when it was moored, unguarded, at night. Maurice later read that a man with whom he had spent time in pubs in Belfast was the culprit – Thomas McMahon, who had been a participant in the Bastille Day meeting in 1972 that condemned the paras' slaughtering on Bloody Sunday and discussed plans for bombing Claudy. McMahon was sentenced to life imprisonment.

In the face of condemnation around the world, the Provisional IRA defensively claimed that the Mountbatten killings were simply part of its campaign to focus attention on the plight of the North's Catholics and on the need for the province to become part of the Republic.

Sinn Fein Vice President Gerry Adams, lately out of jail, said in a formal statement that the furore created by Mountbatten's execution was unfortunate but it demonstrated the hypocritical attitude of the mass media. The IRA had done to Mountbatten, said Adams, what Mountbatten had been doing all his life to other people.

Adams declared, 'I don't think he could have objected to dying in what was clearly a war situation. He knew the danger involved in coming to this country. In my opinion, the IRA achieved its objective – people started paying attention to what is happening in Ireland'.

Maurice could not find what, if anything, the likes of Adams or McGuinness said when it was revealed in public that Mountbatten had wanted a reunification of Ireland.

His disgust grew when he saw that, on the same day as Mountbatten's slaughter, the IRA ambushed and killed eighteen British soldiers, six of them from a parachute regiment, in Northern Ireland's County Down.

In January '81, three Loyalist paramilitaries sledge-hammered their way into a house in the province's County Tyrone. It was the home of civil rights firebrand and MP, Ireland's Joan of Arc, Bernadette McAliskey, nee Devlin. She nearly died from bullet wounds in the chest, thigh and an arm. Husband Michael was similarly wounded. Maurice was pleased that patrolling paras had arrested the shooters.

These reminders of the Troubles and the recent death threats to him caused recurring nightmares that dramatised Maurice's dark days in Belfast. He was sometimes prostrate and defenceless back in the gloomy attic, a bomb ticking nearby, the IRA shooting holes in the door, the UDA firing a tommy gun through the window. His yelling sometimes woke him in the dead of night, dripping sweat.

He wrote home to Birmingham from Tasmania's capital city, Hobart, expressing his love, asking how his parents were faring. The reply was a brief and menacing letter from his mother, Ellen. Her eldest son still disgusted her, she wrote. He had been a rotten English soldier, then a spy, definitely to blame for Kieran's likely death.

Maurice had long known she had changed since that touching farewell at the front door, giving him the medallion as he left to join the army. She was now a provocative brawler, a serial complainer, thanks no doubt to the brutality she had suffered from his now-repentant father, who probably had not been shown Maurice's letter.

Mother Ellen's note said she was heading to Tasmania to say what she thought of him. Amazed that the old woman would travel around the world to abuse him, he knew she would be a disrupter at the home he shared temporarily with friends while selling vending machines.

Maurice was committed to move to Sydney to keep appointments and expand his business. Soon after arriving unannounced at the Hobart home, Ellen lashed out at the couple living there and placed a curse on their two young daughters. The big woman went to the magical city's major Hadleys Hotel and assaulted two women customers. She was lucky just to be ordered out and not arrested, Maurice's Hobart friends wrote.

Fuming Ellen flew to Sydney, failed to find her son, and returned to Birmingham. He is regretful today that he did not see her, and try again to patch over her virulence.

Maurice received another phone threat, from an IRA fanatic, and again changed his accommodation. His mother's enquiries at Irish pubs had alerted the hunters that he was in Sydney, he guessed.

He was fascinated to read that Martin McGuinness had become a leader of Sinn Fein with Gerry Adams and, in 1981, was elected the organisation's MP in the North's Assembly in Belfast for the seat of Mid Ulster, in Derry County.

Despite some awful moments of Marty's obsession with regaining the North for the Irish – the planning of scores of atrocities, as did spy Tansey – he had grown to like the man. Marty was driven by religious and patriotic fervor, which sank to emotional violence when he was young. Marty's mind had matured impressively in Maurice's last year in Belfast. McGuinness now, he felt, would not be a killer. Like his mate Gerry Adams, Marty surely was heading for new heights in politics.

Troubled Maurice read that the Troubles boiled on. Amid regular rioting and bombings in the North, on 12 October 1984, the Provisional IRA planted a long-delay bomb which exploded at night in the multi-storey Grand Hotel at Brighton in an attempt to kill Prime Minister Margaret Thatcher and her Cabinet. They were staying at the hotel for a Conservative Party conference. Thatcher was not hurt, but part of her suite was destroyed.

Three women and two men at the hotel were killed. Other guests were wounded. Thatcher and her husband spent the rest of the night in a police station.

Claiming responsibility, the Provisionals said in a statement: *Mrs. Thatcher will now realise that Britain cannot occupy our country and torture our prisoners and shoot our people in their own streets and get away with it. Today we were unlucky, but remember we only have to be lucky once. You will have to be lucky always. Give Ireland peace and there will be no more war.*

The statement added that the Provos would try again to kill her.

The main bomber, a guest in the Grand Hotel under an alias, was Provo Patrick Magee. Maurice remembered him as a keen bomb maker and exploder, a fresh-faced 21-year-old, a quiet regular in Provo hangouts in Belfast.

Magee had been a Provo for three years when Maurice gave London the bomber's name. He had ignited sixteen bombs around England – in Coventry, London, Southampton, Manchester, Liverpool – when arrested in Glasgow while on another bombing mission. Magee received eight sentences of life in jail.

In June 1985, Maurice was living on Queensland's semi-tropical Gold Coast, promoting his vending machines and establishing a colour-copying and laminating business, when he received a letter forwarded from his old address in Hobart. In was his mother Ellen's reply to his note of a year before, sent when feeling guilty for not seeing her in Australia.

She wrote tersely and briefly that both his father and Uncle Matt had died. Nicholas had not recovered from injuries from a road accident early in the year. Matthew had choked on his own vomit in a boarding house in Birmingham after a drinking session. Ellen, Maurice assumed, would remain alone in the family home. He mourned for the three of them.

He bought a two-bed campervan and went alone in it to Australia's tropical far north. Wearing a green scarf at a modest celebration of Saint Patrick's Day at a popular tavern in Townsville, he got to know a gorgeous, green-eyed beauty from the Irish Republic who was running the place. She had recently come to Australia to help her sister manage the tavern after her sister's husband was hospitalised with cancer.

Maurice and Joan got along famously. He became a resident in Joan's apartment above the tavern. It was, they now declare, love at first sight. Partly to get himself fit again, he sold his business and took a job that involved working for hours with jack hammers at building sites under a scorching sun.

He read that the Troubles flared again on 8 November 1987 when an IRA bomb killed eleven civilian Protestants, some of them children, in Enniskillen, County Fermanagh, west of Belfast. They had gathered at the war memorial for a Remembrance Day service honouring British soldiers from the North who were killed at war. Maurice had spent many days in the picturesque town. The reckless slaughter brought wide condemnation of the IRA, even from Sinn Fein's Gerry Adams.

Maurice left his job after a few months and helped Joan run the popular tavern, where two bands performed a few times a week. The couple did not like but tolerated a long-standing arrangement for band members and customers regularly to go out the back for sessions of smoking marihuana. While doing a stock-take, he found that the drinks stock was far smaller than it should be.

He discovered that the tavern's two big bouncers, settlers of regular fights, opened the door to the cold-store twice a week and sneaked cartons of beer and spirits outside to the druggies in return for a share of the dope.

The bouncers decided against taking on the big co-manager when Maurice loudly sacked them and other night staff who were part of the racket, which included selling drugs and heaping free drinks on friends at the bar.

Joan had been told only that Maurice had been a paratrooper and left the army in disgust to live in Belfast, from where he had migrated with his then-wife and the two boys. He did not want to burden her with knowledge of his spying or the fact that he was in hiding.

Joan's sister Kathleen, one evening at their apartment while Joan was in the shower, asked him why he had migrated to Australia. He told Kathleen he had left the province after a career with the British Army.

'*What?* Fighting the IRA?'

'Of course. Also fighting the militant Loyalists. Trying to keep the peace.'

Kathleen's friendliness turned to frost. Maurice did not know that she was due to go to Ireland soon to attend a wedding. Because of his admission, it was she who planted the poison, he realised months later. Kathleen's husband Sean, back from hospital, bluntly told Joan that she should not be with that former soldier, killer of IRA heroes.

If she remained with Tansey, her Quirke family would disown her. Joan declared that she would not leave the man she loved.

'Well, you two are out of here,' said the man whose illness had caused Joan to come to Australia. 'You no longer work at the tavern and you can find somewhere else to live.'

The couple rented an apartment in Townsville. Joan dismissed her brother-in-law's conduct as a sick man's silly hysterics. She had ten Quirke siblings. Keen to see them, she also wanted to sell her empty home. It was in Limerick County's Abbeyfeale, close to the border with Kerry. Maurice agreed to go there with her. It ought to be safe enough there, way south of Belfast.

On the way, the lovebirds diverted to Wiltshire to spend an afternoon at Stonehenge.

In November 1989, lugging luggage, they left the bus from Limerick City in front of a hardware store in Abbeyfeale owned by her brother, Liam. Maurice stayed outside with the bags while Joan went into the store to greet Liam and ask him to drive them to Joan's home, about a kilometre away on the Killarney Road.

As she ran to her brother with open arms, he backed away. 'I know who you've come here with,' he said. And no, he would not drive them to Killarney Road. 'No way, Joan, will I be seen in the company of that big bloody fighter for the English in the North. You oughta be ashamed.'

'But Liam, Maurie's not a soldier. He's a Catholic. He left the army because he was disgusted with it. There's no taxi in Abbeyfeale and it's a long walk, carrying our bags.'

'Please leave,' she was told.

The Quirkes, owning many businesses there, were influential in the town, a teary Joan explained on the walk to her house. It was sited between her late parents' home and that of her brother Tim and his family. Tim's wife gave her a cool reception when Joan collected the key to the house from her. Tim would discuss an important matter with her, she was told, when he returned from work.

Joan went alone in the evening to see brother Tim. She was told again that it was disgraceful that she lived with a former British soldier. So long as she remained in the company of that man, the family wanted nothing to do with her. Joan was devastated. She told a concerned Maurice about it. He thanked the Lord that the Quirkes, not even Joan, knew he had also spied on the IRA. Should he tell them he had been an IRA heavy? 'Should I go back to Australia?' he asked her.

'Absolutely no, darling. Don't go without me. As soon as we return, I want to marry you.'

The attitude of her brothers and sisters, nieces and nephews, ranged from cool to hostile. It mattered little that Joan had been a tireless worker for them, helping her siblings and their children when they were ill. She had gone to Australia only to help her troubled sister, whose husband was in hospital. It demonstrated to Maurice the depth of the prevailing Irish bitterness against historically-marauding Britain.

Maurice's childhood love of the Republic's countryside was refreshed. They enjoyed strolls along farm lanes and day trips to old Limerick. Seeing robin redbreasts in the countryside, he was reminded of toddler Maurice's prompting of Uncle Matt to shoot one of them in Galway. Of his subsequent tearful anguish, making a grave for the shattered bird, when he realised that robin redbreasts were Catholic symbols of the crucifixion of Christ. That the red on their breasts came from Christ's blood.

The couple had been in Abbeyfeale a few weeks when Joan suspected and confirmed that she was two months pregnant. They jubilantly decided to marry there instead of back in Townsville.

She tried to sell the house, to which she had clear title. The Quirkes, however, used their influence with a couple of local solicitors, a property agent and even the bank to prevent a sale. The family was convinced she had returned to Ireland to sell the house at the urging of the money-grabbing ex-soldier. In a dodgy set of procedures, Joan received a small down-payment based on a low valuation. A brother took over the house's title.

The couple moved into the town's Devon Hotel and arranged to be married in the Church of the Assumption, opposite the convent where Joan had been a student. This event might heal the family rift, they hoped. It was the marrying season and they had to wait for two months for the church to be available.

There was no problem about Maurice being a divorcee. His marriage to Carol had not been in a Catholic church, so it was not recognised.

Their wedding was a happy event on Saturday, 8 September 1990, Joan in white, the 43-year-old groom in a white jacket and pink bow tie, attended by sixty of Joan's friends. The sole Quirkes there were a sister-in-law and a niece from Dublin. Their gratitude to Joan over-rode the risk of unwinding their already-loose ties with the family in Abbeyfeale.

Maurice was reminded of the day he left Northern Ireland, standing at the stern of the Larne to Stranraer ferry, as the crowd sang *Far away in Australia*... He did not share the sentiment of another song at the reception, *I Wish I were in Carrickfergus*... That was where ICI and the attic were.

Tralee businessman Don Wynne, Maurice's new friend for whom Joan was once his secretary, had taken on the role of giving away the bride. During a break by the small band at the reception, Don sidled up to Maurice.

'Mate, Joan's family was warned not to come to the wedding,' he said quietly.

'Warned by *who*?'

'The local IRA, the silly twits.'

A bolt of fear jumped into the groom's head. Someone in town might know he had also spied on the IRA. A bomb might be ticking nearby. A tommy gunner could charge in. He saw to it that the event ended quickly. The couple, showered by confetti, went to their hotel room upstairs.

Fearing for Joan, who still did not know he had been a spy, Maurice felt uneasy in the town. Still, he was not going to yield to fear now and, in a panic, leave the lovely Republic. He was tempted to seek out the local IRA and tell them he had been a senior Provo, had saved Provo lives when he spied on the British Loyalists. That he came from a family of Republicans in Galway and, through Uncle Matt, relatives in America were important donors to the IRA's coffers. But that, he soberly decided, could backfire. Them checking with Belfast would get a mob of assassins to Abbeyfeale.

Joan's heartbreak about alienation from her family lessened a few days after the wedding when she spent some time with them. Later, all was remorsefully forgiven, by both sides.

Joan and Maurice had a brief honeymoon in Hawaii on the way home to Townsville. They moved north in the campervan and rented a house in Cairns. Maurice worked as manager of the golf course at the then Palm Cove Travelodge resort.

In March '91, they had a gorgeous daughter. Their Irishness prevailed and she was named Roisin, pronounced Row-sheen.

22. Safer, farther from Ireland

From March 1991

At the age of 44, Maurice's dome was balding. He shaved off much of the rest of his sparse head vegetation, making the former bearded long-hair of Belfast nearly a skinhead. Despite their love of exploring the Great Barrier Reef and the highlands west of the coast, tropical heat and a drenching and mouldering wet season caused the couple born in the cool of England and Ireland to move to the temperate magnificence of Tasmania, across Bass Strait from Melbourne.

Not thinking of New Zealand, they believed the peaceful and picturesque isle was the most distant home from Ireland of English speakers. To Maurice, it should be a safe hiding place.

He knew that, a few years earlier, disillusioned former MI5 Assistant Director Peter Wright sneaked down there and wrote with a journalist the autobiography *Spycatcher*, which in 1987 Margaret Thatcher's Conservative British Government notoriously tried to suppress. Maurice had been riveted to read how a young Australian barrister named Malcolm Turnbull had beaten in court the best lawyers the Brits could find to enable sales of the book in Britain. Brilliant Turnbull, of Sydney, was destined to be the Leader of the Federal Liberal Party for a while and then a Federal Government Minister.

Wright the ex-spymaster had gone to live in the far south of the southern isle. His revelations about top British Intelligence officers who were in fact spies for the Soviet had confirmed some of Maurice's suspicions about MI6. Was the presence there of traitors responsible for the ignoring of so many of his alerts, then his final plight in Belfast?

Surely, he hoped, his MI6 assigner Bernard was not a Soviet plant. Maurice planned to consult Wright until, in April '95, he read that the old spook had died.

Nearly every Irishman, Maurice was aware, knew of Tasmania by its colonial name, Van Diemen's Land. They learned of it at school as the far-flung place to which England transported the more famous of its patriotic political prisoners, then called Irish rebels, in the 1800s. The convicts included Young Irelanders William Smith O'Brien and John Mitchell.

The couple discovered a splendid little town, where they rented a large home surrounded by trees and a garden. Joan gained a secretarial position and Maurice worked with a house-painting contractor.

Continuing strife in Ireland caused by the IRA and Loyalists made headlines even in this far-flung, friendly, forested and mountainous isle. It is a bit smaller than the Republic, more than five times bigger than Northern Ireland. He knew that about a quarter of its half million residents were descendants of Irish colonial convicts.

In October '93, after the couple's third wedding anniversary, an IRA bomb had exploded in Belfast's Protestant Shankill district, leaving eleven dead. A week later, Ulster Freedom Fighters made a gun attack on a Catholic pub in Greysteel, County Derry, killing seven. The UFV was the mob who murdered the founder of the North's Social Democratic and Labour Party, Republican Senator Paddy Wilson. Maurice still wondered why there was no evident result from his alerting MI6 well in advance of the UVF's plan to kill the senator.

Maurice was interested to read that in the same month his old boyhood friend, Labour Party luminary Roy Hattersley, had held meetings with Sinn Fein leader Gerry Adams. The two had argued heatedly when they met secretly in a former factory in Belfast. Adams lost his temper when Hattersley criticised the Sinn Fein heavy for being a pall-bearer at the funeral of IRA Ardoyne thug Thomas 'Bootsy' Begley.

A bomb Begley set in a fish-and-chips shop in the Shankill Road district was intended to eliminate UDA heavy John Adair. It blew up prematurely, killing Begley and nine civilians. Hattersley said Adams' pall bearing had sacrificed all hope of forgiveness of Sinn Fein by Shankill Road Protestants. Two of their children had been killed by the bomb.

Hattersley had said, 'The driver nominated by Adams to ferry me to and from the secret location did his best to justify Adams' conduct. If he hadn't carried the coffin, they would have killed him. For the peace to hold, Adams has to keep the savages under control.'

Maurice had keenly supported Sinn Fein's Gerry Adams' efforts to get American support for a united Ireland. Adams had applied for a U.S. visa. British Conservative Prime Minister John Major stridently opposed him getting one. He said Adams was a declared terrorist. He should not go to the U.S. and certainly not visit the White House.

For a week in February '94, President Bill Clinton, a tolerant Southern Baptist, repeatedly telephoned Major, evidently wanting to hear why Britain had branded Adams a terrorist.

The CIA, America's equivalent of MI6 and long-time sharer of intelligence with the British, had not been able to enlighten the President, Maurice assumed. Despite, the new Tasmanian understood, the CIA now having spies planted in Northern Ireland. It was another thing he had in common with the agency, born the same year as Tansey – 1947.

He knew Major's hatred of the IRA would have been sharpened by the Republicans' firing of three home-made mortars at 10 Downing Street on 7 February '91 while Major presided over a meeting there of his Cabinet to discuss the Gulf War.

Two shells had over-shot the PM's official residence and did not explode. The third blew a hole in the building's garden. Two of four people injured policemen. When condemning the attack, Major had said, 'Democracies cannot be intimidated by terrorism'.

But it was rampant violence that had delivered Northern Ireland to Britain, former Red Devil Tansey mused.

Despite what Winston Churchill described as a 'special relationship' between the two countries during and after World War II, their close liaison through the Cold War and the Gulf, Vietnam and other conflicts, Major refused to answer the calls from Clinton, who had famously said, 'I'm a great Anglophile'.

Maurice was pleased soon after when the Americans gave Adams a visa. The Republican leader made an official visit to the U.S., spending two days in New York City making useful contacts. A month later, in March '94, the IRA attacked Heathrow Airport with two more mortar bombs. Maurice was sure it was their retaliation against Major's abuse. He had hoped the Troubles were settling. The catalyst of the continuing strife, it seemed, was still mostly Britain.

Adams was back in the United States in '95. Keen follower of Irish news Tansey knew Adams had visited Irish support bases in Boston and finally celebrated Saint Patrick's Day in the White House with President Clinton. An official statement implied that the Irishman had talked there only with White House officials. PM John Major objected again.

Less than a week later, a ceasefire that looked like being permanent was brokered between the North's Loyalist cadres and the assorted gangs of the IRA. Hopes were high, despite the Loyalists' killing of a Catholic man in Belfast a month earlier. Even John Major visited the province, lifting the ban on visiting mainland Britain that had been imposed on Adams and Martin McGuinness. Adams was soon back in the Oval Office, Washington DC.

The uneasy mood of harmony was fractured when violent street protests followed the release from jail on 3 July '95 of paratrooper Private Lee Clegg, after serving only two years for shooting dead an innocent Catholic joy-rider in a car in Belfast.

Republican and even Loyalist prisoners in Long Kesh and elsewhere, jailed for lesser alleged crimes years before Clegg was convicted, were still behind bars. Protesters, who would never forget Bloody Sunday, claimed the soldier was released because he was related to British Liberal Democrat politician (soon to be Deputy Prime Minister) Nicholas Clegg.

Republican fury rose when the Rev. Ian Paisley insisted that Orangemen march on 12 July '95 with their usual fanfare of incitement through a Catholic area to celebrate England's victory at the Battle of the Boyne in 1690.

'Their right to march through Garvaghy Road is a matter of life and death,' said Paisley. 'A matter of Ulster or the Irish Republic, freedom or slavery, light or darkness.'

The march proceeded, but with the bands silent. Not silent, though, were the local residents.

Maurice was heartened for a while to read about the Good Friday Agreement signed in 1998, also called the Belfast Agreement and the Stormont Agreement, endorsed by public ballots in the province and the Republic. This could truly terminate the Troubles, he hoped, when it came into force in 1999. The 21st century might see peace at last.

But he was sure that the more venomous bastards on both sides of the province's long war would be livid about the Agreement.

Loyalist sociopaths would want the IRA in all its guises, even all Catholics, driven out of the place or slain. IRA hardliners would see the Agreement as a humiliating defeat, a betrayal by their former heroes like Bates and McGuinness, who had disarmed their fighters. They had voted for continued rule from London.

The Republican extremists' war would end only when Northern Ireland as such ceased to exist – when British rule ended, when the whole island was run from Dublin, when militant opponents of that Valhalla were exterminated.

There would be pocket gangs of greens and Orangemen determined to see that the Good Friday Agreement was remembered as a brief and pathetic stalemate, like all the accords of the past. Maurice anticipated that the death toll would rise as surely as tomorrow's sun. And for a long time he had been puzzled about why the alleged anniversary of Christ's crucifixion was called Good!

He knew that the relatively few psychopaths on both sides were out and out terrorists, using sectarianism as their cover for getting a kick out of inflicting pain and grief, spilling blood.

And the slaughterers prevailed.

22. The Secret Service: serial bunglers

August 1998

Maurice Tansey sat over his breakfast cereal, appalled as he read about what the BBC described as Northern Ireland's 'single worst terrorist atrocity', delivered by the Real IRA, a new group objecting to the Good Friday Agreement.

The Reals had splintered from the Provisionals and car-bombed a busy street in Omagh, County Tyrone, on 15 August 1998 – four months after the Agreement was signed. Twenty nine were killed and 220 seriously wounded. The dead included Catholics, Protestants, Mormons, Jews. Nine were children. Plus twins growing in their slain mother.

He bitterly knew that violence always flared in the wake of the Orangemen's marching in July. Despite some restrictions, the Agreement had not really tempered their provocative parades.

Prime Minister Tony Blair called Omagh 'an appalling act of savagery and evil'.

What the hell did the Reals think they'd achieve by that slaughter? Maurice wondered. *Only publicity? Frighten Britain enough to surrender the North to the Republic?*

The Omagh blast surely outraged most Irish Catholics as well as alienating world opinion. It would generate Loyalist retaliation.

In the wake of experimental spy Tansey, he expected the Secret Service now to have new spies in the IRA, surely able to warn London that the Omagh horror was coming.

He had long tried in vain to wipe Northern Ireland from his mind. But the news from Omagh prompted a diligent research program which, furthered by your author, continued for years.

Late in 1999, Maurice received a package containing many Tansey family papers and a letter from Mary Collins, a friend of his mother in Birmingham, announcing that Ellen had died. No will. The enclosed death certificate said it had been caused by, 'Deep depression and pneumonia'. As with his father and Uncle Matt, the funeral had already taken place.

Mary had found Maurice's address in a letter he had recently sent his mother. Mary's letter said she did not know how to contact Maurice's married sister, Maureen. Nor did Maurice. He would go and look for her one day.

When his sorrow had settled and the research resumed, a startling rogues' gallery of spooks for Britain emerged. MI5, MI6, the army and the RUC Special Branch had assigned them to the dangerous business within the IRA soon after Tansey left Michelin, probably the province.

He was not surprised to learn late in 2005 that one of the spooks was his long-time Provo mate, genial little Denis Donaldson (discussed late in Chapter 10).

Denny had confided to Maurice that he was sickened by some IRA torturings, criminal robberies and its protection rackets. The worst of the brutes should be in jail, Denny believed. Maurice had agreed with that.

MI6 and the Special Branch of the RUC had recruited Denny during what he termed a vulnerable time in his life in the mid 1980s. In 2001 the RUC had been replaced by the Police Service of Northern Ireland. The RUC, Maurice was surprised to read, had had 8,500 officers and 4,500 reservists when he was a spy.

Other rumbled spies were Willie Carlin, Frank Hegarty, 'Steak Knife' Freddie Scappaticci, Kevin Fulton, Paddy Dixon, Martin Ingram, Michael Bettany. Eight of them, counting Donaldson. His cloak-and-dagger replacements.

Spying must have spawned in the North after 1974. When their covers were blown, all of them courted or copped considerable publicity, which Maurice had carefully eschewed.

The French had arrested Denis Donaldson in 1981 at Orly airport with the IRA's Billy 'Bluey' Kelly for using false passports when returning from a guerilla training camp in Lebanon. In 1983, Donaldson was Sinn Fein's candidate for Belfast East in the general election, when Gerry Adams was elected to the Commons.

Donaldson went to Lebanon again in the late 1980s for talks with Shia militias, Hezbollah and the Lebanese resistance detachment, Amal, trying to free Irish hostage Brian Keenan. He represented Sinn Fein in the United States, branding as liars hard-line IRA supporters such as Martin Galvin, a Bronx-based Irish-American attorney. Galvin claimed that he had warned the Republican leadership that Donaldson was a secret agent for the Secret Service.

Donaldson was group administrator at Sinn Fein's Northern Ireland Assembly parliamentary offices at Stormont in October 2002 when the offices were raided as part of a police investigation into an alleged Irish Republican spy ring. The raid precipitated what was dubbed Stormontgate.

In a blaze of publicity the police generated, they claimed that they found revealing evidence at the offices, plus thousands of incriminating papers at Donaldson's home, which Tansey had visited many times. Donaldson was slung back in jail.

Also imprisoned were his daughter's husband Ciaran Kearney, father of two young girls, and former parliamentary porter William Mackessy. They were released three years later when the investigation was abandoned, on the grounds that proceeding with it was not in 'the public's interest'. A euphemism, it was, for a Secret Service cover-up, Maurice felt.

The general opinion then in the province was that the raids of the Stormontgate Affair were a baseless offensive by the police, perhaps also the North's Government heavies, to discredit Sinn Fein, which had gained public support.

Soon after Donaldson's release late in 2005, Sinn Fein president Gerry Adams told a news conference in Dublin that Donaldson had been spying on the IRA and Sinn Fein in the pay of British Intelligence for more than twenty years. Maurice, however, was certain that Denny was not a spy in the 1970s.

British security interests confirmed Adams' assertion by 'outing' Donaldson. He admitted on radio in Belfast soon after that he had been recruited by the British Secret Service during a vulnerable time in his life, putting himself at high risk of death. Then he had been 'compromised', and stopped spying. He said he was disgusted with Britain's spy masters but did not reveal the nature of the compromise.

Maurice assumed it was some slack act by the Brits. When arrested during Stormontgate, Donaldson, like M. Tansey, had got no help from London at his time of need.

Maurice was prompted to try to contact Donaldson, the sole activist in Belfast he had truly trusted. But Denny had never known that Tansey was a spy. They could compare notes. Astute Denny would be well informed about current events in the North and the Republic. He might be able to help with the on-again, off-again researching.

Maurice remembered the phone number of the cottage that was the Donaldson family holiday retreat at Glenties, in Donegal. He might be hiding there from blood-lusting IRA extremists and Loyalists.

An intrigued and sparkling Denny was at the cottage when Maurice rang, not revealing where he was in Australia. The amiable little charmer already knew from Sinn Fein top brass, he said, that his former cards and dominoes partner Maurice had also been a spy. He had feared Maurice had been executed.

Donaldson described his wretched years in jail. Maurice then spent many minutes relating some of his own experiences. He told his mate why he, too, bitterly regretted ever working for the careless and callous spymasters in London. 'But, Denny, I still dearly wish for a united Ireland. For an end to the killings.'

As did Donaldson, who remarked that Maurice had lost a lot of his accent of the North; sounded like a real Aussie.

'Denny, I've spent years trying to blot it all from my mind. But atrocities lately like Omagh, the need for recording the truth about the Claudy bombings and what I told London well in advance of Bloody Sunday and other horrors, have made me start putting together my own file of it all. Could you bring me up to date on a few things?'

Donaldson became a keen and astute helper, receiving several calls from Tasmania over a few weeks. The little man in Donegal repeatedly urged 'gutsy' Maurice to write a book about what he called Maurice's pioneering, astonishing days of spying. 'Sock it to MI6,' he added.

Maurice said he was still thinking about whether he would embark on such a risky undertaking.

Donaldson said on a crackly line, 'The way London let you down, my friend, never acknowledging all the lives you saved, your information that ensured the capture of a heap of militants, their failure to act on so many of your tip offs, is bloody awful.'

Maurice related details of more atrocities by Provos and Loyalists that a forewarned Secret Service had evidently ignored, their refusal to give him a means of contact other than by letters, which they never acknowledged.

'That cost well over three hundred Irish lives,' said Donaldson. 'What did they pay you?'

'Not a cracker.'

'*What?*'

'Not a cracker.'

'Amazing. And amazing that you went there in the first place and you kept on at it. They just exploited your determination to save lives. I don't think I could have taken the risks I took for them without my control in Belfast and the pay I got. The money was pretty good, actually.'

'How much?'

'More than I got working full-time from Sinn Fein. But I didn't do it just for the money and I still regret it. Your story has to be told to the public, Maurie. MI6 should be shamed publicly for not even rescuing you when your cover was blown and you had to hide in that attic. You were in more danger then than I was when they failed me.

'It's no thanks to them that you and your wife and the boys survived, that you beat that charge of assaulting the UDA gang at the Rangers Club. I never copped any violence from either side, apart from some rough stuff from the police when I was arrested.'

Maurice told him of the promises by his MI6 assigner Bernard and the army officers of protection from prosecution or retaliation from the enemy if his cover was ever blown. Their assurances that any crimes he committed while undercover would be acts of a soldier at war.

'Another amazing job you've done is keeping your former spying a secret,' said his friend. 'Unlike me and the other snoops who followed you. It's a wonder some journalist or historian hasn't found out about Tansey. Now's the time to go public.'

The new Tasmanian promised to keep the name of his research helper a secret. But soon afterwards there was suddenly no point in that.

Kevin Fulton was the alias of Peter Keeley, a Catholic from Newry city, County Down, south of Belfast. The British army trained Keeley for spying after he joined the Royal Irish Rangers aged 18. Then, like Maurice, he was discharged from the army. As a civilian, he infiltrated the Provisionals, for whom he became a bomb maker. Maurice assumed Keeley had learned that skill from the SAS. And he might have been despatched by Bernard.

In July 2001, after his cover was blown, Keeley, using the name Fulton, caused public dismay when he revealed that he had warned his MI5 handlers three days beforehand that the Omagh bombing of 1998 was coming. He said he had reported the name of the Provo making the Omagh bomb and pinpointed its current location and also where it would be planted.

Maurice Tansey had a flood of horrid memories as he read Keeley's assertion that MI5 did nothing to prevent the catastrophe. Sir Ronald Flanagan, then the North's chief of police, branded the claim 'an outrageous untruth'.

How could the man possibly know that Keeley was telling lies? Maurice wondered. The police chief was simply defending the silvertails of London. When spying from Michelin, Maurice had considered Flanagan a thinly-veiled Orangeman. What else would the policeman say about Keeley's revelation? Flanagan stated, however, that his own service was not forewarned about Omagh.

Maurice saw a transcript of a statement by blown spy Paddy Dixon to his police handler, John White. Dixon, who stole cars for the Provos to blow up, recalled saying well in advance that, 'Omagh is going to blow up in their faces'. Policeman White did not disagree with the claim. The conversation was recorded in January 2002, soon before Dixon fled from Ireland.

Four months beforehand, blown key spy for Britain, Willie Carlin, confirmed the claims of British Intelligence's slackness, notably about Omagh. Carlin revealed that Northern Ireland Police Ombudsman Nuala O'Loan (later Baroness O'Loan of the House of Lords) and her inquiring associates also had learned of British Intelligence's failure to prevent the Omagh bombing. The ombudsman made her own statement to that effect.

She had good reason to detest the IRA. She had been lucky to survive a bombing in the province in 1977 that cost the life of her unborn babe. Under pressure from London and Belfast, an Ombudsman's Office spokesman would not confirm or deny Carlin's and O'Loan's assertions.

Maurice smelt the reek of cover-up when Hugh Orde, Chief Constable of the Police Service of Northern Ireland, said, '... security services did not withhold intelligence that was relevant or would have progressed the Omagh inquiry'.

Orde added that the Republican dissidents MI5 investigated after Omagh were in cells of which the bombers were not members. Oh, yeah? Maurice contemplated. How could that be? Keeley had told them exactly who made the bomb, who would set it off, when and where.

The BBC's trusted *Panorama* television program reported that the GCHQ, the Cheltenham-based electronic eavesdropping centre able to tap into any phone, had a special unit monitoring Northern Ireland. Maurice knew that from his SAS days.

Panorama claimed that the unit recorded phone conversations between the men planning the Omagh bombing, and further that the GCHQ's secretiveness, their reluctance to let even allied organisations know the extent of their snooping abilities, caused them to keep the information to themselves. Despite, as *Panorama* revealed, the GCHQ working 'closely' with MI5 and MI6.

So London had continued its bungling, sloppy ways, Maurice concluded angrily. With the late Peter Wright in mind, he again wondered if some of Britain's top spooks, men who called the shots, were in fact spies for the Soviet Union. If they did not care much about the Troubles. If, hopefully, pollution of Britain's intelligence agencies had ended when the Soviet collapsed in 1991.

Perhaps British Intelligence ranked its secretiveness, its reluctance to reveal how much it knew, higher than the business of saving lives.

Maurice confirmed that his letters to London had prevented well over two hundred, perhaps five hundred deaths. Also a thousand or more injuries. He counted 39 dead and 183 badly injured, many of them crippled for life, in just four of the scores of tragedies to which he had alerted an evidently non-responsive MI6.

He remembered the eight-year-old girl blown up in Claudy, the two young sisters he saw after their legs were blown off in the Abercorn. Omagh added 28 dead and 220 injured.

For the sake of the dead and their mourners and the injured, the people of Claudy in particular, the investigators still of Bloody Sunday, the truth had to be revealed, Maurice now decided. The only way he could think of was to get a book written. Risky, revealing the extent of his spooking to vengeful killers, but he should do it.

His revelations would be denied, of course, pointing to an absence of a file on him after a quick burn in the SIS archives store and computer files were deleted. But his story, which they would know was true, might sharpen up today's Bernards of Britain.

All the later spies Maurice read and was told about had been paid for their work. They had direct liaison 'control' officers. It seemed that a few things, bloody obvious ones, had been learned from experimental Tansey.

Peter Keeley, alias Fulton, had spied via the Force Research Unit, a covert branch of Britain's Ministry of Defence, formed in 1980. It allegedly colluded with Loyalists to assassinate fourteen or more Catholics in the North. When Maurice was investigating Keeley, the man was in London, suing the Crown. He claimed his British Intelligence handlers had abruptly cut off contact with him, and payments.

The ex-spy further claimed that MI5 ignored his alert in March 1992 of a coming IRA attack on a police armoured car that killed a woman officer and badly wounded a man who was in the vehicle.

Keeley had been jailed for a while in London, without charge, for allegedly designing the firing mechanism for IRA mortars, using a skill Tansey had also learned from the SAS.

It looked now as if the Ministry would provide Keeley with an army pension. He and his family would also get new identities and other benefits that were promised before he began spying for them.

Maurice Tansey had never been promised the likes of that. 'Still, good luck to you, Peter Keeley,' he said to himself. He had a firm notion that Keeley was the Kevvy Fulton he knew in Provo pubs in Belfast before the man took up spying.

Queen's Royal Irish Hussar, Willie Carlin, was recruited by MI5 and/or MI6 to infiltrate the Provisionals and Sinn Fein in 1974, when Maurice was hiding in the attic. After six years, Carlin became a key personal aide to Martin McGuinness, who had readily accepted the man, 'discharged' from and claiming a loathing of the British Army.

He became Sinn Fein's treasurer in Derry, handling fortunes from bank robberies and extortion by the IRA. All this time, he regularly passed on information to British liaison handlers around Limavady, north of Derry city.

Carlin claimed McGuinness himself, who had no idea that his aide was a spy, had formed some sort of loose arrangement with MI6 after 1974 (after Maurice left) to make himself acceptable to stand for political office.

The pro-London plant confessed to handling McGuinness' allegedly fraudulent election to the Northern Ireland Assembly in 1982.

Evidently to ingratiate himself in 1985, British spy Michael Bettany told Patrick Magee, Brighton bomber and near-killer of Margaret Thatcher, that McGuinness' close collaborator Carlin worked for MI5. Magee told Sinn Fein, probably Gerry Adams.

Carlin fled from the country ahead of a Provo hit squad. McGuinness was reportedly shocked and alarmed that his trusted aide for years was a British spy. He even complained to his MI6 liaison officer, then evidently ended his loose link with the agency.

Maurice and his Provo recruiter Marty had been close mates for years, notwithstanding the tyre maker's leaking to London. The redhead from Derry had told Maurice many things that were kept secret from all other Provos in Belfast. Maurice was sure that if Martin had a notion to contact MI6 when the two were buddies, Maurice would have known.

From his rural retreat across the world, Maurice was tempted to ring Martin and warn him that, in the interests of truthfulness to the public, everyone being made aware of the cost of the Secret Service's costly slackness, he was considering public revelation of the crimes they had committed together. But the law of libel would restrict that. One-time fellow MI6 spy Marty's reaction to that would be interesting.

Maurice could not recall one bit of carelessness on his own part that would have exposed him, apart from telling the Australian Immigration

Office he had been a paratrooper. Had his cover not been blown, would he be there today? Maybe, he thought, a revelation by brother Kieran soon before his evident murder was the catalyst.

From *his* place of hiding, Willie Carlin had lately condemned the fact that, despite the Good Friday Agreement and related amnesties that freed many convicted mass murderers in the North, like multi-bomber Patrick Magee, there was no amnesty, nor formal pardon, for former undercover soldiers who had committed crimes for Britain.

A notable receiver of an amnesty, Maurice remembered, was the Rev. Ian Paisley.

Fred 'Alfredo' Scappaticci was a highly-placed agent for British Intelligence, code-named Steak Knife. The law graduate and son of an Italian immigrant in Belfast worked with Carlin and spy Frank Hegarty at the core of Provo activities, mainly in Derry, from the late 1970s to 1990.

Gerry Adams had been a fellow jail mate prior to Scappaticci's release in 1974 after a term for criminal/political offences. Scappaticci allegedly became an investigator with the RUC Special Branch. British Intelligence recruited him from there and trained him in the ways of spying through the army's Forces Research Unit. Contacts made in jail enabled Scappaticci to infiltrate the Provos in Derry from 1978.

A fellow spy, alias Martin Ingram, reported when his own cover was blown that by 1980 Steak Knife was second in command of the internal security unit of the Provos' Northern Command. His work included vetting potential IRA recruits. A few killings were later attributed to him.

When Scappaticci's spying for MI5 was discovered, he hurried to Italy ahead of a pursuing hit squad. Scappaticci later recorded at least one interview about his times with the Provos. He, too, said British Intelligence failed to act on some of his vital information, costing lives. He survived a heart attack in Italy in 2005.

Martin Ingram did two tours of spying duty in the North for Army Intelligence from 1981 to 1990. He was aware that some of his 'colleagues' in the IRA really worked for MI5 and MI6. Ingram, whose real name Maurice was not able to find, retired after a subsequent term with the Defence Intelligence Staff in the Ministry of Defence in London.

British spy Frank Hegarty, code named 3018, was murdered while on the job. He was reputed to have been the first to tell MI5 that the IRA was getting massive supplies of arms and munitions from Libya. Maurice scoffed at that, remembering that he told London about it, even where and when shipments from Libya arrived, a decade earlier.

For months, neither Carlin nor Scappaticci knew that Hegarty, working with McGuinness, was a fellow snoop. Hegarty was given the job of superintending the Provos' vast cache of weaponry. The warm and friendly man scarpered from Derry after, inebriated, he allegedly blurted to the wrong person, a true Provo, that he was a spy.

In a telephone conversation with McGuinness, evidently recorded by the GCHQ, Hegarty was induced to return to the Provo fold. Soon after his return in 1986 – amid suggestions that other spies there feared 'blabber-mouth' Hegarty would betray them – he was killed.

24. The demise of Denny

From March 2006

Maurice in Tasmania and Denis Donaldson in Donegal kept in touch by phone nearly every week. But over many days well into 2006, Maurice's phone calls to Denny were not answered. Then came a disconnection message.

The last time they spoke, late in March, his old mate had said with some alarm that journalist Hugh Jordan of the Irish Republic newspaper *Sunday World* had found and talked with him at the hideout cottage and wrote about it in the paper.

Denny had told his friend in the Deep South that the Gardai had warned him then that his life was at risk, and offered him protection. He and the Gardai exchanged phone numbers. He appreciated but declined their protection, he had told Maurice. So, Maurice assumed, that news report had driven Denny from his hideout for a while. Good.

He was shattered to learn soon after that Denis Martin Donaldson was dead. He recalled their good times together in pubs, clubs and restaurants, the celebration of Denny's 21st birthday. And the man's misgivings about Provo robbers and extortionists.

Denny had said in a phone call he made on New Year's Day that he hoped to get together again with Maurie some time soon. It would be Denny coming to Australia, or them connecting in Dublin or farther south in the Republic. Maurice would never return to Northern Ireland.

On the evening of April 4, '06, a cyclist who had ridden past Donaldson's cottage reported to the police that the place had a smashed window and front door. Police found Donaldson shot dead in the cottage. Dressed in his pyjamas, he had died from shotgun blasts to his chest and head that also ripped open his right arm. Two spent cartridges were found by the front door. Shots had been fired through it, evidently as Donaldson tried to bolt the door.

Northern Ireland's Secretary of State, Peter Hain, called it 'a barbaric act'. Irish Prime Minister Bertie Ahearn said he was horrified by 'the brutal murder'.

The Provisional IRA quickly issued a statement of one line, claiming it had 'no involvement whatsoever' in the murder, which was condemned also by Gerry Adams. Democratic Unionist Party leader Ian Paisley dismissed that. He blamed Republicans. 'Eyes will be turned towards the IRA/Sinn Fein on this issue,' Northern Antrim's MP in the House of Commons charged. Paisley had been in the Commons for 36 years.

The year 2006 also marked the death, aged 81, of General Sir Anthony Farrar-Hockley. Maurice's alert to MI6 that Provos planned to assassinate the general had caused him to flee Ireland. Maurice was pleased to have saved the life then of the man who went on to be Commander in Chief of NATO in Northern Europe.

On 12 April 2009, the Real IRA claimed responsibility for Denis Donaldson's murder. An inquest into the slaying was adjourned five times over four years. No one was charged, although in April 2011 two men were arrested, questioned about it and released.

The Donaldson family issued a statement accusing 'British security agencies' of having a role in Denis' murder. The family demanded more action to bring the killers to justice. The authorities refused that, deeming that an inquiry would 'not be in the public interest'.

Again, Tansey interpreted that term to mean not in the interests of Denny's former spy masters. He quietly hoped that British counter-espionage agents had not analysed Denny's telephone activity and learned of the murdered one's long contact with his old mate hiding at the other end of the world.

In April '06, two little penguins left the calm sea and waddled towards him as Maurice sat in the evening at the top of a beach near his home, grieving at the loss of his genial mate.

The penguins halted ten metres away, seemed to consider him warily, clicked beaks at one another like snapping twigs and diverted around him, within an arm's reach, to their overnight burrows in the dunes under marram grass.

After reflecting on the brutality of the Real IRA, or whoever it was who killed Denny, the otherwise sublimely-happy husband and father had some uneasy moments of ambivalence about telling all in a book. He well knew that, to the hard core of haters on both sides of Northern Ireland's conflict, the notion of forgiveness, moving on, was alien. His revelations of truths they tried to bury would also infuriate the Secret Intelligence Service and MI5. And the army.

He felt sure that spy masters and militants on both sides lived by intrigue, deceit and denial of old and recent history. His early death might suit all of them, as well as the militants. With Joan and daughter Roisin in mind, he felt he ought to burn that research file.

The Tanseys bonded with their rural community, free of religious, political or social disharmony. The main interests of their gossipy little farming town were the weather and sport.

Roisin completed her schooling and began studying computer science. Joan's and Maurice's large circle of friends banded together to help when any citizen of the town was in difficulty.

Not a soul had a notion that their quiet, golf-playing, bike-riding neighbour was once a spy. He had not received a phone or mail threat since he moved to the magnificent island.

He became a fan and close friend of Charlie Landsborough, prolific British writer and singer of folk ballads, sometimes even rock-n-roll and gospel songs, when Charlie visited the island state. Much of his music has a flavour of Ireland.

Maurice gave Charlie his treasured medallion, blessed by a Pope. Landsborough carries it in his guitar case. Their close friendship, with regular phone calls, surpasses the links that Maurice the music lover had as a youngster with Simon & Garfunkel.

James Martin Pacelli McGuinness, Maurice read, now had four children. He was on the verge of marrying Bernadette when he and Maurice were last together in 1974.

The Tasmanian was not surprised that Martin had further succeeded in politics, continuing to represent Mid Ulster in the Northern Ireland Assembly and was appointed the North's Minister for Education.

Maurice was gobsmacked to read, though, that Martin had become Deputy First Minister for Northern Ireland. Alongside, of all people, First Minister and Democratic Unionist Party boss, the Reverend Ian Paisley – who most Provos had wanted to be dead.

Martin had had a meeting in the Oval Office in 2011 with U.S. President Obama. Topics discussed included the president's part-Irish ancestry. Martin reported back home that Obama firmly believed all of the isle should be governed by the Irish. In October that year Martin played the peace card to run as Sinn Fein's candidate for the presidency of the Republic. He was narrowly beaten.

Maurice had been pleased to read then-PM Tony Blair's apology for Britain not doing more to relieve suffering during Ireland's 19th-century potato famine. It was high time, the southern islander believed, that Britain also apologised for the vicious nature of its conquests of Ireland over the centuries. And for recent horrors like the paratroopers' mass murders on Bloody Sunday, now also called the Bogside Massacre.

The Tansey experiment, he felt, had worked. But it would have been a lot better if the puppeteers in London had phoned the army in Belfast more often.

He was still woken at night by his yelling at visions of bloodshed. Para thugs, Loyalists, Provos and his ruthless spymasters spectred the nightmares.

Joan often asked what caused those horrors of the night. With a book again in mind, he spent hours telling his astonished, then horrified, wife about his spying days in the IRA and the UDA. Perhaps the public should be told about carelessness or recklessness by MI6, he told her.

Irish beauty Joan at first pleaded with him to forget about telling the story of his life to an author. She feared it would wave a red flag, make him a sitting duck for both the Catholic and Protestant Irish who had threatened him, caused their move to the land farthest away from Ireland. He dropped the subject. The nightmares continued.

Joan later opined, however, that informing the public might be the ideal therapy, exorcising his demons. Sure, he would have to revisit those awful times, but once it was done the corridor of horrors might close.

Who could he tell? Who could write it? Or want to? Could he do it without revealing his name or whereabouts?

Joan typed as he dictated the basics of it. Revelations traumatised her at times. But her love for and pride in the British Irishman she had married blossomed all the more. 'He was now my and daughter Roisin's absolute hero,' she says.

He hesitantly enquired to an agent about getting a book published but, reluctant then to be named in a book, putting his family at risk, he terminated the idea.

Maurice had been concerned for years about the whereabouts and welfare of his sister Maureen, who might not know that her parents, and probably Kieran, were dead. She would not know that Maurice was now a family man in Australia. He flew to England to find his sister; his sole sibling.

At Manchester airport, the terrorist-conscious returner was startled to have to hand his Australian passport to an immigration officer whose face was largely hidden by a black burqa.

'This says you were born in England,' she said in a Middle Eastern accent. 'Why do you have an Australian passport? This looks suspicious.'

'I'm a naturalised Australian!' he announced angrily, stamping a fist on the desk. 'It's part of the British Commonwealth. I'm a former British soldier. What the hell's the matter? I'm here for a family reunion.'

Brown eyes glared from the slit in the black cloth. 'You are a rude man. You will not be allowed into this country.'

The noise attracted the attention of another immigration officer, who was British. He and the woman argued for several minutes, the burqa removed, before Maurice was permitted to proceed.

But, being Australian, he had to go through the alien gate. Maurice was not amused to see a group talking in German swagger unchallenged through the Common Market gate. So Australia, colonised by Britain and its vital ally that had sacrificed thousands of lives fighting for Britain in so many wars, was a land of aliens! It then also seemed odd to him after his years in equal-status Australia that most of Britain's residents were called commoners.

He enjoyed his stay in England but, despite his inquiring at all sorts of government offices, he did not find Maureen.

Back in Tasmania in November 2009, Maurice learned of a Loyalist bomb attack on the home of 20-year-old international bowls champion Gary Kelly in old Ballymoney, in County Antrim.

Dazed Kelly, a Catholic, soon after found a note in his mailbox. It said, 'Your Republican connections will not go unnoticed'.

During a picnic, Maurice, Carol and young Allen had marvelled at Ballymoney's massive slabs of rock that were Neolithic tombs of Irish tribal leaders and warriors about 5,000 years ago.

Remembering that holiday break, mixing with peaceful and gregarious citizens, brought a smile to Maurice, then nearly 61. It had been a rare time of euphoria, even marital harmony, during his years in the North.

He had added to his list of recent horrors the fatal bombing in Ballymoney in July 1989 of the three Quinn brothers, aged three, nine and eleven. The Ulster Volunteer Force had attacked their home a week after the boys' Catholic mother and her partner moved into a predominantly-Protestant part of town.

The homes of many other Catholics there were also attacked but most of the residents avoided death. Many moved to another county. It seemed to Tansey that the UVF wanted to drive all Catholics from the town that was in politician the Rev. Ian Paisley's constituency.

He read that fourteen had been killed in little Ballymoney during the Troubles since he left the province. Seven were victims of Loyalist gangs, four more of the IRA and three more of the British Army.

25. Spurred by Bloody Sunday and Monday

From June 2010

Maurice's disillusion thundered back in 2010 when he read about an official inquiry into Northern Ireland's Bloody Sunday of 1972, when paratroopers shot dead 13 unarmed civilians and seriously wounded 13 more.

The Widgery Tribunal, which he knew of long ago, had continued for 25 years, costing more than £200 million. He had not known that the investigation went on after he finished spying. He put that down to his isolation in the attic.

Had he known, even when living in Tasmania, he would have run the personal risk and joined the 2,500 who gave evidence. The importance of public exposure of what was behind the slaughtering by the paras was paramount. If the Secret Service had really wanted full revelation to the tribunal, they would have found him easily enough and arranged for him to testify. After all, he had contacted the army in 1979 to get his Record of Service updated.

The Widgery findings reported what Maurice already knew. But not all he knew. Not, for instance, that its own spy had told MI6 well beforehand that the march the soldiers opened fire on would be peaceful.

The tribunal effectively cleared the paratroopers and British authorities of blame, but described the shootings as 'bordering on the reckless'. Jonathan Powell, chief of staff to former PM Tony Blair, branded the findings a whitewash.

Maurice learned that the Saville Inquiry, chaired by Lord Saville of Newdegate, was established in 1998 to reinvestigate the same day of havoc. It heard 900 witnesses and reportedly cost £195 million. Unlike Widgery's, its findings were expected to bring on criminal investigations into the conduct of the soldiers who erupted from their vehicles with guns blazing.

Lord Saville's report said not one of the people shot was armed. It described the shooting of 26 mostly fleeing civilians, the slaughtering of half of them, by soldiers of 1 Para who 'lost control' as 'unjustified and unjustifiable'. British soldiers had concocted lies in their attempts to hide their barbarism, Lord Saville found.

Contrary to prior established belief, none of the soldiers' firing was in response to petrol bombers or even stone throwers. The civilian marchers did not pose any physical threat.

Prime Minister David Cameron formally apologised on behalf of the United Kingdom. Thinking of Scotland, Wales and half of Northern Ireland, Maurice wondered how united the kingdom was.

Major-General Julian Thompson, a commanding officer of the Royal Marines in the province when Maurice was spying, said that if Saville found troops guilty, 'Let's prosecute the IRA as well, men like McGuinness. How about drawing a line under this unless we want to go and prosecute all the IRA guys who murdered as well? It's ironic that these guys (British soldiers) could be prosecuted and the people who've murdered twenty times more than they have are being allowed off.'

Colonel Richard Kemp, a veteran of Northern Ireland, said that prosecuting soldiers so long after the event would be a serious error. 'And let's not forget,' he added, 'that we have had IRA murderers let off and not prosecuted and brought into government. Let's open an investigation into some of Martin McGuinness' activities, shall we?'

Sir Reg Empey, leader of the Ulster Unionist Party, criticised the inquiry's 're-living the darkest hours' of Northern Island's history nearly 40 years after the event. He contrasted the Saville inquiry into 13 deaths with the absence of any inquiries into the deaths of 3,600 people at the hands of paramilitary gangs.

Politicians were reported as fearing that if soldiers were prosecuted it would generate huge problems, hindering the 'peace process' in the North. Former Ulster Unionist party leader and Nobel peace laureate, Lord Trimble, said the Saville findings stated firmly that soldiers would be tried for murder or manslaughter. But Maurice read that Lord Saville did not recommend any specific prosecutions. No soldier was charged.

An ex-paratrooper who testified to Saville had been under a witness-protection program, living for ten years in fear of being gunned down by former soldier colleagues. The man, called Soldier 027, told the inquiry that the night before Bloody Sunday he and his colleagues had been given what was tantamount to an order to 'get some kills'.

So, Maurice concluded, the army surely had not been told that the demonstration would not be violent.

Then came a report on a spectre that still caused Maurice a lot of grief. It was the day when the eight-year-old girl was blasted to death in Claudy – Bloody Monday, six months after Bloody Sunday. Eight others were killed. Many more were badly wounded. Shops were destroyed. Five of the dead nine were Catholics. He regarded Claudy as the worst case of London ignoring his bulletins.

Derry Social Democratic and Labour Party politician Ivan Cooper revealed that, within a couple of days of the Claudy bombing, 'A man lurked like a scared rabbit outside one of my constituency offices. He told me the IRA was behind the bombing and I had every reason to believe him.

'He gave no names and I asked for no names. That is the way it was then. It was dangerous to know too much. But several months later, I became aware of the identities and I have absolutely no doubt that Father Jim Chesney was involved.'

Maurice read that the Derry Brigade of the Provisionals, in the face of Cooper's revelations, again denied any participation.

The tanning Tasmanian fumed at this public accusation against the Derry priest not being made until twenty years after Chesney, still a cleric, died peacefully in Donegal, aged 46. Also, as Maurice knew from Denis Donaldson, a poster was plastered on a wall in Belfast in 2004 that showed a priest wearing a balaclava and holding a bomb beside the word CLAUDY.

He knew nobody was ever convicted for the Claudy outrage. From the outset, even UDA men told him the killers were Chesney and priests who were fellow Provos.

A website claimed that months after Claudy, the then Bishop of Derry, Neil Farren, and later his successor, Bishop Edward Daly, questioned Chesney, who staunchly denied any involvement.

In 2002, the Northern Ireland Police Service found documents showing that Secretary of State William Whitelaw had discussed with Cardinal William Conway the alleged planting of the bombs by Chesney and Catholic priests John Barnes and Patrick Fell.

Maurice remembered a Provo saying before the bombings that one or two of Chesney's collaborators would be priests.

The cardinal reportedly had told Whitelaw that Chesney was 'a very bad man' and he (Conway) would see what could be done. He raised the possibility of transferring Chesney to Donegal.

When he heard about that, RUC Chief Constable, Sir Graham Shillington, wrote, 'I would prefer his transfer to Tipperary'.

No one seemed to query why the army was not on patrol at Claudy. Maurice wondered how he could quickly inform the investigators that MI6 knew of Chesney and Claudy well in advance, tell them that the Provisionals had supplied the three bombs. On 24 August 2010, after eight years of investigation, the province's police ombudsman Al

Hutchinson published a report. It concluded that the Catholic Church and the British Government had conspired to cover-up Chesney's alleged bombings.

The report stated that, 'The arrest of a priest in connection with such an emotive atrocity at a time when sectarian killings in Northern Ireland were out of control and the province stood on the brink of civil war was feared by senior politicians as likely to destabilise the security situation even further. A deal was therefore arranged behind closed doors to remove Father Chesney from the province, to Donegal, without provoking sectarian fury.

'The RUC's decision to ask the government to resolve the matter with the Church, and then accept the outcome, was wrong. The decision failed those who were murdered, injured and bereaved. The police officers who were working on the investigation were also undermined.'

Hutchinson's report added that 1972 was one of the worst years of the Troubles and that the arrest of a priest might well have aggravated the security situation. 'Equally, I consider that the police failure to investigate someone they suspected of involvement in acts of terrorism could, in itself, have had serious consequences.'

The report said detectives believed Chesney was the IRA's director of operations in southern County Derry. That he was a prime suspect of running paramilitary violence other than Bloody Monday. Another finding was that the Assistant Chief Constable of the RUC Special Branch had refused a detective's request for permission to arrest Chesney.

A memorial to the dead and injured erected in Claudy in 2000 included a bronze figure of a kneeling girl. The eight-year-old who perished, Maurice assumed. Five years later, unknown people knocked the statue from its plinth.

Martin McGuinness in 2002 told the BBC Northern Ireland current affairs program *Spotlight*, 'I have never met Father Chesney, nor do I have any knowledge of him other than from media reports'.

Maurice recalled a much different story he had heard from the Provo leader at the Claudy planning session in the pub after celebrating Bastille Day.

In September 2010, the province's MP again denied any involvement or prior knowledge of Bloody Monday by himself or the Provisionals. He repeated that he did not know the priest before the Claudy bombing.

However, McGuinness admitted that he had met Father Chesney not long before the priest died. 'I was told he was a Republican sympathiser,' McGuinness told an interviewer. 'Would I go and see him and meet with him in County Donegal? There was no mention whatsoever of the Claudy bomb (sic). He just talked to me about his support for a united Ireland.'

Maurice wondered to himself if the interviewer was also expected to believe in the tooth fairy.

Deputy Prime Minister Nick Clegg told the House of Commons that the government at the time should have carried out an investigation. 'The Government is profoundly, profoundly sorry that Father Chesney was not properly investigated for his suspected involvement in this hideous crime at the time.'

MI6, Maurice grimly noted, was a part of that government. That agency, he was sure, would not be sorry. And what about the other two priests?

He expected that Clegg's statement would prompt MI6 to examine its file on its solitary spy in the province at the time. Its people would find Tansey's alert to Bloody Monday, sent some two weeks before the event, reporting that the Provisionals had supplied the three bombs. They should also find his reminder to them afterwards that the prime bomber was Chesney.

Continued claims of sweet innocence, the prevailing uncertainties about Claudy, Bloody Sunday, other bombings and shootings he knew about, reignited Maurice's simmering disgust with the suited spooks in London and his desire to publish what he had experienced. He would now bare all. Sure, vengeance seekers and MI6 would be riled. But to hell with it. Setting the record straight about his part in Ireland's history was more important.

***

Maurie Tansey had known me, Mike Tatlow, for years as a local resident, former national newspaper editor, TV producer, historian and author. He invited me to lunch in a Hobart restaurant and told me about his days as a Red Devil and a spy. He gave me the biographical notes Joan had typed.

He was pleased to learn that I had often visited Ireland, had studied its history, had Irish ancestors who included a colonial convict sent to this far-flung island. And that I was once, like him, an altar boy who was caught sneaking a drink of altar wine. We clicked.

Our researching confirmed that most of the 3,600 or more slain in the more-recent Troubles in the province – population 1.6 million – were Catholics. The toll would have topped 4,000 if Maurice had not gone spying, we calculated. He dearly hoped, but was not confident, that the Troubles would really end in his lifetime.

But he was mortified to learn that the new splinter group of former Provos, the Real IRA, had made forty significant attacks on national security targets in the North in 2010, rivalling the violence of the 1970s.

Many people, mostly English, had lightly mentioned to Maurice 'the luck of Irish'. Really, he felt, no other nation had been so damned inflicted for so many generations. We two knew the phrase came from the gold and silver mining rushes in the California, where some lucky fossickers were Irish. We share the view of Liverpool's Beatle John Lennon, who told young journalist Tatlow in Sydney in 1964, 'If you had the luck of the Irish, you'd be sorry and wish you were dead'.

***

The flaring Reals

Continued flaring of the Troubles was confirmed by a car bombing in Culmore Road, Londonderry, on the evening of 4 September 2010. More atrocities followed. The Real IRA, killer of 29 civilians when it bombed Omagh in August 1998, claimed responsibility for the Derry blast. Militant Republicans struck again with guns and bombs early in 2011.

On March 28 that year, police found a gigantic live bomb in a road underpass near the border of Northern Ireland and the Republic. As the 225-kilogram horror was being defused, the police figured that its IRA deliverers were planning to undermine Northern Ireland's forthcoming election.

The Real IRA claimed the killing in April 2011 of police constable Ronan Kerr, aged 25, with a bomb under the officer's car.

Relations between at least the Irish Republic and Britain improved in May when Queen Elizabeth II risked a brief visit there. Despite some minor bomb scares, mobs of protesting locals, Maurice was pleased that the visit went quite well amid unprecedented security measures.

The Queen expressed sorrow and sympathy for the generations of victims of violence, but did not apologise. No British monarch had been to the land across the Irish Sea in 100 years.

A few days later, President Obama wowed the Irish, and visited a village in the Republic where his great, great grandfather was born.

The Queen and Prince Phillip visited the Northern Ireland in June 2012 and met victims of bombings at Enniskillen. The couple met Northern Ireland's Deputy First Minister, Martin McGuinness. He told the queen her visit was 'a powerful signal that peace-building requires leadership'.

A month after the royal visit, nine policemen were wounded by petrol bombs in the Catholic area of Ardoyne during the Orangemen's yearly parade to glorify the ancient Battle of the Boyne. Violence flared again in 2013. A mass murder was avoided in March when police found four primed mortar bombs in a van near a Loyalist centre in Londonderry. Three Republicans were arrested.

The July 2013 orange parade along streets in Belfast caused the eruption of vicious riots for three days and nights, injuring at least forty marchers and protesting Republicans.

Maurice pondered. Would the hatred and killings in the North ever end? For the lifesaver and his family, the days of fear might never pass. When the book came out, would it be prudent to leave their rural retreat in Tasmania and live in another Australian state, perhaps another country? With another name?

To hell, he decided again in his 66th year, to hell with the merchants of hate who might try to slaughter him. And he was still a pretty good trooper. His secrets had to be bared.

Printed in Australia
AUOC02n1057190115
265359AU00008B/8/P

9 780994 177841